Territoriality and the Westernization Imperative

Antecedents and Consequences

Claude V. Chang

University Press of America,® Inc.
Lanham · Boulder · New York · Toronto · Plymouth, UK

4501 Forbes Boulevard
Suite 200
Lanham, Maryland 20706
UPA Acquisitions Department (301) 459-3366

Estover Road
Plymouth PL6 7PY
United Kingdom

Printed in the United States of America
British Library Cataloging in Publication Information Available

Library of Congress Control Number: 2007940655
ISBN-13: 978-0-7618-3981-1 (paperback : alk. paper)
ISBN-10: 0-7618-3981-X (paperback : alk. paper)

™ The paper used in this publication meets the minimum requirements of American National Standard for Information Sciences—Permanence of Paper for Printed Library Materials, ANSI Z39.48—1984

Contents

Preface

(*"Jen shin ping ping, tenshia tai ping."* When there is peace in the human heart, there is peace in the world. – Chinese Proverb)

This book in very many ways parallels the evolving events in the Middle East since the invasion of Iraq in March 2003; not by design but rather in consequence of the seemingly heuristic approach to foreign policy by the Bush administration in its attempt to link Iraq to al-Qaeda and to weapons of mass destruction as the basis for the invasion that was planned before the heinous acts of September 11, 2001.

With "victory" in Iraq proving to be an illusive proposition after four years of rationalization and politicization; the sworn goals now conveniently situated within the "global war on terror"; and the White House chant of Israel's right to defend herself curiously all but a murmur since its failure to destroy Hezbollah in the summer of 2006, one cannot help but wonder what it was all about. What was it, for example, that compelled the Bush administration to provoke so much dissatisfaction at home and abroad and effectively to squander America's well-earned respect and moral authority?

It surely was not the events of September 11, 2001. The whole world became American and stood side by side in consequence. It surely was not for want of intellectualism in the President's team nor was it ineptitude as so many have simplistically suggested: many team members have had distinguished academic, military, and business careers; many have served in previous American administrations. There had to be something more; something beyond the mundane; something rooted in what we perceive to be "our way of life" unmistakably supported by the exercise of power. Hence, while there are numerous scholarly expositions on the several issues from discrete perspectives, a holistic perspective comes from synthesizing Robert Ardrey's notion of territoriality and John Kenneth Galbraith's discourse on power.

This synthesis of Ardrey and Galbraith provides a unique framework for the critique of the many values we cherish or are told we should cherish. It compels re-examination of some of the forces behind our value system and our relationship with one another and with the wider world from a pluralist perspective. In this functionality, therefore, the selection of information is not entirely value-free.

Not to Praise Caesar

Given the emotional and therefore contentious nature of the issues addressed—which is unavoidable in a book of this kind, more especially in the times in which we live and the sensitivity surrounding the Arab–Israel conflict—it should be clearly understood that this book is not intended to advance any one position or to lend support to the methods employed by those whose reactions manifest in violence, whatever its form. Rather, its purpose is to examine both actions and reactions in context of the territorial imperative as an alternative to rhetoric and polemics which increasingly have come to be accepted as scholarship in popular news media. Indeed, it is simply not possible to find justification in any act of terrorism against innocent people. Only the demented, to be sure, would find justification in perpetrating and supporting acts of terrorism against fellow countrymen. Such acts, as observed by Sir Michael Astill in the trial of the five British nationals accused of plotting to do harm to their fellow countrymen in the name of al-Qaeda, can only be considered a betrayal to their country; more than that, their actions are not acts of martyrdom but rather in consequence of Faustian pacts and must be condemned as such.

As an overarching comment, it should be noted that this book, this perspective, by its very construct is born out of freedom; not unbridled freedom but the freedom to information, to question, and to expression; freedom that could only be fully understood and appreciated by being an American. It is a privilege which ever so often has been abused since the adoption of the US Constitution; but a privilege that has been enshrined and thus endured as the essence of Americanism. Indeed, it is a credit to the Founding Fathers that, despite periodic assault on this bastion of Americanism, this great country continues to be, in the words of the late President Gerald R. Ford, a country of laws and not of men. It is in the spirit of the framers and a comfort to ordinary Americans that the US Supreme Court should pursue decisions on the basis of principle and not on politics. It is also an attest to the wisdom that obtained two hundred and thirty years ago that ordinary citizens should be the ultimate arbiter of right and wrong by way of choice, arguably the greatest freedom of all, as evidenced by the results of the Congressional Elections of November 2006. But, alas, it is a country that seems to have reached too quickly the point of critical-vulnerability in consequence of its unparalleled if aggressively achieved economic standing and its even greater success at upholding the principle of individual rights and freedom, as the infamy of 9/11 so rudely and cruelly reminded us.

This openness to governance and public accountability, one of the corner stones of America's moral authority of which Americans are rightly proud is now so tightly woven into the fabric of American society that contrivance as a policy approach however well-intentioned is rejected as un-American even when the national interests are threatened. Yet, ever so often the confluence of events does at times make contrivance irresistible to opportunists and necessarily manifest in philosophical inconsistency in domestic and foreign policy, the latter to the chagrin of a pluralist and still-conflictual world whose expectation is for moral leadership.

An oft overlooked and somewhat contradictory American characteristic is the belief that patience as a virtue is for the other person, and that "winning isn't everything, it is the only thing." It is this commitment to winning that has worked well to make America great in its short history; but it is also the impatience with the slow pace of change coupled with the insecurity attendant unrivalled success that bring it into conflict with older and more mature cultures—some dating back to B.C.E.—in the twenty-first century, where "old" is still a desirable quality and change a very slow and deliberate process even in an age where information transfer is instantaneous. Every so often we are reminded of the abiding tension attendant this false dichotomy; most recently by the attempts of former Secretary of Defense Donald Rumsfeld to draw a distinction between "old Europe" and "new Europe" and, of course, by Secretary of State Rice's notion of a "new Middle East." In contrast, it is instructive that the Chinese Premier Zhou (Cho) Enlai thought it too early to offer an informed judgment on the French Revolution.

As a general comment, while this book challenges conventional wisdom with respect to many of the issues examined, it does so in the interest of presenting an alternative perspective and not with intent to disparage or belittle the contributions of the several eminent scholars whose dispassionate specialist analyses are indispensable to a better understanding of the several discrete challenges in a post 9/11 world. It further comes free of any malice against any elected official, at home and abroad, whose actions irrespective of their motivations are acknowledged as representing their honest beliefs. It moreover recognizes the freedom of everyone to pursue their "right to have rights" and unhesitatingly supports policies and initiatives that foster coexistence in a pluralist world.

Finally, I would like to express my sincere appreciation to those who have gladly lent their support to the research and publication of this manuscript. However, their contribution does not in any way absolve me of full responsibility for any errors of facts, which are unintentional, or contestable opinions contained herein.

Claude V. Chang
Pompano Beach, Florida
September, 2007

Part One

Territoriality and the Westernization Imperative

Chapter One

Territoriality and the Westernization Imperative: Overview

Introduction

This book offers a perspective derived from critiquing the interchangeable use of condign, compensatory, and conditioned powers as instruments of territoriality by the more powerful states operating within a global political and economic framework that is premised on Western ideology and institutionalized in international charters and covenants. It is a perspective informed, in general, by the evidence relating to the growing pressure on the Western economies in the twenty-first century in consequence of an emerging China as change-agent to the geopolitical and geo-economic order, and in particular, by pursuing this primary question: Is the crisis in the Middle East a convergence of American and Israeli territorial imperatives or is it reflective of a *clash of civilizations* (see Huntington, 1996)? Arising from this primary question are the following subsidiary questions: Is effective international relations in a pluralist world premised on notions of goodwill and fairness or on relative power? To what extent does the westernization imperative of the United States (US), and thus the West, manifest in conflict with the primal instinct to survive typical of traditional societies, in particular Middle Eastern communities whose way of life is anchored in seventh-century Islam but whose oil resources are essential to Western prosperity? Are compensatory and conditioned powers in the form of foreign aid and trade agreements used by rich countries to bridge the socioeconomic divide between rich and poor countries or are they instruments of political and economic asymmetries? Last but not least, are aid-recipients victims or astute players in the frenzied game of territoriality?

These questions are the principal concern of this inquiry; and when approached as interrelated issues and in context of the larger geo-economics and geopolitical issues attendant an emerging China the answers are likely to convey a very different understanding of the Bush foreign policy as is being played out in the Middle East.

Looking Past 9/11

While many of the above questions have been analyzed from discrete specialist and, to be sure, interested perspectives, the experiences since 2000—looking past the heinous acts of September 11, 2001 (9/11) perpetrated by al-Qaeda, whose activities up until then were largely discounted by the Bush administration (see Brietweiser 2006; Clarke 2004)—suggest an underlying interconnection between the several issues raised above. But beyond addressing the trauma of 9/11 and the actions of the Bush team in constructing and advancing the case for invasion of Iraq, and its consequences, few scholars have ventured to address the issues in context of an overarching neoconservative grand strategy; hardly any in the wider context of territoriality.

That this is so is perhaps because the social conditioning arising from embracing and proselytizing Western culture and ideology as the ideal is accepted as *the* reality; or perhaps because specialization and thus discrete narrowly-focused analyses are the hallmarks of a superpower; or perhaps because the exercise of freedom of speech and expression guaranteed by the First Amendment to the *Constitution of the United States of America* as a form of conditioned power are constrained by other instruments of power—such as the Patriot Act—ingeniously contrived by the Bush administration in its declared war on terror to restrict the protection afforded by the First Amendment.[1] But, while many of the security steps taken are absolutely necessary and should be fully supported, as Seifudein Adem (2005: 27) rhetorically asks: "Should scholarly judgment be perverted by excessive concern with political correctness?"

In addition to the Patriot Act which many have argued violates First Amendment Rights under the Constitution, there is, to be sure, evidence to suggest that Fourth Amendment Rights also are being violated by the government.[2] In hearings conducted by the US Senate, it was revealed that the *National Security Agency* (NSA) has been engaged in data mining with the cooperation of several telecommunications companies, even before 9/11. According to the *Electronic Frontier Foundation* which filed a law suit against AT&T in 2006, about ten percent of domestic internet traffic of AT&T customers in about 15 to 20 locations nationwide was being diverted to the NSA's secret monitoring devices.[3] There are other telecommunications companies that allegedly complied with the NSA's requests for data. These alleged violations of the US Constitution, according to Bruce Fein and John Nichols, rise to the level of "high crimes and misdemeanors" and are impeachable offences.[4] Bruce Fein, it should be noted, drafted the Articles of Impeachment against President Clinton.

There are of course other constraining influences on freedom of expression that are psychological: the overwhelming flow of information and the influence of the news media in shaping their use (see McNair 2005); the crafting of a new security discourse premised on the "Axis of evil" and "global war on terror" as replacement for "evil empire" (Luke 2005); and last but not least, the effective media management by the White House, what Compton (2005) labels "the convergence of military and media discourse", the subject of *Bill Moyers Journal.*

Whatever the reason, given the Bush administration's attempts to use 9/11 as the catalyst for launching its neoconservative grand strategy—as revealed in accounts of meetings prior to 9/11 (Suskind 2004: 96–7) and in declassified memorandums obtained by "*Frontline*"[5] in which the Vice President is shown seeking to make a link between al-Qaeda and Iraq as a pretext for invasion—taking a holistic approach to the issues is a necessary first step to looking past the rhetoric; and to ascertaining the *raisons d'être* for the conflicts in the Middle East which may not necessarily be what they seem or what we are told they are and which keep changing to reflect the changing conditions on the ground.

In Search of a Justification

For most dispassionate observers the changing justification for the Iraq war comes too glibly to the Bush administration and arguably betrays a hidden agenda which this book seeks to explore. For example, in an *ABC* televised broadcast on November 18, 2001 the then First Assistant Secretary of Defense and Chairman of the Defense Policy Board Richard Perle told his interviewer: "Weapons in the hands of Saddam Hussein plus his *known* contact with terrorists, including *al-Qaeda terrorists*, is simply a threat too large to continue to tolerate." Also, when asked by Wolf Blitzer of CNN: "Next phase, Saddam Hussein?" Perle replied: "*Absolutely*, we would be seen as liberators in Iraq."[6]

For over a year following 9/11, efforts were directed at finding a justification for war against Iraq. It became a matter of shaping the reality to suit the prediction. But according to the former Director of the Central Intelligence Agency (CIA) George Tenet: "We could never verify that there was any Iraqi authority, direction, control and complicity with al-Qaeda, with 9/11, or any operational act against America, *period.*[7] Evidently, Mr. Perle's parallel intelligence operations at the Pentagon took precedence over the CIA. Mr. Perle, it should be noted, has proclaimed that the neoconservative agenda is alive and well despite the apparent set backs in the Middle East.[8]

With no weapons of mass destruction (WMD) as the "smoking gun" and the quagmire the US finds itself in Iraq four years after "mission accomplished", Perle's reasons for being in Iraq morphed into: "We are in Iraq to *help* an elected government *battle terrorism*. It has become a *central front* in a much larger war [emphasis added]."[9] That Iraq has become a central front is not because the terrorists were provided safe harbor by Saddam Hussein but rather in consequence of what the *Time magazine* characterized as "Cowboy diplomacy" of the Bush administration. Indeed, as many analysts observed, the longer the US stays in Iraq the greater the opportunity for al-Qaeda to gain support from the growing hordes of disaffected Iraqis. Moreover, the White House conveniently denies its earlier attempts to link Saddam Hussein with al-Qaeda as part of its effort to portray the war on Iraq as a just war. However, there are numerous news clips of the Vice President and others on the Bush team making or seeking to make just such a link either directly or indirectly.

A "Just War"

St. Augustine (354–431) defined just wars as "those that avenge injuries, when a nation or its citizens should be punished for failing to right a wrong done by its citizens, or to return what has been taken away unjustly" (Sigmund 1988: 65). On the basis of this definition few if any would find fault with the US for attacking al-Qaeda and its Taliban supporters in Afghanistan. Indeed, the whole world stood with the US and shared the grief of all Americans. No one offered any objection to the American response even though it resulted in the loss of thousands of Afghan civilian lives; it was totally in keeping with St. Augustine's notion of just war and, therefore, was fully embraced by the world.

However, 9/11 created an opportunity for implementing the neoconservative grand strategy. Riding on a full sea of support for the war on al-Qaeda in Afghanistan, the Bush team sought to portray the war in Iraq that was clearly planned before 9/11 as a just war from its inception. However, with no WMD and no proof of any prior connection with al-Qaeda, one is left to ponder the question: Does the invasion of Iraq rise to the same level of the just war against al-Qaeda who have injured Americans, or against the Taliban who have provided safe haven for the perpetrators of 9/11? More fundamentally, is the invasion of Iraq and the resultant killing of hundreds of thousands of innocent Iraqi civilians the consequences of a just war as defined by St. Augustine or, as is clearly being interpreted by extremists, no less cause for a just war against the perpetrators of such perceived wanton death and destruction?

It is precisely to avoid addressing this moral contradiction in US foreign policy posed by these questions that the Bush team furiously seeks to establish a link between al-Qaeda and Iraq; or at the very least, have a logically-defensive reason—for example, bringing freedom and democracy to the Iraqi people—for invading Iraq. But it is a moral contradiction that cannot be explained away by logic or contrivance. Indeed, as observed by the Chinese philosopher Lin Yutang, to be logical is not always to be right and that, truth is a part of human nature; it cannot be proven or explained by logic. In this vein, 1970 Nobel Laureate Alexander Solzhenitsyn's take on truth is equally instructive: "One word of truth shall outweigh the whole world."

Contrivance

On the flip side of the just war-contrivance dichotomy, as defined by Galbraith (1983: 129):

> Contrivance is a business on which truth does not impinge.... Scholars and publicist who deal in social interpretation and description take account of their audience, and assess the quality of their own ideas, by the extent and volume of the reputable applause.

It is an all too familiar spectacle post-9/11. Indeed, a discernible phenomenon in discourse on the Middle East crisis is the idea that if something is repeated often enough some of it will stick; it does not have to be truthful. This has never been more evident than in the run-up to the invasion of Iraq in March 2003 and since. Evidence the chant by President Bush and his team that Saddam Hussein posed an imminent danger to the world and possessed WMD. In his address to the Veteran of Foreign Wars on August 26, 2002 Vice President Cheney declared: "Many of us are convinced that Saddam Hussein will acquire nuclear weapons fairly soon". This was followed up by the then National Security Adviser Condoleezza Rice who, appearing on CNN on September 8, 2002 pronounced: "The problem here is that there will always be some uncertainty about how quickly he can acquire nuclear weapons, but we don't want the smoking gun to be a mushroom cloud." The President also echoed the so-called threat posed by Saddam Hussein: "We cannot wait for the final proof. It could come in the form of a mushroom cloud"[10]. Moreover, the performance by the former Secretary of State Colin Powell at the Special Meeting of the UN Security Council to hear the US case for war on Iraq was compelling to a non-suspecting world.[11]

According to former Secretary of State Powell: "Our conservative estimate is that Iraq today has a stockpile of between 100 and 500 tons of chemical weapon agents. What we are giving you are *facts* and conclusions based on *solid intelligence.*" Armed with aerial photographs that showed mobile chemical labs and information on Saddam Hussein's attempts to acquire nuclear weapons, proving the case was a "slam dunk" in the narrative of the Bush team.

All Americans and the world believed them. Who better to know? After all, Saddam Hussein indeed had used chemical weapons with US help against Iran in the 1980–8 Iraq-Iran war.[12] There are published pictures of Donald Rumsfeld and Saddam Hussein shaking hands and conveying a sense of achievement. Moreover, as highlighted by Bill Moyers in his exposé on the American media's complicity to the deception, no one asked the hard questions of the President; and Mr. Bush's press briefings were often contrived, with the White House national press corps validating the charade.[13] With few exceptions, the entire national media networks with connection to Washington sheepishly complied, with the *Weekly Standard* headed by the neoconservative William Kristol leading the way.[14] But this is not a new phenomenon or unique to the Bush administration. According to Compton (2005: 40), there is research that chronicles "how US news media have largely downplayed critical perspectives on military actions" in the past.

No one entertained the thought that public sentiment would be manipulated or that the evidence would be contrived; not with the country still in mourning for the victims of 9/11. And even though the majority in the UN Security Council pushed for giving the UN Weapons inspection team headed by Dr. Hans Blix time to complete the task, Mr. Bush and British Prime Minister Tony Blair were not only adamant in their assertions that Saddam Hussein was seeking WMD but were insistent on immediate exercise of condign power. In his 2003 State of the Union Address, Mr. Bush was deliberate in his assertion: "The British government has learnt that Saddam Hussein recently sought significant quantities of uranium from Africa." This questionable assertion has proven not to be true, and despite a relentless and costly—about US$750.0 million—search for WMD after the invasion, no WMD were found. David Kay and Charles Duelfer who were dispatched to Iraq by the Bush administration separately confirmed there were no WMD to be found. Indeed, after a sixteen-month exhaustive search Duelfer found no chemical or biological labs; only that Saddam Hussein "aspired" to possessing WMD.[15] Even so, Mr. Blair whose government as it happens contributed to the contrivance maintains that WMD will one day be found.[16] It should be noted here that, according to Larry Johnson, British intelligence regarded the American claims with respect to WMD as "cooking the books".[17]

On the national political scene, contrivance continues to be the option of choice for the administration and its supporters, and for Richard Perle, one of the widely believed architects of the Iraq war, whom one anti-war activist labeled "a weapon of mass destruction"[18]. With respect to the administration, as revealed in testimony to the *US House Oversight and Government Reform Committee* chaired by Representative Henry Waxman, the death of Corporal Pat Tillman was knowingly misrepresented as arising from engaging the enemy and died defending his comrades; in fact he was killed by friendly fire from a distance of about 300 meters. Similarly, Jessica Lynch whose rescue was filmed by the Army as a public relations exercise denied in testimony the US Army's claim that she was shot and that there were Iraqi soldiers in the hospital at the time of her rescue. Both accounts were used to mislead the American public into supporting the war in Iraq.[19]

Contrivance is also a prominent Republican Senator and surge-supporter, fully armored-clad, arriving at a public market square in Baghdad which had been secured prior to his arrival, with over 100 troops and two attack helicopters overhead providing a secured area for him, returning with the message to the American people that the "surge" is working, it is now safe to walk about in Baghdad. A few days later 150 Iraqis were killed by four car bombs, and the carnage continues unabated. Months later, in his report to the Senate Foreign Relations Committee, Comptroller General David Walker testified that of the 18 benchmarks set out as objectives for the surge, only three were fully met.[20]

Perhaps more egregious, is Richard Perle's manifest obsession with power. Having failed to sell the invasion of Iraq as a just war, and the right to interfere in the working of other states such as Iran, he callously invokes the idea that "there has got to be some advantage of being a superpower."[21] That notion was quickly rejected by Patrick Buchanan, a conservative Republican and former White House staffer, as evidencing "democratic imperialism". Perle found similar rejection of his rationalizations for the Iraq war from Ambassador Richard

Halbrooke, former US Ambassador to the UN. Not to be deterred, Perle tried to get the former Prime Minister of Bosnia Haris Silajdzic to denounce the UN. What he got instead was:

> You cannot let one country decide what's wrong and what's right ... that country may be led by a government that is not able actually to be really discern and choose between moral guidance and its own interest.

Perle did find support in an Iranian student dissident who "escaped" from Iran while on his way to sit an examination at the university in Tehran and now wants the US to send in the Marines.

Interestingly, while most analysts have since concluded the crisis in the Middle East reeks of "incompetence" at the planning and administrative levels, Jon Stewart suggested if somewhat cynically that, the incompetence portrayed by the Bush team possibly could be deliberate, designed to distract from the true purpose of their strategy. As explained by Stewart, if the objective is to increase sales of lemons, rather than advertise lemons directly you simply promote stronger lemon-scented detergents by preying upon the vulnerabilities of users of detergents.[22]

"Incompetence" or "ineptitude" notwithstanding, it is the contention of this book that, hidden in the phrase "a much larger war" is something at play that is much larger than fighting terrorism in the Middle East. As noted earlier and in other parts of this book, the planning for invading Iraq was well on its way before 9/11. Indeed, the early rumblings were that the status quo—"stability"—in the Middle East was not an acceptable condition for the Bush administration; the region had to be brought into conformance with the Bush imperative of universalizing freedom and democracy: the Westernization imperative, if you will.

Whatever the rationalization or its form, the Bush narrative speaks to a heightened state of US territorial imperative seemingly made urgent by an emerging China when examined in context of Sino–US relationship, past and present. In other words, Jon Stewart's "lemon" of the Bush administration's strategy is to prolong America's hegemony by containing if not eclipsing China's emergence. While some are likely to question this supposition, it would be the height of naivety to buy into the patronizing grand assertions of the Bush administration and not look past attempts at managing thought, especially in America.

Conspiracy Theory or Opportunity?

As will become clear, there are potential beneficiaries contributing to this strategy. Their grand assertions are not only equally patronizing but also speak to their respective territorial imperatives. In this regard, a discernible theme in Mr. Blair's narrative does indeed border on the existential: Survival of Western

European ideology. With a born-again Christian George Bush as President of the US—supported by Christian fundamentalists—a Tony Blair concerned for the survival of Christian values and British influence as British Prime Minster, and the ever-present Israeli desire for a return to and control of the Promised Land of King David[23] converging as it were at the turn of the century, proved too good an opportunity to pass up in the wake of 9/11. It was the neoconservative dream of what makes for an irresistible combination: threat and opportunity; a full sea, with the current serving.

But contrivance is not the exclusive domain of the neoconservative Bush administration. In the run up to the First Gulf War of 1991, the daughter of Kuwait's Ambassador to the US appeared on national television networks to falsely bear witness to the kidnapping and killing of Kuwaiti babies by invading Iraqi forces. Her performance rivaled those of Oscar winners. It was the performance that launched a thousand bombs. Before then, of course, was the contrivance of Saddam Hussein for invading Kuwait and for declaring war against Iran in 1980; and before that, the incident in the Gulf of Tonkin that led to the unleashing of one of the most unrelenting bombing campaigns in history; and before that, Hitler's rationale for the Holocaust, the most immoral of all, and so on. Contrivance is clearly the last haven of politicians and those seeking hegemony and territorial expansion, as evidenced by the conquest of the American West. It separates humans from animals in the play-out of territoriality; the latter taking territory not by deception but by the laws of nature.

Contrivance in Economics

Contrivance is not the exclusive domain of the political either. Contrivance manifests in legislations that almost always speak to interested perspectives. Indeed, contrivance as a way of American corporate and political life is manifest in the ever-increasing number of lobbyists in Washington DC and in regulations that speak to an interested viewpoint if not financial rewards. One has only to carefully listen to the debates in Congress a few times before recognizing the importance of contrivance to "our way of life."

In international economic relations, contrivance translates to institutions such as the *General Agreement on Tariffs and Trade* (GATT) and its successor *World Trade Organization* (WTO) that until recently almost exclusively served the interests of the Western economies; to the *International Monetary Fund* (IMF) and *World Bank* which since the 1980s morphed into instrumentalities of the powerful; to asymmetrical trade agreements; and to foreign aid which until recently were designed to compensate in asymmetric agreements rather than provide sustainable development in conformance with the self-determined socioeconomic needs of aid recipients. These will be discussed more fully in Chapter Four on compensatory and conditioned powers.

Territoriality Broadly Defined

While most of the terms used in this book are defined within the text, the terms territoriality and territorial imperative are explained in some detail below for a better understanding of the discussion that follows. As the reader will discover, foreign policy initiatives necessarily manifest in the exercise of power—whether condign, compensatory or conditioned—and as such they reflect territoriality.

As defined by Robert Ardrey (1961: 10–14), "territoriality—the drive to gain, maintain, and defend the exclusive right to a piece of property—is an animal instinct" which he attributes to humans who as part of the natural world possess as do all other species a genetic territoriality drive; and that, "hierarchy is an institution among all social animals and the drive to dominate one's fellows an instinct three or four million years old." In the extreme, "the territorial imperative is as blind as a cave fish, as consuming as a furnace, and it commands beyond logic, opposes all reason, suborns all moralities, strive for no goal more sublime than survival" (Ardrey 1966: 236).

As the ensuing chapters seek to show, this primal instinct of survival is latent in all humans, civilized and the not-so-civilized, and will manifest in the extreme when all else fails. As William Golding reminds us in *Lord of the flies*, the veil of civilization is so thin it can be broken at any time. The Donner party resort to cannibalism in the Sierra Nevada in 1846 (Stewart 2002), and the survivors of a plane crash in the Andes in 1972 (Read 2005) speak to this instinct. Less to the question of individual survival and more to the issue of terrorism as a geopolitical tool is the alleged resort to cannibalism by some African peoples in their struggle against their respective colonial masters. Hence, though abhorrent to civilized man, the resort to suicide bombing in Iraq, Afghanistan, Pakistan, and Israel, is no less a manifestation of the survival instinct for the "terrorists" as alleged cannibalism was for some Africans and South Asians; the territorial imperative, if you will.

In "civilized" societies, the territorial imperative is played out in the decision-making processes within institutional frameworks that speak to a hierarchal political and socioeconomic order both domestic and international, despite liberalizing influences: the apparent preferred mode of dispute settlement by those who control the decision-making processes. For example, at the international level, as a condition for admission to the EU the essentially Muslim-Turkey must recognize Cyprus as a sovereign state which is already a member of the EU and must acknowledge the Armenian genocide allegedly committed by Turkey in 1915. In addition, the EU has threatened cancellation of aid to Turkey if it does not allow Cyprus access to its ports. Even then, the leaders of both Germany and France are opposed to having a non-Christian state as a member of the EU. These conditions and reservations speak unequivocally to territoriality.

Clearly, man has not evolved beyond his basic nature despite the passage of time, the influence of cultural interaction, and his technological achievements. Relationship with one another is still based on the primitive notion of a hierarchical social and political order, with the dominant power equipped with the military means to enforce compliance as and when required. Hence, Thucydides (1934: 334) observation, "right must give way to might; the strong will do what they can and the weak what they must"[24] is as much a characteristic of contemporary international relations as it was of Peloponnesian socio-political order.

Territoriality in Capital Accumulation

As recognized by Ardrey (1961; and 1966), land is not the only form of property that is open to constant dispute. Indeed, an ideology predicated on the endless accumulation of capital derives the capitalist world economy and attendant institutions (see Wallerstein 2005), and thus extends the notion of territoriality to access to and maintenance of property rights necessarily. Within the context of this broader definition, then, trade disputes and the various trade agreements and institutions that mediate international economic relations, not necessarily in equitable terms as one might like to think or is led to believe, are more about territoriality than about equity. In this regard, activist Vandana Shiva of India sees the WTO as an "instrument of corporate unilateralism."[25] In the same vein, the IMF and the World Bank are still widely regarded as instrumentalities of the Washington Consensus (see Chang 2006) notwithstanding the shift in emphasis from structural adjustment to poverty reduction.

While economic theory speaks of *Pareto Optimality* (see Sen 2004), reality speaks to asymmetries in agreements for economic cooperation and the exercise of compensatory and conditioned powers (see Krueger 1993; Bhagwati 1988; Galbraith 1983) by those who control the decision-making processes. It is only when entrenched Western economic interests are threatened that the notion of "level playing field" becomes part of the narrative and then only from a self-interested perspective (see Lentner 2004). For example, from America's perspective it is always the other country that is not playing by the rules, as with respect to certain Japanese and Chinese commercial and financial practices, and of competing imports from developing countries that threaten entrenched domestic interests.

In keeping with such rationalizations, leveling the playing field from an American perspective translates to imposing sanctions and other instrumentalities such as, for example, the International Labor Organization's (ILO) labor standards or other treaties even when the US has not signed on to them (see Dillon 2007). It also means raising public concern about quality and standards of imported products from countries it wants to target. From the perspective of a French wine producer, on the other hand, leveling the playing field is removing regulations and restrictions placed on French vineyards. But France's hegemony is no longer a factor despite the rhetoric for domestic consumption.

And then there are the former Russian republics as the more recent entrants to the capitalist world economy, jostling for control over access to resources and markets, both theirs and others, and attempts by the US and the EU to influence their decisions so as to protect established advantages. Russia, of course, is as much part of the fray as the US and the EU, seeking to ensure its access to markets for Russian energy resources and exercising its leverage as needed to protect its perceived rights and sphere of influence. Developing countries are not exempt either: The survival instinct in many instances often manifest in individual self-interest which tends often to take precedence over community or national territorial interests; a psychosocial flaw attendant the institution of slavery and later colonialism, and, thus, exploited by the powerful as observed by Ali Mazrui (Adem 2005: *xxvi*).

Understanding the Issues of Territoriality in the Twenty-first Century

In human interaction at the international level, there are two discernible components to territoriality: the geo-economics and the geopolitical. While both have been approached as discrete theoretical and operational issues, they are mutually reinforcing and often indistinguishable having found common expression in foreign policy. Be that as it may, the thesis of this book suggests that the geopolitical is derived from the geo-economics, with the former as instrumental rather than substantive notwithstanding that "political power" is often pursued for its own sake. Hence, as significant and all-consuming as the events in the Middle East are to the region and indeed to Americans, there is the nagging suspicion that looking beyond the play-out of self-fulfilling prophesies in Iraq, they are largely the result of the initial stages of an overarching grand strategy gone awry; a strategy that was hatched by the neoconservatives during the Reagan years (see Grandin 2006), and has as its long-term objective the containment of China's economic growth and growing geopolitical influence (see Peck 2006; Shambaugh 2005); arguably through controlling China's access to Middle East oil supplies.

Evidence of Western Anxiety

The anxiety over China's emergence as an economic rival to the West is becoming increasingly manifest in academic papers and in economic and financial presentations and policy proposals, Gerald Segal (1999) perspective notwithstanding. To be sure, apart from the crisis in the Middle East, there is no other contemporary issue more talked about than the perceived challenge posed by China in the twenty-first century (see Dillon 2007). Evidence the observation by Howard Schultz, Chairman of *Starbucks* that China's competition for energy supplies will reach critical mass in five years[26]; thus adding to other similar expressed concerns. Evidence further the increasing Western concerns expressed over China's modernization of its military and its achievements in space, and further, the announcement by British Prime Minister Blair that the UK will reintroduce the use of hard power as an option in its international relations framework. It is, therefore, no accident that the BBC in a commentary on the crisis in the Middle should refer to China's emerging hegemony in Africa and its increasing energy demands and rhetorically ask whether the *real conflict* is still to come.

Arab–Israel Conflict

Given the drive to gain, maintain, and defend manifest at the very basic level in wars among neighbors, man or beast, it is not out of definition to see the Arab–Israel conflict of the 1940s–1960s and the Israel–Lebanon issues in terms of the territorial imperative. For the most part they are all about historical lands previously walked upon by both Jews and Muslims—a bond between man and the soil if you will, despite 1800 years of absence for the Jews—that came under Arab control for centuries after the Jews were expelled by the Romans. As part of the "Promised Land", Israel clearly wants to keep as much of what it has captured in 1948 and in 1967 (see Eldad 2007: 143), whilst the Arabs would like to have it all returned to them, having paid too much in blood and dignity under European colonialism.

However you slice it, both Arabs and Jews have historical claims to settlement in the Holy Land; and the final borders eventually will be approved if not drawn by the UN. Indeed, many of the nation-states in the region are creations of colonial powers past, with their borders having no historical or legal significance other than that accorded to them by the UN and informed by Western notions of nationalism and nation-state. All either gained or declared their independence from colonial rule at about the same time. Hence, they all exist at the will of the international community that created them, as embodied in UN Mandates and Resolutions. It is therefore this perception of fluidity of borders in the region that arguably provides Israel the opportunity to challenge their legitimacy and to explore the willingness of those in control to have them redrawn. In this connection, Israel has been encouraged by European and British emotionalism (see Thatcher 1995: 372–9) and, of course, the Westernization imperative. With this in mind and given the significance of Israel's territorial imperative, the Israel–Palestine issues together with the Israel–Lebanon issues are examined more fully in Chapter Nine.

Afghanistan

The battle for Afghanistan is no less evidence of territoriality, in this instance between the Taliban and the West. Indeed, the conflict reflects the extent to which the threatened would go to gain, maintain, and defend: The West, its security and peace of mind, and very likely a foothold and thus control of oil and gas reserves in Central Asia, whilst for the Taliban it is about their historical lands, their pride, and their traditional way of life made vulnerable by the harboring of the terrorist movement al-Qaeda. It is a classic confrontation of military might on the one hand and the primal instinct of survival on the other that dates back to Alexander the Great. Evidence the words of British Prime Minister Tony Blair: "Here in this extraordinary desert is where the future of world security in the early twenty-first century is going to be played out" and "they want to test the will of NATO ... we've got to prove to them that our will is greater than theirs."[27] Forgotten in this exhortation, however, is that the battle of will is taking place in Afghanistan and not in a NATO-member country and that those under siege know it is a matter of their survival; they have been there before. Hence, while individualism reigns supreme in the West both in thought and deed, the less civilized are more likely to act in the interest of kith and kin for, as Confucius observed, men of integrity in such cultures do things differently: "a father covers up for his son, a son covers up for his father—and there is integrity in what they do." Indeed, it is instructive that the increasing death toll of Afghan civilians has prompted calls from the Afghan Parliament for negotiations with the Taliban. Also, as reported, President Karzai is finding civilian deaths from NATO bombings—reportedly over 1,600 as of May 2007—to be unacceptable and is threatening to seek a withdrawal of NATO from Afghanistan.[28]

With respect to Tony Blair's exhortation to the British troops in Afghanistan, some may be tempted to draw a parallel between the Falklands war of 1982 and the British military engagement with the Taliban: The Northwest Frontier has never really been brought under British control during the heady days of colonialism. Indeed, to many who have experienced colonialism, and to the Muslims in particular, Mr. Blair's rhetoric borders on the neo-colonial.[29] It is noteworthy also that none of the 19 terrorists that attacked the US on 9/11 was Afghan although they all had refuge and some form of training there. Nonetheless, it is well recognized that providing safe haven to terrorists is tantamount to subscribing to their ideals and in this regard the Taliban are no exception. Therefore, the desire for their destruction is an act of territoriality in the twenty-first century.

The concerns expressed over a possible resurgent Taliban and the perceived threat of a spring 2007 offensive that had the US and the UK seeking to shore up defenses from a position that was touted as offensive serve not to motivate the troops but to embolden the Taliban. In this vein, it is equaling telling that the US Vice President on his visit to Pakistan in February 2007 should "lean" on Pakistan's President Musharraf—to whom the job of fighting the Taliban in the tribal areas has been outsourced—to take on al-Qaeda[30], an organization that was pronounced all but defeated and is now believed to have formed an alliance with the Taliban.

That al-Qaeda has re-emerged as a threat in Afghanistan is seen by Zahid Hussain as not entirely in consequence of laxity on the part of Pakistan but also of US neglect.[31] In fact, the threat of terrorism rather than diminished has morphed into cells comprising recruits from the middle and educated classes in Pakistan. According to Hussain, President Musharraf's policy of appeasement towards the tribal leaders in the *Federally Administered Tribal Areas* has contributed to providing the Taliban sanctuaries where they can regroup and train to fight another day. Adding to the problem of containing al-Qaeda is the apparent lack of democratic progress and the failure to alleviate the plight of the poor in Pakistan despite annual economic growth rates of eight percent and huge debt-forgiveness by the West. However, despite these challenges, Pakistan in the eyes of Ambassador John Negroponte remains "a very committed partner in the war on terror" for obvious reasons.

Iraq

Similarly, the battle among the various factions in Iraq although billed as "sectarian violence" by those who seek to avoid the classification of "civil war" is about control over territory and rights by disparate tribal groups brought together in the early twentieth century in consequence of British imperialism. Then as now, the issue is all about territoriality; then as now, access to oil reserves in the region by the West is the prime motivation for creating and maintaining a secular Iraq premised on Western modalities; then as now, the politics of off-setting interests is the name of the game: combining the interests of the Kurds and Sunni–Arabs as counterbalance to the majority Shia–Arabs with religious ties to Iran ensures control by a power other than Iraqi.

The planners could not have been more wrong both then and now. Iraq, like Yugoslavia and Czechoslovakia, as one of the "diplomatically convenient artificial states" was destined to fail. As observed by Thatcher (1995: 525): "In the Middle East, attempts to create a unified Arab state based on an Arab nationalism that owed too much to socialism and not enough to Islam [and indeed to Sunni–Shia schism] have always come to nothing." A prophetic observation to be sure if only one would listen. As played out, the minority Sunni-Arabs in Iraq became the dominant group, capitalizing upon what Vali Nasr (2006: 108) characterizes as: "the heady days of the 1960s, when Arab nationalism was at its height ... [and] ethnic identity was a measure of loyalty to the Arab cause."

The dislike for Shia-Arabs and Iranians by Sunni–Arabs in Iraq, to be sure, manifested first in waging war against Iran so as to gain control of the oil reserves in Western Iran. Such a war was considered to be in the strategic interest of the West and thus was supported by it, particularly the US. Secondly, the mass murder of Shia–Arabs and Kurds by Saddam Hussein after having been driven out of Kuwait in the 1991 Gulf War on a change in US foreign policy was yet another example of Sunni–Arab power. However, with the collapse of the Soviet Union, Iraq under Saddam Hussein was no longer an asset to the

West; indeed he became a threat to the economic and security interests of the US and, therefore, had to be removed in keeping with the territorial imperative as perceived by the Bush administration (see Suskind 2004). Moreover, having been degraded by the first Gulf War Iraq posed no real challenge to the US military. Indeed, the sentiment expressed by members of the Bush administration was that they will finish the job the First Gulf War failed to do (see Woodward 2006).

The lack of understanding of the importance of territoriality in Iraq is evidenced in statements such as: "We gave them a government"; "we want them to be an ally in the war on terror"; and "what is needed is for the Iraqis to come together." Indeed, the general refrain is that the Kurds, Sunnis, and Shias must come together. These statements reflect the US short-term imperative for a quick solution to the crisis in Iraq and to extricating itself as quickly as possible so as to salvage the remains of its moral authority. Analyzed, they betray little or no understanding of Middle Eastern history and culture; or at the extreme, a total disregard for them. Why would the Kurds who are not Arabs, with a distinct language and way of life want to come together with Sunni–Arabs who have in recent memory committed acts of genocide against them? No one has yet offered an acceptable reason for these disparate groups to come together other than the inevitable conclusion that doing so would serve to validate a form of governance imposed from the outside; and, then, if only temporarily as history has shown (see Nasr, 2006). Moreover, if the solution were to be found in a "unitary Iraq", why should not a single state for Jews and Palestinians be the solution to the Israel–Palestine issue? Why propose the creation of a separate state for the Palestinians? The Kurds are no more Arab than the Palestinians Jewish; and the Israel–Palestinian conflict has been going on for decades whilst the crisis in Iraq is in its infancy. Hence, what we have in Iraq is the disintegration of a highly formularized neoconservative game-theoretic model where "outcome" has now been substituted for "method."

Other Locations

There are, of course, other areas around the world where territorial disputes continue to inform foreign policy: India and Pakistan over Kashmir; Armenia and Azerbaijan; Ethiopia–Eritrea; and Turkey and Greece over Cyprus, to name a few, with Cyprus interestingly yet another former British colony whose status is disputed by Turkey. The break away of East Timor from Indonesia and the continuing battle between the Tamil Tigers and the Sri Lankan government that is now over two decades old in which over 60,000 lives have been lost up to the end of 2006 are other examples of the legacy of imperialism and seemingly disinterest of the Western powers; arguably for a lack of strategic significance. The break-up of Yugoslavia and the Balkans War also were about territoriality. Interestingly, the hatred between the Serbs and the Bosnian Muslims survived four hundred years before finally erupting in separation and the mass murder of 8,000 Bosnian Muslim men by the Serbian military, the worst in Europe since the Holocaust.

Purpose and Approach

This book does not pretend to have any specific answers to our contemporary geopolitical dilemmas which must come necessarily from our individual, collective national and international introspection for, as observed by Socrates, "the unexamined life is not livable for a human being." This need for introspection has been made urgent by the events in a post 9/11 world. As observed by John Ikenberry (2004: 324):

> For the first time since the dawn of the Cold War, a new grand strategy is taking place in Washington.... America is to be less bound by its partners and to global rules and institutions ... [and] will use its unrivaled military power to manage the global order.... No coalition of great powers without the United States will be allowed to achieve hegemony.

In consequence of this and other similar observations, then, this book seeks to awaken our collective consciousness to the dangers of excesses rooted in notions of superiority and in the abuse of power in an age of growing dissatisfaction with the existing socioeconomic and political world order. To this end, it seeks to provide a 360-degree looking glass for those who would look: Highlighted, are inconsistencies in policy premised on falsehoods and ambitions, and the growing aversion to patronizing rhetoric.

It is fully expected some "experts" would readily find disagreement with the arguments advanced in this book, especially as they relate to US policy in the Middle East and to the territorial imperative imputed specifically to the US and Israel. As noted above, many would readily consider it another conspiracy theory. But interstate alliances with their secret meetings are just that: conspiracies.

Approach

In pursuing the questions posed above, this book analyses the several concerns, issues, and events past and present in context of territoriality from the perspective of the powerful and the not so powerful. The analysis is largely informed by American and Israeli narratives together with specialist reports on the play out of strategies in the Middle East, supported by scholarly expositions as necessary. As part of the exercise, it reaches back into history—albeit not exhaustively so—as a means to providing a historical context and to filling-in some of the gaps found in narrowly defined analytical models and frameworks designed around constraints of one sort or another and manifest in many high-minded academic analyses, policy papers, and more blatantly in polemics which, as noted above, have come to define discourse in the twenty-first century.

In addition to examining the conflicts in the Middle East and their consequences, it examines the rationale behind economic and financial aid, and other arrangements with state and non-state actors, overt and covert, and their outcomes and seeks to show the causal relationship with the territorial imperative. To this end, it draws a connection between "the endless accumulation of capital", the *sine qua non* of modern capitalism, and economic backwardness exemplified by the number of poor developing countries existing on the periphery and representing the low end of the socio-economic continuum. Particular attention is drawn to the pursuit of asymmetries by the more powerful states in an interstate system that has been founded on a European value system, laws, and political philosophy, and has by its very design operated to advance the fortunes of its members over the centuries. Indeed, as recognized by Lady Thatcher (1995: 524):

> The concept of the "nation" is something which makes little or no sense outside Europe, because it is itself rooted in and a construct of a long and distinctive European history.... Nationhood has to be understood in a somewhat different way in the Middle East or Far East or Africa—or even in North and South America—from in Europe.

Clearly, then, such pursuit as discussed, takes several forms: some subtle while others are less so depending on the agendas of the occupants in seats of power; all manifest in the exercise of condign, compensatory, and conditioned powers as dictated by the territorial imperative.

Organization

While a conscious attempt is made to establish some form of logical ordering to the material, each of the remaining chapters may be read independently albeit within the context of the underlying theme of territoriality and its instrumentalities: condign, compensatory, and conditioned powers. With this in mind, Part Two explains certain fundamental concepts, providing context to the analyses that follow in the remaining parts. Chapter Two draws on Newton's Third Law of Motion as it applies to human interaction. It offers a window to the exercise of condign power and the countervailing responses it elicits dating back to B.C.E. The exercise of condign power is shown at its most brutal. It offers snippets of history that have been largely ignored in current discourse on the conflicts in the Middle East and indeed in our international political and economic models but which are essential to a better understanding of our contemporary dilemmas and to freeing ourselves from our ignorance, our fears, and our prejudices. It shows that actions and countervailing reactions are inherent attributes and are no less a law of nature as Newton's Third Law of Motion is of the physical sciences. It examines the use of power and its consequences, good and bad. Emphasized is the ability of humans to look adversity squarely in the eye and to react in unpredictable ways that are often missing in game-theoretic models: the unknown unknowns, if you will. Chapter Three follows on where Chapter Two leaves off. It examines the exercise of condign power and countervailing responses to include the current conflict in the Middle East. Chapter Four examines compensatory and conditioned powers as alternatives to condign power. In this context, the extent to which compensatory and conditioned powers serve the Westernization imperative is examined primarily in context of the politics of international economic relations, with a geopolitical twist albeit. As part of the exercise, foreign aid is examined as are trade agreements and their supporting institutions. It draws a distinction between humanitarian aid and official 'development' aid, and seeks to show that official foreign aid arises partly from benevolence but primarily from self interest. The perverse side to aid is critiqued to show aid recipients as trading their competitiveness and economic independence for preferential treatment in trade agreements, grants, and other aid tied to social infrastructure. The extent to which some aid recipients have become adept at extracting aid from the developed countries and have made it the *sine qua non* of their governance is also touched on as an aspect of the process.

The emergence of China is discussed in Part Three. While it does not pretend to be an exposition on China, Chapter Five traces China's return to internationalism and to reasserting itself in the region and the wider world. It further serves to support the supposition, however improbable to some, that driving US policy in the Middle East is the perceived consequence of an emerging China which, as Huntington (1996: 313) observed, would be "contrary to American interests as they have been historically constructed."

Central to the inquiry, as would be expected, is the US experience and the Bush administration's foreign policy which are the subjects of Part Four. As articulated by the US president, it is a policy premised on the utopian idea that, "the best hope for peace in our world is the expansion of freedom in all the world"[32] which, ironically, has been described around the world increasingly as dangerous for world peace; not because freedom is inherently bad but because the Bush narrative is increasingly proving to be philosophically inconsistent and unaccommodating of "Other." Indeed, the Bush narrative has come to reflect the neoconservative notion that to predict the future you have to shape it by whatever means, including the use of force. It thus raises concern around the world; even by those it considers friends. Evidence the remarks of Russian President Putin:

> Nations are witnessing an almost uncontained hyper use of force in international relations.... One state, the United States, have overstepped its national borders in every way.... This is very dangerous. Nobody feels secure anymore because nobody can hide behind international law.[33]

Interestingly, seven months earlier in July 2006, Mr. Putin was equally unequivocal about where he stands on the Bush doctrine of preemption: "I made it clear [to Bush] that I would not be a party to any crusade or holy alliance."[34] Curiously, this response was little reported in the US, if at all, even though it clearly suggested that Mr. Bush was seeking to recruit Mr. Putin to his plan for creating a new Middle East and to supporting the declaration of war on Lebanon by Israel on 12 July 2006. These and other similar observations to the extent they speak to territoriality are examined with particular reference to US policy in the Middle East and to trade issues with the wider world. The American experience is therefore examined in Chapter Six, with an emphasis on an American economy struggling to remain number one, and is offered as a precursor to the Bush foreign policy of preemption which, in addition to exploring the notion of a grand strategy to contain China, is critiqued in Chapter Seven. Chapter Seven also provides a reasoned contemplation of the circumstances contributing to the inability of the US and its allies to successfully effect the phases of the grand strategy by way of game-theoretic models in the Middle East. In Chapter Eight, the confusing messages of the Bush administration are linked to the ever-changing conditions not only in Iraq but also in the Arab-Israel conflict of which the Palestinian issue is central.

Part Five offers a perspective on the territorial imperative of Israel, America's most important partner in the Middle East in its bid to contain an emerging China. In Chapter Nine, the Israel experience is included not as an historical account necessarily—there are numerous scholarly works available to the reader—but rather as representing a convergence of imperatives: economic and political dominance in the Middle East for the US and the West; occupation and control of the Holy Land for Israel in keeping with its long held dream, articulated as the "*Baltimore Program*" at the Baltimore Hotel in New York City in 1942 and reaffirmed by the *Atlantic City Resolution of 1944*, and adopted by the *World Zionist Organization* in London in 1945. It examines Israel's confusingly-constructed narratives on Arab–Israel peace as both supporting and feeding off the American imperative embedded in the Bush narrative.

Part Six offers a plea for tolerance of "Other" by way of a paradigm shift in the thinking of the West, in particular the US. Hence Chapter Ten argues that, despite territoriality is an instinct no less in man than in animal, human evolution and aspiration for a kinder, gentler world dictate that the combined wisdom of the peoples of the world irrespective of race, creed or color be brought to bear in the preservation of our common humanity. It rejects the narrative of hate and violence, and calls upon those in power to seek not only a better understanding of the natural forces that are at play in the twenty-first century but also to find the political will to overcome the destructive forces that have been unleashed by an aberration of history. Moreover, it calls upon the US to recognize, understand, and embrace the values and responsibilities of leadership in a pluralist world order.

NOTES

1 See "News War: Secrets, sources and spin", *Frontline*, *PBS*, February 13, 2007
2 Neumeister, L., "Judge strikes down part of Patriot Act" *Associated Press*, http://news.yahoo.com/s/ap/20070906/ap_on_re_us/patriot_act_lawsuit
3 "Spying on the home front", *Frontline, PBS.org*, May 15, 2007
4 Interview by Bill Moyers, *"Bill Moyers Journal"*, PBS.org, July 13, 2007
5 'The Dark side', *Frontline*, PBS.org
6 "Wolf Blitzer Reports: Is Iraq the next target?", *CNN*, November 19, 2001
7 '60 Minutes', *CBS News*, April 29, 2007
8 "The Case for War: In defense of freedom", included as part of "America at a Cross-roads", *Frontline*, April 17, 2007
9 Ibid.
10 Televised broadcast, October 7, 2002
11 Address to UN Security Council, February 5, 2003. Secretary Powell, who has since claimed to have been misled to his credit has apologized for misleading the world at that meeting.
12 Dickey, C., "Death of a Tyrant", *Newsweek*, January 8, 2007, p. 22
13 "Buying the War", *Bill Moyer Journal, PBS.org*, April 25, 2007
14 Ibid.
15 "The Duelfer Report on Iraq Weapons: Key Findings", October 6, 2004
16 "Blair makes Partial Iraq Apology to Win Back Party", http://news.yahoo.com/s/nm/20040928/wl_nm/britain_blair_dc
17 "News Hour", *PBS.org*, April 30, 2007
18 "The Case for War: In defense of freedom", included as part of "America at a Cross-roads", *Frontline*, April 17, 2007
19 "Accuracy of Battlefield Information", House Oversight and Government Reform Committee, *C-SPAN*, April 24, 2007
20 "Iraqi Benchmark Report", US Foreign Relations committee, *C-SPAN*, September 4, 2007
21 "The Case for War: In defense of freedom", included as part of "America at a Cross-roads", *Frontline*, April 17, 2007
22 'Bill Moyers Journal', *PBS.org*, April 27, 2007
23 See Mearsheimer and Walt 'The Israel Lobby', Letters, *London Review of Books, Vol. 28, No.9*, May 11, 2006
24 "The Peloponnesian War", (NY: Modern Library)
25 Salmon, P., "Globalization", News Hour, *PBS.org*, March 23, 2007
26 "American Perspectives", *C-SPAN*, January 16, 2007
27 Televised News Conference in Afghanistan, November 20, 2006
28 Woodruf, J. , 'News Hour', *PBS.org*, May 9, 2007
29 Khouri, R, American University of Beirut, *BBC World*, May 9, 2007
30 Graham, S., "Cheney asks Musharraf to fight al-Qaeda", *The Associated Press*, February 26, 2007
31 "New American Foundation", *C-SPAN*, March 19, 2007
32 Excerpt from the President's Inaugural Address in January 2005.
33 "Putin attacks 'very dangerous' US", *BBC World Service*, February 10, 2007
34 Joint Bush/Putin televised Press conference in St. Petersburg, July 10, 2006

Part Two

Fundamental Laws, Precepts, and Concepts

Chapter Two

Fundamental Laws and Precepts

Introduction

In addition to the notions of territoriality and the territorial imperative, there are three principles or beliefs that serve to inform this book. The first is the importance of language in defining self and others, and in conveying meaning to others; the second is Newton's Third Law of Motion; and the third, is the Buddhist belief that we seek knowledge to free ourselves from our ignorance, our prejudices and our fears. This chapter seeks to show that language often betrays our agendas and that understanding Newton's Law of action and reaction goes a long way to satisfying the Buddhist knowledge-imperative and to ameliorating the impact of language in conflict situations.

Our Vocabulary Reflects Our Interests

Despite the feel-good rhetoric, we do appear to be living in interesting times and, therefore, as Wallerstein (2005: 1) admonishes us: "We need to confront directly how we have come to think the way we do so that we can begin to liberate ourselves to think in ways that permit us to analyze more cogently and more usefully our contemporary dilemmas." To this end, as Honi Haber (1994) reminds us, our vocabularies being products of our culture and conditioning almost always reflect our interest and therefore mirror our political perspectives. Moreover: "Our prejudices become dangerous only when they are dogmatic, kept hidden from view and not open to discussion." In this regard, two excerpts of Prime Minister Blair's rhetoric on the Iraq war are instructive: "In the end, it is not our power alone that would defeat this *evil.* Our ultimate weapon is not our guns but *our belief*"[1]; and "the mission is a struggle between *freedom and democracy* on the one hand and *terrorism and sectarianism* on the other.... And it is a *noble* mission.... And it is important for *our world* that it succeeds" [emphasis added].[2]

Clearly, the differential logic of language could hardly be missed in Mr. Blair's expressions. Indeed, the binary distinction evident in his statements forecloses accommodation of an alternative perspective, that is, if you are not for "freedom and democracy", then you are for terrorism; strangely enough, not dissimilar to Mr. Bush's "either you are with us or you are for the enemy." Moreover, Blair's pronouncements, with religious undertones not dissimilar to the Bush pronouncements, cross the boundary between the purely private and the public in political discourse, and evidences the extent to which personal value systems permeate public and foreign policy; or at the extreme, the extent to which religion has been accessed as a source of power in the Westernization imperative. Either way, as with Mr. Bush's binary distinction, Mr. Blair's language draws a false distinction in context of the current international political framework that recognizes "difference"—race, ethnicity, religion, short, tall and the like—as fundamental to a pluralist world and thus has been largely rejected.[3] In addition, we need to recognize that in the fast-paced and competitive world in which we live, the errors we make in our thinking are often if not the result of contrivance then certainly of curtailing the all important dialogue in our quest for significance. In other words, the *clash of civilizations* as implied in the existential narratives is a self-fulfilling prophesy of those who wittingly or unwittingly situate the current crisis in the Middle East in a clash of culture.

The above notwithstanding, given that language is "potentially an infinite system of signs" the narrative construction of "freedom"; "democracy"; "capitalism"; and "victory" to name a few, could always be re-described in terms of alternative perspectives. Thus we arrive at "socialist democracy", "multiculturalism", and the like when there is accommodation in our language. Even in perceived existential cases, the possibility for re-description exists. For example, "victory in Iraq" has since been re-described by the Bush administration as "success in Iraq" and, therefore, indicative of accommodation of something less than the earlier declared desired outcome. Indeed, many would point to the arming of some Sunni–Iraqis to help fight al-Qaeda in Iraq as just such accommodation; others, on the other hand could interpret the change as a manifestation of weakness in terms of offense-defense theory (see Van Evera 2004: 46).

Newton's Third Law of Motion

Newton's Third Law of Motion that says every action has an equal and opposite reaction is an immutable law. Although it is a law not of nature but of physics it is applicable to human interaction, albeit not always to the same degree of certainty or indeed predictability. Indeed, as observed by Galbraith (1983: 74):

> We may lay it down as a rule that almost any manifestation of power will induce an opposite, though not necessarily equal, manifestation of power. Any effort to bend people to the will of others will encounter in some form an effort to resist that submission.

Hence, when examined in context of territoriality there is a discernible symmetry between instruments of enforcement and the degree of resistance, with winning for the powerful—survival for others—as the ultimate determinant as discussed below.

The Role of Oppositional Politics

Interestingly, changing one's perspective appears not to be automatic. Rather, it is seemingly derived from oppositional politics. President Bush accepted the second version of the Iraq War Funding Bill—having vetoed the first—not entirely because time-lines for troop withdrawal were deleted (it was only one of his objections to the first Bill); rather, it was because of the growing perception that the war in Iraq in the words of Senator Chuck Hagel, is a "disaster", and the equally growing opposition to it from members of his own political party.

Similarly, Prime Minister Olmert's recent overtures to the Arabs—albeit conditioned, as usual—is not because he truly wants to bring the Israel–Palestinian conflict to an end at any price; rather it is because he is under siege at home—with a nine percent approval rating—for failing to secure the freedom of the two Israeli soldiers captured by Hezbollah in the summer 2006 despite a massive military assault on Lebanon. For Mr. Olmert, the "adventure" in Lebanon was a costly mistake as discussed more fully in Chapter Nine.

Yet another example of oppositional politics is the agreement reached with North Korea, one of the "Axis of evil". One could attribute the substantial progress made in resolving the North Korean nuclear issue to the interplay of oppositional politics: The North Koreans get their US$25.0 million unfrozen by the US, delivery of food and other aid, and though unwritten, respect and a possible peace treaty; the US gets the "shut down" of North Korea's nuclear reactor in a framework of multilateral negotiations, as opposed to a bilateral agreement.

From these examples, it is clear that in terms of hostile interaction, as observed by Van Evera (2004: 47): "When conquest is hard, states are dissuaded from aggression by the fear that victory will prove costly and unattainable." Recall that, Fatah was considered a terrorist organization, with several of its members either in Israeli prisons or are identified as wanted terrorists, yet Israel is now prepared to negotiate with the umbrella *Palestinian Liberation Organization* (PLO). In the case of North Korea, trading insults at the highest levels has given way to establishing bilateral working groups, in the face of a nuclear-armed—however primitive—North Korea, lending credence to deterrence theory.

There are, of course, other accounts of the effectiveness of oppositional politics in reversing seemingly entrenched and unbending positions. One has only to review the history of opposition to colonial rule, especially in Africa as well chronicled by Ali Mazrui in *The Africans,* and the scholarly works of Samir Amin (2006) to fully understand and appreciate the importance of oppositional politics in international relations, from the perspective of the oppressed.

Opportunity for Good

The discrepancy between action and reaction or between power and countervailing power, if you will, presents dominant states with a window of opportunity for good or evil in their relationship with others; the choice of either depends crucially on intentions on the one hand and the capacity and willingness to actualize them in either direction, on the other. History has enshrined numerous accounts of both capacity and political will notwithstanding attempts at rewrite and in some cases erasure of the evidence at various points in time. It is for this reason alone that many countries have legislated against the denial of the Holocaust which exemplifies intention, capacity, and political will at their very worst in human interaction.

With respect to good intentions, the natural expectation is for reciprocity as a reaction which usually is forthcoming. Good, then, often begets good and becomes the basis for community formation and good neighbors. While the vogue of opportunists in America since 9/11 is to demonize Muslims and Islam, it needs remembering that although southern Spain, in particular Granada, was under Muslim rule for centuries, Christian, Jews, and Muslims lived in an environment of relative harmony that would be envied by many so-called pluralist societies in the twenty-first century. That it came to an end was not because the Muslims wanted absolute power as is being asserted in rewrites but partly because of the fall of the Caliphate in the Iberian Peninsula and partly because of the later ambitions of Ferdinand and Isabella who capitalized upon the vulnerability of the Church and created an imperial Spain (see Craig, 2002). Curiously, the Jews fought with the Christians against the Muslims with the expectation that they would be integrated into a Christian-Spain; they were later expelled by the Spanish who wanted an all-Christian society. Jewish conversion to Christianity was maliciously revealed as a sham, rendering the "new-Christians" to expulsion.

There are numerous examples of Western goodness resulting from what is often referred to as a good decent Christian upbringing: Many in the Christian West have responded to the needs of others while many still have sacrificed in the name of humanity. That Americans as a rule are generous people has been proven time and time again. But, in a world in which the endless accumulation of capital is held out as paramount even good deeds are often viewed as weaknesses and, therefore, are seen as opportunities to exploit if not to plunder, especially when "difference" informs judgment. These latter consequences of good intentions speak to Max Weber's observation that, it is not whether intentions are good or bad but the consequences that matter.

The New World

As recognized by St. Augustine some 1600 years earlier, "even if a war is initiated by a legitimate authority and its cause is just, it can become unjust because of evil intentions" (Sigmund, 1988: 65).

The New World was founded on the good Christian intentions of saving souls. In reality, it was essentially a case of Spanish adventurers first exploiting the generosity of the vulnerable natives and later destroying their communities because they were different and thus were regarded as savages. In North America, such exploitation was couched in the vocabulary of racial supremacy: the Manifest Destiny of "Euro-Americans ... a people chosen by God" to control the lands between the Atlantic and the Pacific, bringing "civilization and democratic institutions to a wilderness" (Heidenrich, 2007: 75). In this pursuit, Anglo-American imperialism was rationalized as a "right to defend"—a still familiar phrase in the twenty-first century—while the reality was a systematic destruction of the weak and eventual confiscation of their lands attendant conquest. The Tall Grass Prairie was settled by white settlers in consequence of the Blackhawk War of 1832. The "Bear Flag Incident" as retold by Chicana/o historians, in particular Antonia Castaneda, "provided a counter-narrative to romanticized stories of the mission era and to the still dominant narratives of Manifest Destiny." (Heidenrich 2007: 76).

The massacre at Wounded Knee in 1876 contrasts most vividly and poignantly with the romanticized Hollywood version of the *Alamo*: as Brown (2001) tells it, it was the last desperate attempt by the great Sioux nation led by Chief Sitting Bull to escape annihilation. Equally poignant, is Chief Joseph's last desperate attempt to get his people to safety across the US–Canada border in the middle of winter. It is also in the continued belief that Native Americans are a conquered people that, in 2007, according to Senator Bryon Dorgan of North Dakota, Chairman of the *US Senate Indian Affairs Committee*, they are subject to "healthcare rationing" and suffer from diseases such as tuberculosis and alcoholism in numbers four or more times greater than non-native Americans[4]. American notion of frontier went beyond the boundaries set by the Eastern rim of the Pacific Ocean as evidenced by the Philippine–American war in the last decade of the nineteenth century (see Silbey 2006).

Returning to the defense of the Alamo, when stripped of the romanticism invested by Hollywood, it was in reality in support of a break-away Mexican state which later was over-run by Anglo-Americans, as indeed were the other south-western states and California. It is also from this early violent history—despite attempts at erasures which is a corollary of conquest—that the US sees itself as continuously vulnerable to attack. Hence, it is in this rationalized if mythological notion of being on the right side of history that the Bush doctrine of preemption arguably resides. But, it is this psychological make-up of a country largely in denial of its own territorial imperative and in a perceived hurry to be the epitome of history that compels it to walk a thin line between competitiveness and unilateral aggression in a world that expects respect for international institutions and for diversity. It is this "schizophrenic self" that arguably is America's that brings it into conflict with older, matured, slower, and assumed backward societies. Not surprisingly, as observed by Temple University David Silbey: "We go to great lengths of creating conflicts."

In South America and beyond, it was Christianity proselytized by the Conquistadors with the Bible in one hand and the "sword" in the other. Either way, whole societies were dehumanized, degraded or destroyed by European invaders in search of riches to fund their wars with one another whilst ostensibly saving the souls of savages (see Heidenrich 2007). Hence, while Columbus Day is celebrated in the US, Hispanic Americans treat it as a day of veneration to their ancestors. Similarly, Native Americans view Thanksgiving not as a day of celebration but as a day of mourning: Plymouth Rock represents to them the beginning of the end to their society, their forgotten way of life.

Asia and Africa were not spared from European deception and conquest either. The British gun boats sailing up the Yangtze River to force the Chinese to become dope addicts—the Opium War (1839–42)—and the plunder of Africa are all well documented. Almost every imperial European nation sought to control a piece of China and Africa; first through friendly overtures and later by the proverbial sword. Returning conquerors were showered with honors and titles in recognition for their contribution to empire; plantations were later established and manned by slaves to ensure the free flow of precious stones, gold and other minerals, sugar, and other raw materials to fuel the industrial revolution. Hence, whilst Adam Smith in 1776 correctly assessed the contribution of the market to the wealth of nations, the contribution from colonization as a political and economic system is likely greater. This is the reality of empire.

Clearly, Newton's law failed to apply to the early adventures of the Europeans. There was no native response equal to Spanish muskets and the repeating rifles and Gatlin guns of the "Blue Coats" that dropped Native Americans like flies; or indeed to the British and French fire power, not to mention the diseases that accompanied invasion. Not that there were no inter-tribal wars on either continent or indeed elsewhere in the world. Far from it! There are numerous accounts of tribal wars but these were largely among foes of similar if not equal means and no doubt temperament and approaches, with their own rules of engagement. Often, the enemy was manifestly evident, not clothed in pretensions of goodness, the Peloponnesian Wars notwithstanding. Moreover, many such wars were fought to unify factions as a means to nation-building. Examples of such wars are those waged by the Chinese Emperor Qin (Ch'in) some 2,500 years ago, the several internal wars in England and France and, of course, the US Civil War, to name a few.

Opportunity for Evil

Just as there are windows of opportunity for good, there are windows of opportunity for evil in the imbalance between action and reaction in human interaction. Philosophies have been written in support of ruthless pragmatism, chief among which is Machiavelli's *The Prince*: "When trouble is sensed well in advance it can be easily remedied; if you wait for it to show itself any medicine will be too late because the disease will have become incurable." Destroying the opposition before it becomes a "disease" has become embedded in Western culture, especially in American culture, and arguably informs the doctrine of "preemptive strike" which the US reserves to itself but which is increasingly being questioned in international organizations such as the UN despite being threatened to be made "irrelevant". Yet, as is fully recognized by other stakeholders in a pluralist world and by dispassionate scholars within and without the US, such predisposition to the abuse of power as exemplified by the US-led invasion of Iraq in March 2003 speaks to the need for national and international political accountability as a first-order requirement. As observed by Harvard Professor, Father Bryan Hehir: "When you have a super power of enormous capability, it is not a bad idea to place it in a framework of law and policy, moral argument and legal argument and force it to justify what it should do." More direct was the late Arthur Schlesinger's observation in 2004 that the Bush administration's resort to the doctrine of preemption places it in the position of "judge, jury and executioner."[5] Schlesinger is not alone. G. John Ikenberry (2004: 325–6) likened the Bush doctrine of preemption to Israel's bombing of the Iraqi nuclear reactor at Osirak in 1981: claimed as self-defense by Israel but condemned in the UN, even by the US, as "an act of aggression."

Triumph of Truth over Politics

But even when there is an international framework of law and policy in place, such as the UN Security Council, the ability to hijack the process has been clearly demonstrated by either threatening the existence of that body as noted above or by compromising the integrity of the process by securing acquiescence if not compliance through resort to an over-sized line of credit. Even at home in the US where law and policy are institutionalized, acquiescence is secured arguably through a process of intimidation and attempts at disparagement. Hence, the narrative that seeks to divide Americans and the world—"either you are with us or you are with the enemy", a binary distinction invoked to secure support for the invasion of Iraq by preying upon emotional vulnerability and patriotism—will not escape the annals of history as evidencing intimidation on the one hand, and opposition, albeit delayed, on the other.

While every one in America supported the Bush administration in its assault on the strongholds of al-Qaeda in Afghanistan, the known perpetrators of 9/11, few at home and abroad suspected the falsehood of the administration's claims, supported by faulty British intelligence, that Iraq had WMD and the assertion by the then National Security Adviser Condoleezza Rice that Iraq poses the threat of a "mushroom cloud" over US cities. More egregious to concerned-Americans is the Bush Republican campaign assertion in 2006 that, "a vote for the Democrats is a vote for protecting the terrorists" and the oblique accusation implicit in the statement: "Not that they [the Democrats] are unpatriotic, they are just wrong".

It should be of no surprise that the Iraq Study Group (ISG) should emphasize a political and diplomatic approach to solving the crisis in the Middle East. These events and the loss of control of the House and Senate by the Republicans on November 7, 2006 and thus support for the Administration's Iraq policy, represent the triumph of truth over politics. Once again, Ardrey (1966: 237) sheds some light on this time-recurring phenomenon: "While the master politician seems acutely aware of how far the forces of outward antagonism will go toward unifying his own people in support of his rule, history offers few evidences that he is equally aware of what the same forces will accomplish with his enemies"; so it was with the Vietnam War, and so it is with Iraq in 2007. Indeed, one of the analects of Confucianism is: "The moral power of the gentleman is the wind; the moral power of the people is the grass. The grass will always bend in the direction of the wind. Hence, if you yourself desire what is good, the people will be good." It is perhaps ironic that Captain America, the famous comic strip hero who embodied the virtues of Americanism, should die in 2007; he was created during World War II in response to the tyranny of Hitler.

Terrorism is not Uniquely Muslim

Since the tragedy of 9/11, terrorism has been made a household word in America, with Americans encouraged to believe that all Muslims are either terrorists or potential terrorists. Indeed, the opportunists with personal and public agendas anchored in nationalism and capital accumulation, have sought to capitalize upon this American tragedy by seeking to fan the flames of hate against Muslims. In consequence, in the same way "Cathar" became synonymous with "heretic" in early thirteenth-century Catholic France, "Muslim" is fast becoming synonymous with "terrorist" in twenty-first century America. But as discussed below terrorism is not uniquely Muslim, neither is the majority of Muslims potential terrorists. Nonetheless, this misperception remains, indeed often utilized perversely for political reasons; and in this the American people and the notions of pluralism are ill-served. More importantly, the so-called ideological war of the twenty-first century is a self-fulfilling prophesy of the Bush administration. To understand this we need to look back in history; beyond rhetoric, beyond polemics, beyond hate; and beyond media sound-bites.

According to Walter Laqueur (2004: 450), terrorism can be traced throughout the ages to, "fanatical believers driven to despair by intolerable conditions" with the objective of sowing fear and panic, not as an end but as a means to bring about political change (see also Jenkins 2004). In this regard, the *Irish Republican Army* (IRA), the Basque separatist group ETA, and the Sri Lankan-Tamil Tigers are no less terrorist organizations than Hamas or Hezbollah. Timothy McVeigh was a home-grown American Christian terrorist whose act of terrorism was directed at the system; his grievances according to Laqueur (2004: 451) were: "the grievances of *The Turner Diaries*, of America taken over by foreigners and degenerates, of the holy duty of all patriots to cleanse the country in a river of blood—in short, the worldview of a virulent form of fascism." Hence, what is discernible is that the methods of terrorism as countervailing responses have evolved in keeping with the available means: McVeigh used chemical fertilizer whilst the Muslim terrorists resort to suicide bombs; the effects are the same (see Jenkins 2004); neither is acceptable in a world of laws and justice.

There is, however, one fundamental difference between the terrorists of yesteryear and the terrorists of the twenty-first century: whilst the former were basically localized, the latter are internationalized and, according to Jenkins (2004: 79), pursue terrorism not to commit mass murder but rather to "inspire and manipulate fear to achieve a variety of purposes" and, as such, supports a theory of international terrorism. Strangely enough, in keeping with this definition, many would consider "Shock and Awe" by its very construct—psychological intimidation of the opponent—as a form of terrorism to the extent that its intention is to destroy the opponent's will to fight by means of a spectacular and overwhelming display of military might (Compton 2005: 44).

In seeking to demonize Muslims, some "experts" have pointed to the fact that the Prophet Muhammad wielded a sword. Not mentioned, of course, is that the sword was wielded against polytheism, corruption, and evil-doers, in bringing monotheism to the Muslims in the seventh century (see Armstrong, 2006). Moreover, long before Muhammad, St. Augustine some 300 years before wrote: "For the true followers of God even wars are peaceful if they are waged not out of greed or cruelty but for the sake of peace, to restrain the evildoers and assist the good" (Sigmund, 1988: 65). There is much in Muhammad's thoughts and deeds that speaks to St. Augustine's definition of a just war, gainsayers notwithstanding. Also, despite the trend to cast Islam in the darkest light, it should be noted that "forced conversion to Islam was unusual" (Spodek 2006: 376), indeed, the practice was to offer *dhimmi* status to non-Muslims, that is, as worshippers of one God who accepted Muslim rule; and this was only after their "open-door approach" put them in the position of being minority ruler. Jews did not have to identify themselves by wearing yellow crosses or yellow hats or yellow stars as they were compelled to do in a conflicted Christian Europe. While the idea of *dhimmi* status is unacceptable in the modern world, it would be anachronistic to impute twenty-first century notions of democracy to ancient societies. Moreover, democracy developed and flourished in homogenous societies; it is yet to prove itself in a plural society.

Apart from unifying the Muslims in the seventh century in praise of monotheism, it is noteworthy that Muhammad allowed the Jews to return to the Holy City for the first time since they were exiled by the Romans in 135 C.E. (Spodek, 2006: 376). Why? Because, according to Robert Ardrey (1966: 307): "Despite all the indignities heaped upon him, Mohammed out of respect for Jewish and Christian religions decreed him a 'people of the book'." The book is, of course, the Torah[6] which Cyrus II of Persia insisted that Ezra take with him to reinstruct the Jewish people and to ensure they live by it on their return to Judaea in 538 B.C.E. The Jews having been enslaved by the Babylonians were freed by Cyrus II who also restored the gold and silver that had been taken away from them by the Babylonians (Spodek 2006: 136–7). Those who stayed on in Babylonia were equally free to travel and trade along the cultural and trade networks established by the Persians in the sixth century B.C.E. They were also allowed to build synagogues and worship as they please while rebuilding their temple.

Equally noteworthy is that, prior to the First Crusade (1095 C.E.), Muslims, Jews, and Christians lived side by side in peace in the Holy City after it was captured by Muhammad in 638 C.E. Also, Muslims, Jews, and Christians as noted above lived in harmony in Spain for centuries before the Spanish Inquisition of 1478. They would never again live in harmony with the Catholic Christians in Europe despite an eagerness to identify with imperial Spain. Indeed, Jews were persecuted by the Inquisition for centuries, right up to the middle of the nineteenth century even though they banded with the Christians to defeat the Muslims who had for the most part throughout their history treated them with respect. Hence, for most of their history since the death of King Solomon and the splitting of the kingdom of David into two kingdoms—the kingdom of Israel and the kingdom of Judaea—the Jewish people have been a Diaspora and traumatized (See Eldad, 2007).

But despite the several accounts of accommodation and respect accorded the Jewish people by the early Muslims there are those who unabashedly if not maliciously seek to denigrate the Prophet Muhammad and Islam. The most egregious of all, is to insinuate that the Prophet Muhammad was a pedophile by drawing attention to his marriage to a girl under ten years old; an obvious example of anachronism clearly designed to be malicious as if Jewish amity in the twenty-first century depends on Muslim enmity. Ignored, is that some 700 years after the death of Muhammad, child marriage was still a practice even among European nobility. For example, Henry Tudor, who became Henry VII of England in the late fifteenth century, was born to the 13 year-old Margaret who was married to his father when she was nine years old. Sadly, such hate-mongering which finds expression through those who seem unhappy with themselves serves only to cause reflection on their long history of disagreeableness (see Birmingham 2006; Feldman 1978; Ardrey, 1966). Many are still to discover that it is not necessary to hate what you are not to love who you are.

Terrorism and the Territorial Imperative

Almost every nation that pursued an expansionist policy resorted to the most brutal form of violence, if only to, yes, terrorize the opposition. Hence, terrorism has been with us since the beginning of history and is not a singularity of Islam as some are at pains to condition us to believe. Moreover, terrorism takes many forms. The early conquerors: Spartans, Athenians, Attila, the Romans, Genghis Khan, and others embraced brutality in the extreme. To serve the warrior-elite of Sparta, an entire society was conquered and enslaved in 650 B.C.E. In the conquest of Melos in 415 B.C.E. the Athenians killed every male of fighting age and sold the women and children into slavery. The Romans were no exception to brutality as a means to conquest: Their "New Wisdom" of brute force became a policy toward their enemies (Spodek, 2006: 166). The Knights Templar and the crusader king Richard I were no less brutal and "terroristic" in their respective bids to recapture the Holy City of Jerusalem from the Muslims who were themselves unified by Muhammad in the seventh century by, yes, the sword as noted above. Interestingly, it is instructive that, according to Neil Hamilton (1995: 42), David Ben-Gurion, the founder of Israel, "waged a terrorist campaign against the British" in the years preceding Israel's declaration as an independent state.

The Christian Crusades

The early example of sectarian coexistence in the Holy City quoted above lasted for 461 years under Muslim rule until it was shattered when every man, woman, and child—Christian, Muslim, and Jew—was slaughtered by the Knights Templar who dubbed themselves the poor soldiers of Christ. Indeed, the Jews in the Rhineland were the first to experience brutality committed in the name of Christ; the Jewish Chronicles referred to the "*Council of Clairmont*" called by Pope Urban II in 1095 which indirectly authorized the First Crusade, as *Har Afel* ("the Mount of Gloom") (see Murray 2006: *xliii*; Andrea 2003: 185).

The mass be-heading of over 3000 Muslim prisoners of war by the crusader Richard I in the Third Crusade (1189–92) to save on ration in his campaign to recapture Jerusalem was regarded even in those days as equal in savagery reminiscent of the Dark Ages, and committed in the name of God no less. Moreover, in contrast to the humane treatment afforded to crusaders captured by the Muslim *Salah al-Din* (Saladin), Richard I in his attempt to recapture Jerusalem is recorded as having massacred the men, women and children of Acre; more brutal than the Athenians in their conquest of Melos in 415 B.C.E., some sixteen hundred years earlier. About a hundred years later, in 1291, the Muslims recaptured Acre, giving birth to the Ottoman Empire (Slack 2003: 2).

The Crusades to the Holy Land in the middle of the thirteenth century were sponsored by Kings and Emperors, with Louis IX of France, Emperor Baldwin II of Constantinople, and Henry of England as primary sponsors. Indeed, King

Henry took the Crusade vows at Westminster Abbey in 1250 (see Slack, 2003: 112). The unleashing of the Crusaders upon "heretics" in Medieval Europe by Pope Innocent III was equally brutal and, "as among the darkest blots on the record of mankind, revealing a ferocity unknown in any beast" (attributed to Will Durant, "The Age of Faith", p. 784).

To many Muslims whose sensitivity is clearly in overdrive, then, Pope Benedict XVI's reference to a fourteenth-century Byzantine ruler's attribution to Islam the war waged by Arab politicians who took advantage of the exhausted Persian and Byzantium empires to build an empire of their own after the death of the Prophet Muhammad (see Armstrong, 2006)[7] as evidencing the violence of Islam was ill timed; more so since the Pope appeared conspicuously silent on the recorded atrocities of the Inquisitions that lasted from the Middle Ages to the middle of the nineteenth century, and the Christian crusades to the Holy Land. Recall, the First Crusade was initiated by Pope Urban II who for political reasons responded to the call from the Byzantine emperor Alexius I for help to fight the Muslims and re-capture Jerusalem and the Holy Land (see Spodek, 2006: 377; see also Slack, 2003). Also, as detailed in history, the rallying call of the crusaders in all their brutality in hunting down heretics in Europe was "God wilts it" while enriching their coffers and consolidating the power of the Church. While the Holy Father has since sought to appease Muslims, the unintended message of his lecture unfortunately remains with an overly sensitive group, understandably so given the times, and cannot be explained away by logic. Pragmatically, however, when examined in the context of territoriality, the Holy Father's comments convey an equal concern for the waning influence of Western ideology and thus the influence of the Church. In this connection, it is instructive that the Pope should visit Brazil in 2007 in an effort to arrest the decline in the influence of the Church in that country. It is equally instructive that he should seek to draw a distinction between the Catholic Church and popular expositions of Christianity, especially in America.

Medieval History Beyond the Crusades

It should be remembered also, the Jews were driven out of Spain in 1492 not by the Muslims but by the Christian Spanish rulers who had the Roman Catholic Church establish the Spanish Inquisition in 1478 to hunt down both Jews and Muslims even though many Jews had converted to Christianity and contributed to Spain's war against the Muslims while profiting from their status as "new Christians" (see Jones 1998). Under the direction of the first Grand Inquisitor, *Tomás de Torquemada,* "about 2000 [Jews] were burned at the stake" (Spodek, 2006: 379) while the others fled; Muslims too were expelled totally from Spain between 1499 and 1500. It is therefore not surprising that, with respect to the persecution of the Jewish people Ardrey (1966: 307) should observe: "Through all Christian lands his fate was a harsh one; perhaps Christian amity demanded an enemy to complete its own complex." But the Jews were not the only ones persecuted during this period in history.

During the reign of Oliver Cromwell, 3000 Irish were burned to death in the castle in which they sought refuge. Scotland was conquered by the English by an equal measure of brutality with the massacre of 38 members of the Clan McDonald at Glencoe in 1691 by order of King William III as a warning to other clans; both evidence the measure of man's inhumanity to man in civilized societies. On Guam, Chamorro males were put to death by Magellan as a means to removing opposition to Spanish conquest of the Pacific Islands and the Philippines. The US was also born out of violence and recorded brutality on both sides, with accounts of pregnant women bayoneted by the "Red Coats" while similar atrocities in countervailing actions were perpetrated by the "patriots" who would be considered "terrorists" in today's vocabulary.

Twentieth–century Atrocities

Unequalled, and hopefully never to be repeated, although there have been almost close parallels since, is the most heinous crime perpetrated in living memory by Hitler and his civilized German elite against the Jewish people who represented "difference", the "Other", within European society. Hitler's intentions were foretold in *Mien Kamph*—long removed from many bookshelves around the world —with little attention given to it by the victors of World War I. His admiration for the Spartan practice of eugenics manifested in the Holocaust: Much like the reign of terror perpetrated by Sparta's armed youths, Hitler's Brown Shirts terrorized Jews and non-Arians and yes, dissidents. While the US and UK dithered—the British constrained by the acts of violence against Jewish immigrants to Palestine—and refused to accept the European Jews in any great numbers in the years preceding the outbreak of war, it was an obscure Japanese diplomat in Russia who against his government's policy reportedly issued visas to thousands of Jews seeking refuge from persecution and ultimately extermination. As it turned out, it was a drop in the bucket; nonetheless it evidences inaction by those who could have prevented the Holocaust.

Even after the Holocaust, as Ardrey (1966: 309) recalled: "in America immediately after World War II anti-Semitism reached peaks never before attained, despite all Nazi contributions to our universal conscience." To be sure, many Jews in the UK, for example, changed their Jewish names to Christian last names to avoid being identified as Jewish. Ironically, what stunned the world in 1948, according to Ardrey (1966: 309), "were the photographs of dead Arabs, not cremated Jews" and the realization that, "Jews could behave just like anyone else" when the need arises. But even before 1948, Jewish inclination to violence was evident. As leader of Mapai, David Ben-Gurion according to Hamilton (1995: 42): "waged a terrorist campaign against the British" who had restricted Jewish immigration to Palestine as a result of growing Arab violence against Jewish immigrants, even when they were at the Wailing Wall. In addition, the

Baltimore Program of 1942 and the *Atlantic City Resolution of 1944* were unambiguous about the use of force against Arabs, despite denial to the contrary by propagandists bent on dehumanizing Arabs, as more fully discussed in Chapter Nine.

While the West vowed to prevent genocide from rearing its ugly head again, witnessed in 1994 was one of the most brutal forms of genocide committed by one tribe against another on the African continent while the "civilized" world looked on. Over one million men, women, and children were murdered in the most horrific manner in consequence of the misguided notion of empire past; it exemplified the territorial imperative at its most brutal. It also evidences the consequence of inaction by those who have the power to intervene for good. To his credit, former President Clinton accepts responsibility for not acting on a timely basis. According to him, it is one of his regrets as president.[8] He seeks to make amends to the Rwandans by being contrite and to devoting some of his energies towards building a better society for the survivors.

Devine Intervention, Primal Instinct or Historical Determinism?

The above accounts of atrocities notwithstanding, history is replete with extreme cases where conquest was the overarching objective yet failed despite possession of overwhelmingly superior military assets. The most recent example is, of course, the Vietnam War. Despite a bombing campaign that surpassed all the bombs dropped in World War II in quantity and destructive power, the North Vietnamese emerged victorious; victorious simply by surviving as a people, with dignity that allows them to be forgiving to the US as a country largely made up of good people; to be a member of the WTO a little more than three decades after. The Japanese also survived the destruction visited upon them by two atomic bombs, the only use of a weapon of mass destruction and ironically by, yes, the US. The rationalization for the use of such weapons is for the historians to debate; nonetheless, the reader is directed to Louis Morton's chapter, *The Decision to Use the Bomb* in Art and Waltz (2004: 165–180). Suffice it to say that, as the second largest economy in the world Japan also is considered victorious. Moreover, for over 50 years the Japanese embraced peace with the fervor and dedication that is essentially Japanese. One might argue that the Japanese had to be brought out of their isolationist notion of superiority (see Sansom 2004: 153–164); yet, we seem unable to draw any lesson from their mistake.

Returning to ancient times, despite the mass murder of his Muslim prisoners of war and the massacre at Acre, Richard I failed to recapture the Holy City. Although within 12 miles of Jerusalem he could not hold his army together for the final assault on a weakly defended city; he reportedly was also troubled by his own cruelty. As a result, Richard made truce with *Salah al-Din* (Murray

2006: *li*). Before him, in the third century B.C.E. Alexander the Great fresh from his conquest of the Persian Empire could not get his troops to complete the conquest of India (Spodek, 2006: 156). Before Alexander, the Syracusians defeated the powerful Athenian fleet of triremes because of the omen the latter ascribed to the eclipse of the moon; and before that, the much smaller and presumed-weaker Athenian fleet defeated the great Persian Empire on its march to conquest. Similarly, for whatever reason Hitler failed to follow through on his attack on British forces on the beaches of Dunkirk; some have argued he would have broken the spirits of the British people had he done so; but Churchill prevailed. Hitler also failed to utilize the feared and efficient Panzer regiment when he had the clear advantage. One might be tempted to attribute such lapses or failures to Divine intervention while others would attribute them to the overpowering aura attendant the primal instinct in man to survive; others to paranoia, even arrogance attendant superpower; others still to historical determinism. Whatever the reason, what seems certain is the cause must not only be legitimate but must be free of evil intentions, not just in word but also in thought and deed.

Bush's Ideological War

The invasion of Iraq in March 2003 by President Bush reluctantly must be added to the crusades. By his own words, widely reported in the news media and detailed in *State of Denial* by Bob Woodward (2006), he attributes his actions to consultations with "a higher father." Hence, he sees the war in Iraq in existential terms: "The war we fight today is more than a military conflict. It is the *decisive* ideological conflict of the twenty-first century;"[9]"this *crusade*, this war on terror will take a long time"; and "failure in Iraq would be disastrous for the United States."[10] But, the continued occupation of Iraq by the US-led "coalition of the willing" and the unpopular surge in US military forces which has been described by Senator Chuck Hagel as representing "the most dangerous foreign policy blunder in this country since the Vietnam war if it's carried out"[11], puts it firmly under the self-fulfilling prophesy of crusade; and the Muslims are validating it by countervailing actions.

The existential pronouncements by Mr. Bush couched in language that appeals to Christian fundamentalist, when taken together with his strategy to "stay the course" and his promise of "victory in Iraq", evoke eerily the Spartan admonishment, "with your shield or on it" that attended Sparta's "death or glory" militaristic mentality. They moreover provoke countervailing responses equal in tenor, brutality, and psychology if not in military response. As such, they are no less inflammatory than Mr. Ahmadinejad's suggestion that "Israel should be wiped off the map." Both suggest as their ultimate goal the destruction of "Other": Islam, as a way of life for Muslims all over the world, and Israel as a state in the Middle East; both speak to territoriality; both speak to unjust cause for war.

Of course, there is legitimacy in drawing a distinction between Islam and radical Muslims who conveniently and strategically associate their actions with Islam; but the two are incompatible for those who are familiar with the Qur'an. There is also legitimacy in drawing a similar distinction between a peaceful Israel and an expansionist Israel; and between a just America and a unilateralist America who, in exercising its perceived right of preemption has exalted itself above international norms of behavior (see Ikenberry 2004: 325) with intent to subjugate Muslims to American power (see Piscatori 2003). In pursuit of this new grand strategy, "terror" is a metaphor for "radical Islam" and any other reaction the US chooses to so brand whilst Israel's use of its military might against home-made rockets and stone-throwing defenders in Palestine is rationalized as "the right to defend herself"; the statistics, on the other hand, tell a different tale.

"Terror" thus used by the Bush administration and the bandwagon as a whole, is perceived by Muslims as a metaphor for Islam, and "terrorists" a metaphor for Muslims, constants in the Bush narrative, and like WMD and "nuclear weapons ambitions" are used interchangeably to maintain the specter of fear uppermost in the minds of Americans and indeed build antipathy to Islam. But, as observed by the Prime Minister of Malaysia Abdullah Ahmad Badawi, President Bush should get "a better understanding of Islam vis-à-vis the Christian West." Moreover, Mr. Badawi sees "the attack on Iraq and Afghanistan, and the policy in the Middle East which always favor Israel" as adding to the crisis in the Middle East; and were pursued by Mr. Bush in furtherance of another agenda seemingly against Muslims despite the support of Muslims in the fight against terrorism after 9/11.[12] It is perhaps this kind of response around the world that prompted former President Carter to find disagreement with British Prime Minister Blair's support for Mr. Bush: "I think the almost undeviating support by Great Britain for the ill-advised policies of President Bush in Iraq have been a major tragedy for the world."[13]

Any doubts about Mr. Bush's intentions and coded messages to his Christian fundamentalist base—"*you* know what I mean"—are dispelled by his refrain: "Iraq is only a part of a larger ideological war on terror".[14] But it is an ideological war predicated on self full-filling prophesies fanned by the dangerous rhetoric of the Iranian President Ahmadinejad which is no less ill-informed and ill-advised than was the response of the Arabs to the declaration of statehood by Israel in 1948. Then as now, such uncompromising rhetoric provides the required rationalization indeed legitimization for military action against Iran.

Harsh, undiplomatically-informed and confrontational that it is, the Iranian President's assertions are curiously in keeping with Senator Joseph Biden's perception of what is required to get the Bush administration's attention:

> They read the failure to directly confront [them] and openly do it in public view as weakness, not as resolve; that the ability to have a constructive engagement [with them] rests upon direct, serious confrontation; confrontation in the sense of making it absolutely clear where we disagree.[15]

While Senator Biden was clearly referring to the administration's foreclosure on alternative opinions, his sentiments reflect those of the dissenting wider world.

Muslims and the Works of Aristotle

It is perhaps ironic that the very ideology of freedom and democracy which Mr. Bush now preaches in the Middle East owes its existence in part to the wisdom and foresight of Muslims who preserved the early writings of the Greek philosophers, the foundation of Western democracy, centuries before the new world was ever discovered. According to Richard Rubin (2004: 214–5): "The Western world owes a particular debt to the Muslims for preserving the works of Aristotle [whose writings] were translated into Arabic for use by Arabic scholars." Indeed, the Reformation was premised on the scholarly interpretations of Aristotle by Muslim and Jewish scholars. The question then is: why is Iraq a part of a larger ideological war? The answer, curiously, has been offered wittingly or unwittingly by the US Secretary of State Condoleezza Rice.

Getting the Strategic Context Right

In her interview with reporters following her meeting with German Chancellor Merkel on January 18, 2007, Secretary Rice reportedly said: "You cannot negotiate unless you get the strategic context right." Without apparently realizing it, Secretary Rice summed up the administration's foreign policy dilemma in that one sentence.

Ever since the ill-advised unilateral and hastened invasion of Iraq in March 2003, the Bush White House has been trying to get the strategic context right, albeit with much difficulty; somewhat like trying to pick-up mercury with your fingers. What this means, of course, is that the administration's long-determined grand strategy which includes creating a new Middle East in which control of Middle East oil is placed firmly in the hands of US-friendly states, as alluded to by the President[16], has come up against road blocks of one sort or the other, many in consequence of self-fulfilling prophesies. Hence, while the neo-conservatives celebrated "Shock and Awe" and cheered the Bush team on in the early days of the Iraq war, the somber reality of Newton's Law—at least opposite reaction if not equal—is the unplanned opposition to occupation, and the sectarian violence all of which began to take their toll on American military personnel and resources soon after Mr. Bush's now much-decried declaration of "mission accomplished".

President Bush's unrestrained enthusiasm to declare victory after 'Shock and Awe' and to soon thereafter invite al-Qaeda to "Bring it on", characterized as "Cowboy diplomacy" by the *Time Magazine* in July 2006, exemplified a dangerous void in the Pentagon's game-theoretic offence-defense model: understanding of the territorial imperative. That the US should find itself in a quagmire in Iraq suggests that very little consideration was given to the countervailing response, other than military, triggered by invasion. Indeed, in terms of the territorial imperative Ardrey (1966: 5) reminds us: "Man defends his land for reasons no different, no less innate, no less ineradicable, than do lower animals"; the unknown unknowns that are absent in game-theoretic offence-defense models. Hence, notwithstanding Vice-President Cheney's pronouncement that the "insurgency is in its last throes" some two years ago, Secretary of Defense Rumsfeld has ex-post come to the realization that: "There are things we know that we know. There are known unknowns. That is to say, there are things that we know we don't know. But there are also unknown unknowns: things we don't know that we don't know."

As a result of the number of unknown unknowns, rather than "mission accomplished", Iraq has become mission in progress if not mission unaccomplished after four years and counting; and measured in terms of thousands of additional US military casualties and hundreds of thousands of Iraqi civilian deaths and, of course, hundreds of billions of US taxpayers dollars, with no end in sight. But all is not lost in Iraq; there still remains a glimmer of hope. According to John Burns of the *New York Times*, "there is always the possibility this situation [in Iraq] could resolve itself"[17]; the world waits with bated breath.

Meanwhile, success in Iraq, instead of being measured in terms of the expected billions of dollars of oil revenues to be derived from an Iraq freed from the control of Saddam Hussein as envisaged and told to the US Congress by Paul Wolfowitz, has now become whatever the events of the day suggest. In the words of former National Security Adviser Zbigniew Brzezinski:

> Islamic fundamentalism one day is compared to fascism; another day to communism. We are told it is an existentialist struggle that we must win in Iraq because if we don't win in Iraq, somehow or other the people of Fallujah would come over here and attack us in Atlanta."[18]

Not surprising, then, success has been redefined in 2007 by the administration and indeed by the President in terms of: a) "a national reconciliation plan" for Iraq which is dependant upon making concessions to Sunnis[19] who were Saddam Hussein's supporters and thus constitute the insurgency; and b) an Iraqi government that can govern itself, sustain itself and defend its borders. In May 2007, success in Iraq according to Mr. Bush is not bringing an end to violence in Iraq, but bringing it down to an acceptable level; "stability" has now entered the vocabulary of the Bush administration some five years after it was dismissed as an unacceptable condition in the Middle East.

In addition to the flawed offence–defense model that relied heavily upon "Shock and Awe", and the disrupting influences of the ever-present unknown unknowns, the failure of Israel to successfully eliminate Hezbollah from the equation could not have been more damaging to the grand strategy of the neoconservatives. Moreover, Americans are restless, almost five years into the war.

That is to say, Americans no longer buy into the Bush narrative as indicated by the President's less than 30 percent rating in the national polls. As a consequence, the decision of Mr. Bush in January 2007 to progress the "surge" of US troops despite advice to the contrary has elicited the ire of many in Congress, including Republican Senator Chuck Hagel: "This is not a strategy. This is a ping pong game with American lives"[20]. Moreover, the apparent failure of the surge is being rationalized by the administration to the point where on June 25, 2007 Republican Senator Richard Lugar who heretofore had publicly supported the president, publicly criticized the handling of the war and withdrew his support to the chagrin of the administration.[21] Senator Lugar has since been joined by other senior Republican Senators.

A resurgent Taliban in Afghanistan also does not help getting the strategic context right. Indeed, the war in Afghanistan has become a drain on US resources, as evidenced by the Secretary of State's call for greater NATO commitment in terms of manpower and finance[22] and the sending of an additional 3,000 US troops in March 2007. The growing frustration over increasing civilian casualties in Afghanistan is also taking its toll.

NOTES

1 Press Conference with President Bush, June 7, 2003
2 Press Conference with President Bush, December 7, 2006
3 Heneghan, T., "Bush Mix of God and War Grates on Many Europeans" http://story.news.yahoo.com/news?tmpl=story2&u=/nm/20030404/pl_nm/iraq_bush_europe_dc_2, April 4, 2003
4 U.S. Senate records, January 22, 2007
5 "Tribute to Historian Arthur Schlesinger, Jr.", *C-SPAN2,* November 27, 2006
6 The Torah was edited and canonized in 300 B.C.E., 238 years after the return of the Jewish people to Judaea
7 Armstrong, K., "Muhammad: A Prophet for Our Time", *Book TV, C-SPAN*, November 20, 2006.
8 Clinton, W., "Role of Leadership", McLean Virginia Potomac School, *C-SPAN*, May 2, 2007
9 Televised Address on September 11, 2006.
10 Press Conference, January 26, 2007
11 US Policy in Iraq, Foreign Relations Committee, *C-SPAN*, January 11, 2007
12 Interview with Zenab Badawi, *BBC World News*, January 23, 2007.
13 "BBC News", *BBC.org*, May 19, 2007
14 Interview with Jim Lehrer, News Hour, *PBS*, January 16, 2007
15 "Markup of Biden, Hagel, Levin Resolution on Iraq", *C-SPAN*, January 24, 2007
16 Ibid
17 "Charlie Rose", *PBS.org*, January 25, 2007
18 "Carter Presidency Diplomatic Initiatives", *C-SPAN*, January, 2007
19 As testified to the Senate Foreign Relations Committee in January 2007 by the Secretary of State.
20 "Markup of Biden, Hagel, Levin Resolution on Iraq", *C-SPAN*, January 24, 2007

---

21 "The McLaughlin Group", *PBS.org*, 2
22 "US to boost Afghan troops and aid", *BBC News*, 25 January 25, 2007

Chapter Three

Condign Power and Countervailing Response: Then and Now

Introduction

As advanced in this book, condign, compensatory, and conditioned powers are primary instruments of Western territorial imperative in the twenty-first century. Not that they were not of other cultures or in other periods for as discussed in the preceding chapter they defined accession to kingship and to creation of empires. But more significantly, they served to shape political and economic thought and institutions that define contemporary society, imbuing them with a value-system that on occasions speaks to a not-so-tacit ordering of Western and non-Western peoples. This chapter therefore examines the exercise of condign power and attendant countervailing reactions for a better understanding of the reactions of others to the Bush doctrine of preemption and prevention as briefly discussed in Chapter Two.

Condign Power

As used in this text, condign power refers to the ability to threaten physical or emotional pain so as to gain submission from others to one's will (see Galbraith 1983). As shown, submission as an objective has been frequently pursued by the powerful throughout history through the reality of punishment, the barbarism of which is well documented both then as now.

Condign power has been in existence before the Common Era (B.C.E.), to be sure, and defines human interaction no less than it defines the interactions of animals (see Ardrey, 1961; 1966). The great conquests which some societies revered, even romanticized, have been by way of condign power as discussed in Chapter Two. In the Common Era (C.E.) and until recently, the Church and kings embraced condign power as a Devine Right in relation to their respective communities, with the un-translated Latin Bible as the primary instrument of suppression in Medieval Europe. Attempts to educate the people were regarded as heretical and dealt with condignly: Wycliffe who translated the Bible into English was condemned as a heretic posthumously in 1415 and his body exhumed, burned, and scattered a few years later. The Bishops of Medieval Europe relied on instilling the fear of purgatory to elicit submission to their rule, with burning at the stake as the ultimate form of punishment; and for its demonstration effect—terrorism in today's vocabulary—a concept that seemingly still prevails in modern society, indeed in the twenty-first century.

Monotheism was achieved through the exercise of condign power in all three major religions and not just in Islam as some are wont to maliciously convey. Indeed, the records of the Inquisition released by the Vatican in the late 1990s exposed the extent to which condign power was exercised by the Church as a means to imposing its will upon the people, especially in the twelfth and thirteenth centuries. As confirmed by the documents, thousands were burned at the stake for defying the Bishops (see Jones, 1998; Craig 2002).

Morphing of Devine Right

In terms of geopolitics, Devine Right has over the centuries morphed into other expressions of conquest and subjugation: "Manifest Destiny" and the right of preemption implicit in a "moral authority" which the US accords to itself; supported no less than by an unequal arsenal of nuclear weapons. Evidence Richard Perle's expressed belief: "There has to be some advantage of being a superpower."[1] Whatever the motivation or rationalization, they all speak to the exercise of condign power bound up in notions of a hierarchical social order in man, with the ruler or state as omniscient and omnipotent and, as observed by Pope John XXIII (Sigmund, 1988: 169): "as if the relationships which binds them together could be controlled only by force."

Ordained Hierarchy

Some would argue we are witnessing a revival in the belief of an ordained hierarchical social order in the twenty-first century (see Foot et al. 2003). If this were so, it bears remembering the observation by Pope John XXIII: "fickleness of opinion often produces this error: many believe that the relationships between men and states can be governed by the same laws as the forces and irrational elements of the universe, whereas the laws governing them are to be sought elsewhere, namely, in the nature of man." (Sigmund 1988: 169). This observation by Pope John XXIII is no less true for interstate relationships than it is for the relationship between man and state. Moreover, "kingship", whether by an individual within a state or by a state within an interstate system, is considered by many people to be, according to St. Thomas Aquinas: "odious because it is associated with the evils of tyranny" (Sigmund, 1988: 20). Hence, kings who become tyrants or tyrants disguised as kings are usually driven out by the people. This phenomenon is well illustrated in the accounts of history and is no less true in the twenty-first century than it was in Medieval Europe and, of course, elsewhere. Indeed, given the proclaimed embrace of modernity, pluralism, and, yes, freedom of choice, it is remarkable that so many twenty-first century politicians and commentators seem wedded to a framework that supports an hierarchy of order premised on power; unable to extricate themselves from slavery to ideologies that are incompatible with a pluralist world order: a genuine multipolar world. Not surprising, then, is Rosemary Foot's (2003: 3) rhetorical question: "How do we define the legitimate scope of societal difference in the presence of universalizing processes? And who is the 'we' who is doing the recognizing, the promoting, and the defining?" Legitimate questions, to be sure, but point to an even more fundamental question: Is the universalizing of any idea good or bad for a pluralist world or is it pursued merely to serve the interests of the powerful, requiring condign power as means of enforcement? Interestingly, Harvard University Louis Gates made the observation that Descartes' notion of being—"I think, therefore I am"—has been universalized to the point where it is taken as a requirement that one has to think in Western terms (individualism) to "be", thereby marginalizing all other cultures that revolve around community where the whole is still perceived as greater than the sum of its individual parts. Descartes notwithstanding, individualism, strangely enough, is meaningless without community as Daniel Defoe aptly conveys in *Robinson Crusoe*.

Right of Intervention

Given established rules of the game which largely have been adhered to prior to 9/11, the idea that a dominant state should seek to effect change in another by the exercise of condign power infringes upon the rights of the people in the weaker state whose right to make changes in keeping with their notions of order and justice, and, therefore, of community tolerance and methodology (see Roberts 2003: 60–61). Such intervention, therefore, should be seen as rooted in a cause other than pretensions of social justice or human rights. As stated earlier, Iraq was not a creation of the three disparate groups that now constitute it; Iraq is an illusion of colonial rule, made possible by the exercise of condign power. Left to their own devices, the Kurds, Sunni–Arabs, and Shia–Arabs would arguably have established their own rules for interaction; as they have done for centuries before European colonization, one of the less socially agreeable universalizing processes in a hierarchical social ordering of man.

Contrary to the rhetoric, saving souls and spreading freedom and democracy, to be sure, were not the objective of universalizing colonialism. The name of the game bluntly stated was conquest and plunder; to fuel economic development in the West. In this connection, many have questioned the Bush administration's right to impose "freedom and democracy" in the Middle East; for invading Iraq; and to setting the rules for relationship among Iraqis within the artificial state of Iraq, and among its Middle Eastern neighbors: the people of the desert have been there before. Strangely enough, almost four and one-half years into occupation, Secretary of Defense Gates has come to the realization that: "In some ways we probably all underestimated the depth of the mistrust and how difficult it would be for these guys to come together on legislation"[2]; legislation, of course, being used euphemistically. Indeed, as observed by Anthony Cordesman of the *Center for Strategic and International Studies* (CSIS), the election in Iraq was meaningless from the perspective of the Iraqis; the Iraqi constitution came into being "for our political reasons, not their's."[3]

What has been said above about Iraq is equally applicable to societies impacted by colonialism, especially in Africa. Nigeria, Ethiopia—before the break away of Eretria—the Congo, Rwanda, and others carry the stamp of European notions of nationhood: features of the Westphalian state system of sovereignty; all manifesting a total disregard for disparate native culture and customs; all abandoned and left to their own devices when geography became a factor and the effects of countervailing reactions (discussed below) became unmanageable and deemed too costly vis-à-vis the benefits.

Interestingly, many African states still are unable to free themselves from the control of the West; their violent interactions with one another often betray some form of dependency on Western patrimony on the one hand and, indeed, exploitation of Western vulnerabilities on the other. The majority, however, are forced to live within the confines of statehood imposed upon them by outsiders; resorting to violence with no other cultural value to access and no place left to retreat (see Kaarsholm 2006), locked into artificial political boundaries as most of them are. Those who seek to operate outside this *de facto* framework of Westernization are punished, often condignly with the authority of the supreme international institution ready to demonstrate its readiness to bend to the will of its creators; a reality not lost on UN Ambassador in Jerusalem Alvaro deSoto with respect to the Israel–Palestinian conflict[4] or indeed to UN Human Rights envoy John Dugard.[5] In this hierarchical geopolitical framework, the US now intervenes with impunity in places such as Somalia on the basis that, according Pentagon spokesman Bryan Whitman: "The U.S. remains committed to reducing terrorist capabilities when and where we find them"[6], resorting to what Ikenberry (2004: 325) identifies as preventive force, that is, "taking on potential threats before they can present a major problem"; and France could threaten a country with the use of force even though that country poses no security threat to it.

But use of force and threat of force are forthcoming only when the risk of retaliation is minimal (see Van Evera 2004: 44–69). In this latter regard, Israel's peace overtures in July 2007—with full support of the Bush administration—to the Palestinian President Abbas is strictly out of the game-theoretic offence-defense playbook. It allows Israel to isolate Hamas in the Gaza and indeed even to defeat it at some future date, having succeeded in rendering the PLO and the West Bank benign. The inclusion of Jordan, Egypt, and Saudi Arabia to any peace settlement with Abbas would effectively seal the fate of Hamas; hence Mr. Bush's call for an international conference on the Israel–Palestine issue, and the bearing of gifts by the Secretary of State and Secretary of Defense to the major Arab players, which, incidentally, is also out of the same playbook.

Setting Rules for Iraq's Neighbors

In keeping with notions of condign power, the US finds itself free to demand non-interference in the internal affairs of Iraq from others in the region, in contrast to being fully supportive of Israel's interference in Lebanese affairs or Ethiopia in Somalia's,[7] or indeed of its own self-anointed right of preemptive or preventive actions wherever there is a perceived strategic interest; "the extension of the Munroe Doctrine to the rest of the world" as seen through the eyes of Samir Amin (2006: 9). Hence, in addition to rhetoric directed at Iran and Syria, it has stationed its battle carrier group threateningly in the Persian Gulf with supportive rhetoric from British Prime Minister Tony Blair.[8] Meanwhile, the US continues to pressure Syria to break with Iran while Israel tests the defenses of Syria. Moreover, in what appears to be a recant from the ISG's recommendations, the former Secretary of State and Co-Chairman of the ISG James Baker, took the position at a Congressional hearing that the US should be talking to Syria to get them to break away from the influence of Iran. At the same time, however, the kidnapping of Iranian officials in Iraq by the US has been condemned by Abdel Aziz al-Hakim, a top Shia Iraqi official and someone believed to be close to Mr. Bush, as "a kind of attack on Iraq's sovereignty"[9] while attempts by Secretary Rice to garner Arab support in Iraq "drew only tepid endorsement."[10]

With respect to Iran as one of the contiguous neighbors of Iraq, according to Ambassador John Negroponte, "today they [Iran] are looking at the region in a much more assertive way" and have become "embolden" by the "victory of their surrogate Hezbollah in the summer against Israel."[11] However, as observed by Sir Alan Munro in a BBC-hosted panel discussion[12]: "In the Nixon era, Iran was appointed under the Shah by the Americans to be the guardian of the region." In the opinion of Sir Malcolm Rifkind, another participant: "Iran is entitled to expect to be considered a regional power by virtue of its size and its general position in the Gulf." Yet another participant, Clare Short, a former Minister in Mr. Blair's Cabinet until her resignation in protest of Britain's role in the invasion of Iraq, was less diplomatic: "it is really funny for America and Britain to tell Iran to keep out of Iraq when it is its neighbour. Who is it that's coming from far away to interfere in Iraq?"

In referring to the Bush administration's refusal to talk to Iran, the former British Foreign Secretary Lord Hurd in the same discussion observed: "The trouble about the Americans is that they think, under this administration, that talking to somebody is doing them a favour." These sentiments are shared around the world, especially in Muslim countries who given the Bush doctrine of preemption cannot help but feel threatened by the superpower. In the words of the Malaysian Prime Minister: "He [Bush] has a different agenda, and the Muslims know it."[13]

World opinion notwithstanding, obsessed with the notion of power Richard Perle declared: "We would be entirely justified in doing what we have done [even] if no one in the world supported us."[14] But as argued in this book, it is precisely this wanton disregard for the perspectives of others that takes away from everything that is good about America and its people in the eyes of the wider world; and serves to condemn the neoconservative grand strategy to the trash heap of history. It is perhaps this seemingly intoxication with power that prompted former President Carter to bluntly declare: "I think as far as the adverse impact on the nation around the world, this administration has been the worst in history."[15] President Carter has since moderated the tone of his message.

The Israel–Arab Conflict

Few would deny the Israel–Palestine conflict as representing yet another example of the exercise of condign power by the more powerful Israel. Prime Minister Olmert is on record promising and indeed inflicting condign punishment on the Palestinians couched in terms of a right to defend itself. In pursuing such promises Israel has not spared the Palestinians, calling upon its overwhelmingly superior military power to destroy homes allegedly housing rocket launchers, breaking the sound barrier by low-flying jet fighters, and killing several thousands of Palestinian civilians in the process. The Palestinians, on the other hand, not in possession of F-16 jet fighters, attack helicopters or hi-tech tanks or guided missiles have found countervailing responses in alternatives in the name of survival which, incidentally, should be very familiar to the Israelis as discussed in Chapter Nine. That Palestinian methods serve to prolong their survival notwithstanding many are deemed barbaric and offensive to twenty-first century notions of human dignity, speaks to the reality of countervailing actions as inherent in the territorial imperative. Without lending support to the rationalization or the methods employed, it needs to be recognized that the demise of European colonialism was in consequence of countervailing actions of unprecedented barbarism—as defined by the West—by many African leaders, many of whom now sit in high council as the theoretical equal to their former colonial masters.

The same could be said about the relentless bombing of Southern Lebanon and Beirut during the Israel–Hezbollah 34-day war in July 2006. Hezbollah's use of short and medium range missiles during the war while causing civilian deaths in Israel was clearly not equal to Israel's assault in terms of civilian causality and destruction. Indeed, while both sides were deemed in violation of human rights, the world witnessed one of the most brutal attacks perpetrated on a civilian population as a form of collective punishment. As observed by the *Economist*, Prime Minister Siniora's "erstwhile American friends dawdled diplomatically while Israeli bombs systematically demolished the country's infrastructure. Moreover, deadly cluster bomblets, supplied by America, still clutter south Lebanon."[16] Indeed, as reported by the UN, there are still about one million unexploded devises in largely civilian-populated areas in South Lebanon as a result of the use of cluster bombs by Israel in the last two weeks of the war. Also, as observed by *Deutsche-Welle Television* (DW–TV) on February 22, 2007, 40 percent of cluster bombs used by Israel missed their targets while 60 percent of the civilian causalities were children.

Countervailing Actions

It should be obvious by now that countervailing action to the original action although capable of intellectual restraint is a natural phenomenon. While countervailing responses in armed conflicts have largely been condemned as acts of terrorism especially when they are not expected and therefore not factored into game-theoretic offence-defense models, when motivated by the survival instinct they have been instrumental in effecting change to unjust rule as discussed in Chapter Two. For whatever reason, throughout history such acts of desperation do not as a rule conform to expected modes of behavior (see Pape, 2006) and thus become unknown unknowns; and by the very logic of desperation in the long run elicit equally barbaric acts as counter-countervailing, thus creating a vicious cycle of barbarism, even in a twenty-first century world. But countervailing actions do not have to be existential, as the numerous accounts in history testify.

In less extreme cases, the notion of oppositional politics by definition is countervailing-derived, and as suggested in Chapter Two often do result in change. For example, *Magna Carta*, adopted in 1215 was not derived from the goodness or kindness of the English rulers but rather from opposition to their oppression. The Reformation in sixteenth-century Europe though met with condign punishment was similarly rooted in opposition to the authoritarianism of the Church: with the aid of Jewish and Muslim scholars, buying redemption was recognized by the people for its debasing constructs rather than for its promise and as such threatened the very existence of the Church.

Similarly, state constitutions that speak of individual freedom and equality speak to the importance of countervailing actions and reflect oppositional politics firmly nestled in the belief articulated by Pope John XXIII that, "every human being is a person; his nature is endowed with intelligence and free will ... with rights and duties of his own ... which are therefore universal, inviolable and inalienable" (Sigmund, 1988: 169). Success of countervailing actions thus depends crucially upon finding the inconsistency in the belief system of the aggressors and by so doing use their self-doubt to advantage. King Harry (Henry V) of England succeeded in battle against the French and later became king of France not only because the cause was just but also because he and his men were transformed into a "band of brothers"; the French lost despite their overwhelming numbers—about three times as many—because the French king Charles II doubted his own legitimacy to the French throne and this doubt was transmitted to his men. Joan of Arc succeeded in ridding France of corrupt English nobles because her cause was just and her men believed in her; the English nobles had no cause other than their own corrupt way of life. The corrupt Catholic Bishops of Medieval Europe knew of their perverse proclivities and thus doubted themselves, notwithstanding that they had others to do their dirty work; hence the Reformation which, as noted above, was informed by the works of Muslim and Jewish scholars.

Slavery came to an end because of oppositional politics that took aim at the belief-system of the slave-owning establishment. The horrors of the slave trade could not have been more vividly told than by Turner's rendition of the *Slave Ship* in 1840. In the twentieth century, Martin Luther King and the Civil Rights Movement created self-doubt in the minds of the establishment which resulted in the Civil Rights Act of 1964. Indeed, one can state as an unwritten rule that a society that pursues policies which are inconsistently applied and which are counter to its established value and belief systems is a society that is dysfunctional and will implode in the fullness of time. In this connection, US politicians have yet to comprehend fully the effectiveness of the internet in bringing to public notice the gap between rhetoric and reality. One might be tempted to include demise of the Soviet Union: it imploded from self-doubt with a little help from the West; in particular, West Germany's *"Ostpolitik"* that supported a policy of trade with Eastern European countries which helped to foster self-doubt about the superiority of communism as a world system.

Modern societies, then, have come to recognize the cruelty associated with condign punishment and have enacted laws to mitigate its use and effects, both domestically and in inter-state relations; not voluntarily in the case of the latter but in response to countervailing actions. Failure to uphold these laws often elicit condemnation, as evidenced by the outcry of the world against the images of detainees at *Abu Ghraib* and *Guantanamo*, many showing evidence of physical torture while others allege psychological torture and water-boarding; the latter defended by Vice President Cheney as "a no-brainer for me."[17] There are other violations of basic human rights allegedly authorized by former Secretary of Defense Donald Rumsfeld. These and others—rendition, for example—in particular the denial of rights under the Geneva Convention to detainees at *Guantanamo*[18] have been decried by the International Red Cross and other Human Rights groups. These condemnations have resulted in recoil from overt use of so-called "enhanced interrogation techniques" on alleged illegal enemy combatants captured by the US and its allies. By the same token, the graphic display of beheadings and mutilated bodies of Americans is no less an exercise of terrorism design to traumatize a society that has long found such methods barbaric notwithstanding they clearly fall within the definition of countervailing actions attendant the invasion and alleged atrocities by the invading forces. These, too, have moderated since they were condemned.

For those who are wont to question the notion of countervailing actions, consider the outburst by former Director of the Central Intelligence Agency (CIA) George Tenet to the atrocities committed by Osama bin Laden and al-Qaeda on 9/11: "I am going to run you and all your bastards down, and here we come because the *rules are about to change*; here we come, our turn now; *unleashed*." [emphasis added].[19] The outrage was shared by all America and even beyond. What is significant about this expression of anger by the CIA director is that beyond its promise of condign punishment outside the operation of established rules and a resort to maximum force short of nuclear weapons, it is a human response, a manifestation of the territorial imperative. If this is acceptable reaction of civilized man, what should be the expected reaction of the not-so-civilized to similar violations attendant the exercise of condign power by those who found themselves so disposed, who callously believe there has to be some advantage to being a superpower? Is moral outrage an endowment exclusive to Western man? The truthful answers to these two basic human questions make us all equal on the treadmill of the territorial imperative. Indeed, those of us who are unable to get past self-interested perspectives are no more civilized than the uneducated, unsophisticated "men in cave" whose reliance on survival instincts continue to elude quantification as an "unknown unknown" in the neo-conservative game-theoretic offence-defense model.

One of the more egregious examples of condign power in modern history is the enslaving of one race by another for economic reasons. Its effects still reverberate in contemporary societies notwithstanding the embrace of pluralism as ameliorating policies. But, while such policies seek to ensure equal access to opportunities on a going forward basis, they cannot redress for the psychosocial consequences which are deeply embedded into the fabric of Western society and which continue to define inter-racial and inter-cultural interaction in a largely ordered world.

Moreover, the benefits that have accrued to Western capitalism from the exercise of condign power over the centuries serve to foster an inequality gap in terms of resources, knowledge, and other indicators of capacity and capability that cannot ever be bridged by domestic legislative initiatives or by foreign aid to poorer developing countries however well-intentioned. The effects of centuries of deprivation, erasure, and other consequences of dominance, on the one hand, and the benefits from asymmetric relationships compounded over an equal time span, on the other, are too numerous, too embedded to be bridgeable by foreign aid premised on market access. Moreover, as discussed in Chapter Four, foreign aid has been largely predicated on maintaining a core-periphery relationship within the capitalist system, and in consequence operates to exacerbate the polarization of wealth and power, a condition not lost on Samir Amin (2006).

Western societies that are pluralist, such as the US, are regarded increasingly as vulnerable to decline as lamented by Patrick Buchanan; not because of a decline in absolute numbers necessarily but as alluded to by Buchanan because of the racial and cultural mix, with the culture of the new immigrants from the third world permeating the standards achieved by the Europeans. In other words, as Buchanan (2002) tells it, the white races are in decline, signaling the death of the West as represented by the preponderance of Europeans.

Sources of Power and Countervailing Response

A phenomenon of the territorial imperative is that there always will be countervailing responses in keeping with the primal instinct with which humans are endowed. While Galbraith was clearly speaking to the exercise of power in context of economics and commerce, the symmetry between the sources of power and the sources of countervailing response is equally evident in other areas, such as, for example, the conflicts in the Middle East and Afghanistan.

By invoking his religious beliefs in his "war on terror", President Bush has garnered the support of the Christian right or the Moral Majority—all Christian fundamentalist however you slice it—and have relied upon them for his reelection in 2004. However, in couching foreign policy in religious terms, the president has elicited the countervailing response of Jihads—equally rooted in religion—which, as observed by several Muslim scholars and Robert Pape (2006), was initially directed not at the West but at secular Arab states prior to the First Gulf War of 1991 and dates back to the 1950s. It was only after the stationing of US military in Saudi Arabia that bin-Laden turned his hatred on the US (Pape, 2006; see also Dershowitz's letter). Moreover, such countervailing responses may take on barbaric proportions even in today's civilized world when the issue is a matter of survival. To paraphrase the former Secretary of Defense Rumsfeld, you fight with the army you have, not with the army you want. The rag tag army of George Washington did the best they could with what they had against the greatest, most disciplined military in the world two hundred odd years ago. Thus, while offensive to our ideas of civilized behavior we need to bear in mind that to the non-Western man whose existence and essence—however backward to the Socratic West—are perceived to be threatened, sacrificing his life is the most truthful expression of loyalty to a society anchored in antiquity. To the modern Western observer whose reverence for antiquity has been largely replaced by reason and love of things ephemeral, however, such sacrifice is simplistically interpreted as "the enemy loves death more than life." Interestingly, it was Socrates who defined the task of philosophy as "learning how to die" (Bloom 1987: 278). There is no such thing as immortality.

Moreover, there is a discernible denial in the language used to describe truth when it conflicts with things cherished, and as Alan Bloom (1987: 278) observes: "regard as a monster the man who does not care for such things." Hence, in the absence of rationality the resort to the most extreme description, such as, for example, "Axis of evil"; "Islamo-fascist"; "men in cave"; "terrorists", and the like. These terms could not be more derogatory and border on the extreme of contempt for another human being. But more than that, in seeking to dehumanize others such terms betray ignorance, fears, and prejudices. Therefore, while these labels speak to an interested perspective and serve a particular objective at a particular time, they are difficult to climb down from and reflect in aggressive policy until expunged from language. In this latter regard, it is instructive that at the time of writing "victory in Iraq" has been replaced by "success in Iraq" in the Bush narrative. Moreover, "stability" has re-entered the Bush narrative—albeit briefly—this time as an objective for Iraq and not as a discredited policy pursued by prior US administrations.

Even then, few would disagree with the perception that the dilemma faced by the Bush administration in the Middle East is precisely because it is finding it difficult to climb down from its ideological rhetoric that borders on the existential, and from its desire to remain the unchallenged king of the hill come what may as articulated in the new grand strategy (see Ikenberry 2004). Speaking to this observation is the apparent contradiction of objectives between the newly-appointed Middle East Envoy, former British Prime Minister Tony Blair and the Bush narrative. Mr. Blair, for example, advances "stability" as a necessary objective of peace in the Middle East[20] whilst President Bush finds himself once again rejecting the notion of stability in the Middle East as an acceptable outcome. According to President Bush, "freedom" is a God-given right to every man and is thus the objective of his foreign policy[21], with "complete victory" now the stated goal of the US mission in Iraq. But to others, freedom means living without interference, even in caves or trees.

In less extreme examples but none the less evidencing a state of denial is the practice of avoiding recognition of things or events for what they are when they conflict with our prejudices. For example, while the *Economist* acknowledged "Israeli bombs systematically demolished the country's [Lebanon's] infrastructure"[22] it skillfully avoided any direct mention of the high civilian casualties attendant such bombings and the humanitarian crisis visited upon the Lebanese people in consequence.

Interestingly, those who are compel by their sense of duty and honor and indeed sense of morality, are castigated for seeking, and more significantly, telling the truth, as was Bill Moyers, for example. In other examples, General Shinseki was allegedly forced to retire soon after contradicting the Pentagon's estimate of the number of US troops needed to secure the peace in Iraq in his testimony to Congress. Indeed, his testimony to Congress was openly dismissed by the then Deputy Secretary of Defense Paul Wolfowitz. Similarly, Abu Ghraib Prison Investigator Major General Antonio Taguba was told: "I need you to retire" by one of his commanding officer, and, again, "I no longer need you on my team" by another in consequence of his investigation of the atrocities at Abu Ghraib.[23] It is this practice of avoiding recognition and acceptance of the hard facts and to manipulate language in the interest of political correctness or, indeed, an interested viewpoint, that the Israeli writer David Grossman admonishes those in authority to call things by their right names: "a freedom-fighter when he is one, a terrorist when he is a terrorist, and a wall when it is a wall." It is equally instructive that the Oxford English Dictionary defines terrorist as: "a person who uses violence and intimidation in the pursuit of political aims."

Not in Praise of Violence

While some are wont to interpret the above statements narrowly, they are offered not in praise of violence but to state Newton's immutable law of action and reaction and Galbraith's notion of countervailing action; well exemplified by the justifiable response by the US to the heinous acts on 9/11, and, as some would argue, by those who perceived themselves to be resistance fighters in the Middle East but who rightly or wrongly are labeled terrorists. In this latter regard, we are reminded that "al-Qaeda in Iraq" is a creation of the Bush administration. Recall the invitation of President Bush: "Bring it on." Hence, as the argument goes, Iraq is now the central front of the war on terror not because they were there in the first place, despite the Vice President's veiled assertion that all Muslims are terrorists, but because it is what President Bush wanted.

Similarly, we are reminded that the Palestinian Liberation Organization (PLO) was formally organized in 1964 in response to Israel's continued occupation of Palestinian lands in defiance of UN Resolution 194 which calls for the return of Palestinians to their homes or compensation by Israel; that Hezbollah came into being in response to Israel's invasion and use of American-made cluster bombs against the Palestinians refugees and Lebanese people in 1982, whilst the militant group Hamas came into being not in 1967 but rather in 1987 after Israel crushed the 1987 Palestinian *intifada*. While these are now regarded as terrorist organizations, in the language of Galbraith, they are to be sure manifestations of countervailing actions to the exercise of condign power by Israel; the territorial imperative. One may argue that Arab methods are terroristic; others will argue that all killing irrespective of means is barbaric and terroristic. Indeed, the human capacity for brutality has been well demonstrated by both sides. Few however would in good conscious deny that the use of cluster bombs that kill or mutilate long after the war is over is designed for purposes other than winning on the battle field. Curiously, while the death and destruction from such advanced weaponry are greater, they do not convey the same degree of fear as the idea of a terrorist among us (see Jenkins 2004: 79).

While it is true the attack on the *USS Cole* and the bombing of US Embassies in Kenya and Tanzania were unprovoked and preceded the invasion of Iraq in 2003, the existence of bin Laden and al-Qaeda as the leading force behind terrorism were not known to the US until after 1993 (Clarke, 2004: 79; 88). Indeed, based on Clarke's account, it appears likely that the large-scale retaliation to the murder of 18 US commandos in Mogadishu, Somalia "that killed over a thousand Somalis in a day" provided the opportunity for al-Qaeda to emerge on the world scene, testing its capability and geographic reach as an avowed terrorist organization. The question then is: why was al-Qaeda in such a ready-state in the first place; and did it gather momentum from the bombing of what was mistakenly believed to be a chemical weapons factory in Sudan or from the events in Bosnia and Chechnya, as many have suggested?

We are also reminded by Richard Clarke that in 1991, bin Laden was a Saudi dissident, protesting the presence of US military presence in Saudi Arabia after the Saudi King turned down his offer to defend his homeland. He was subsequently banished from the kingdom. His involvement in Afghanistan was as a financier and fighter against the Soviets. According to Clarke (2004: 96), bin Laden was regarded by the CIA as: "a radicalized rich kid, who was playing at terrorism by sending checks to terrorist groups." His link to terrorism was through his association with Hasan al-Turabi, leader of the National Islamist Front that governed the Sudan, to where he moved after he was banished from Saudi Arabia and stripped of his Saudi nationality (see Clarke 2004: 135). Furthermore, according to Alan Dershowitz, "bin Laden was primarily motivated by the presence of American troops in Saudi Arabia"[24]; a perspective shared by most scholars and analysts who have studied al-Qaeda.

Relative Effectiveness

As further observed by Galbraith (1983: 74): "The relative effectiveness of these opposing forces depends [on] the extent and effectiveness of the exercise of the original power." Indeed, according to Van Evera (2004: 47): "Adversaries can parlay smaller gains into larger conquest." Hence, al-Qaeda appeared to have gained an idea of its strength as a result of US withdrawal from Somalia and expanded its operations into other areas. With respect to Iraq, while "Shock and Awe" had a mesmerizing impact, its psychological effect was short-lived for the simple reason that 5,000 years of history have taught the people of the desert to rise up again, like the fabled phoenix, if you will. The failure to follow-up with actions appropriate to building trust and confidence rather than basking in the glory of military achievements, when coupled with the increasing number of civilian deaths at the hands of the US military have allowed the insurgency to devise countervailing responses that have become almost proportional in terms of outcome when public opinion is factored into the equation. As observed by Ardrey (1966: 236–7):

> The enhancement of energy invariably engendered in the defending proprietor; the union of partners welded by the first sound of gunfire; the biological morality demanding individual sacrifice even of life: all of the innate commands of the territorial imperative act to multiply the apparent resources of a defending nation.

To say that "the enemy loves death more than life" is simply to not understand the territorial imperative and to assume that all humans are similarly made up psychologically and culturally; motivated by materialism and individualism; indeed, it says little for the ideology of individualism and materialism. In reality it speaks more to lapses in judgment by the neoconservatives and to theory-practice problematic. In terms of the latter, methodological inadequacies in the exercise of the "original power" first, in Bosnia and secondly, in the invasion of Iraq is seen as having played into the opportunistic framework that is al-Qaeda's. Moreover, as Ardrey (1966: 236) reminds us, we need to "bear in mind that the territorial principle motivates all of the human species. Whether we approve or we disapprove, whether we like it or we do not, it is a power as much as an ally of our enemies as it is of ourselves and our friends." The report that al-Qaeda is manufacturing its own brand of rockets[25] and is able to recruit from every corner of the world speaks to Ardrey's observation of four decades ago and is validated by an evolving countervailing process in Iraq which is grounded in territoriality. Indeed, Pandora's Box has been busted wide open; hence the existential self-fulfilling prophesies of Mr. Bush.

The Internet as an Instrument of Propaganda

What has been said above with respect to US involvement in Iraq is equally true for the Israel–Lebanon war in July 2006: Israel was unprepared not only for Hezbollah's military response but also for the condemnation by the world—despite its well-oiled propaganda machinery—for the death and destruction wrought upon Lebanese civilian by its disproportionate use of force, including the use of cluster bombs.

In terms of public opinion as a significant factor, neither the US in the case of Iraq nor Israel in the case of Lebanon fully considered the impact of the speed by which information is transferred around the world via the internet prior to embarking on their respective misadventures, as some have characterized them. True, the Bush administration attempts at muzzling the news media, especially televised broadcast of the war, reflect the lessons learnt from the Vietnam War where the graphic display of death and destruction turned Americans against its continuance and polarized the country. But no one viewing the pictures or reading of Abu Gharib on the internet—early publication of which the administration sought to discredit—could unquestioningly subscribe to the false dichotomy of "either you are with us or you are with the enemy" imposed upon the American people and the world by Mr. Bush: the disconnect between rhetoric and reality was inescapably visible.

Similarly, few who viewed UN Jan Egeland's spontaneous emotional account of the results of Israel's attack on the civilian population of South Lebanon in July 2006 in response to the kidnapping of two Israeli soldiers and the killing of an additional eight by Hezbollah could possibly thereafter in good conscious buy into the notion that Israel was only acting in self-defense. For many, the attack on Qana on July 29, 2006 brought home the callous brutality with which Israel prosecuted the war against Lebanon: It reminded the world of the 1996 attack by Israel on a UN base in which 100 civilians were killed while sheltering from the Israeli "Grapes of Wrath" offensive. Hence, while Mr. Bush in his Saturday radio address chose to characterize the Israeli attack on Qana as "painful and tragic", and could not resist characterizing it as "also a moment of opportunity for broader change in the region"[26], many around the world condemned the action. To the former British Foreign Secretary Jack Straw the Israeli attacks were "disproportionate."[27] Unmoved by the world-wide condemnation, and secured in the thought that it is only a matter of time before Hezbollah is crushed, Mr. Olmert reportedly advised Secretary Rice that "his troops needed another 10–14 days to finish the Lebanese operations."[28] The world watched the political machinations of both Mr. Bush and Mr. Blair: buying time for Israel to complete the job as promised. They also witnessed the humiliation of the British Prime Minister (Yo, Blair!) in July 2006; they got more than a glimpse of the Bush administration's agenda.

The subsequent reminder that Israel had previously used cluster bombs against the Lebanese people in 1982 inflamed the outrage of the world even more. Nonetheless, such is the relationship between the Bush administration and the Israeli government that the Under Secretary of State Karen Hughes should pen an 'Op-ed' in the *Washington Post*: "Where is the outrage", drawing attention to Israeli civilian casualties which was less than one-tenth of that of the Lebanese; inflicted not from cluster bombs, naval bombardment, and high-tech artillery but by rockets and missiles, the range and accuracy of which were unreliable.

Furthermore, while Israel and the US tried to focus public attention on Iran and Syria as suppliers of arms to Hezbollah, the US was caught sending two air-cargo shipments of "bunker–busting bombs" described as "civilian flights" to Israel through Scotland, which likely would have gone unnoticed had they first secured landing approval from the British government.[29] As the reality of the war became known, ordinary Israelis were equally against its conduct, with 50 percent of those polled in December 2006 expressed concern over the integrity of Mr. Olmert while over 75 percent thought he had no leadership qualities and were largely responsible for the outcome of the war. It is therefore not surprising that Alan Dershowitz should lament: "Israel is not stronger as a result of what happened in Lebanon"; in contrast to President Bush's earlier conclusion that "Hezbollah was defeated."

It is also instructive that US Intelligence Officer, Brigadier General John Custer, should consider the wars in Iraq and Afghanistan, as "a battle field of asymmetrics. Terror counts. There is no frontline of troops... It is a battle of perceptions; and al-Qaeda understands it; and America needs to understand it."[30] But it is an understanding that is being denied the American public by the dissemination of spin. The administration embattled as it, is forced to withhold the unpleasant facts whilst the news media in competition for ratings with few exceptions offer sound bites and polemics as scholarly analyses. Those who dare to seek the truth are decried and ostracized. In the US Congress, as in the UN, special interests lobbies as well as political self-interest dictate what goes into the records. Were it not for live broadcasts by *C-SPAN*, the ability to differentiate between reality and managed information—the latter often manifesting in rewrites of events—would be non-existent. Yet, the administration presses on in it campaign of patronizing the American public.

NOTES

1 Perle, R., "The Case for War: In defense of freedom", included as part of 'America at a Crossroads', *Frontline, PBS.org*, April 17, 2007
2 Baldor, L.C., "Gates: Iraq political reform difficult", *Associated Press*, http://news.yahoo.com/s/ap/20070802/ap_on_re_mi_ea/gates_iraq
3 "U.S. Policy in Iraq", Washington Journal, *C-SPAN*, August 11, 2007
4 Inskeep, S., "Morning Edition", *National Public Radio*, http://www.npr.org/templates/transcript/transcript.php?storyId=11007437
5 Franks, T., "UN envoy attacks Mid-East Quartet", *BBC NEWS*, http://news.bbc.co.uk/go/pr/fr/-/2/hi/middle_east/7044069.stm
6 Hassan, M.O., "Report: U.S. hits militants' Somali base", http://news.yahoo.com/s/ap/20070602/ap_on_re_af/somalia_us
7 "Somalis 'at war' with Ethiopia", *BBC News*, December 21, 2006
8 Reynolds, P., "Blair and the 'strategic challenge' of Iran", *BBC NEWS*, December 20, 2006
9 "Top Iraqi condemns US over Iran", *BBC News*, January 17, 2007
10 Gearan, A., "Rice lobbies Arab for backing in Iraq", *Associated Press*, January 16, 2007
11 Senate Hearing, *C-SPAN*, January 17, 2007
12 'Panel Discussion', *BBC News*, February 6, 2007
13 Interview with Zenab Badawi, *BBC World News*, January 23, 2007.
14 "Buying the War", *Bill Moyers Journal*, *PBS.org*, April 23, 2007
15 CBS News, May 19, 2007
16 "That let-down feeling", *The Economist*, December 2, 2006, p. 29
17 "Buying the War", Bill Moyers Journal, *PBS.org*, April 23, 2007; see also: "The Dark Side", *Frontline*, PBS.org 2007
18 The argument being that Guantanamo is not on US soil. The shallowness of this argument renders the legal status of embassies on foreign soil subject to question.
19 Scott Pelly interview, "60 Minutes", *CBS News*, April 29, 2007
20 "Prime Minister Question Time", British House of Commons, *C-SPAN*, June 27 2007.
21 President Bush's presentation on Iraq War & Middle East, Naval War College, *C-SPAN*, June 28, 2007.
22 "That let-down feeling", The Economist, December 2, 2006, p.29
23 "Abu Ghraib Prison Investigation", Commonwealth Club of California, *C-SPAN2*, June 25, 2007.
24 Dershowitz, A., "The Israel Lobby", Letters, *The London Review of Books*, Vol. 28, No.8, April 20, 2006
25 Youssef, M and Mroue, B., "Al-Qaida-linked group making own rockets", http://news.yahoo.com/s/ap/20070417/ap_on_re_mi_ea/iraq

26 Bohan, C., "Lebanon crisis is part of a broader struggle: Bush", *Associated Press*, July 30, 2006
27 "Straw warning on Israeli action", *BBC NEWS*, July 29, 2006
28 "Dozens killed in Lebanon air raid", *BBC News*, July 30, 2006
29 "More US arms deliveries for Israel expected in Scotland", *BBC News*, July 29, 2006.
30 Interview by Scott Pelly, "60 Minutes", *cbsnews.com*, 4 March, 2007

Chapter Four

Compensatory and Conditioned Powers: Then and Now

Introduction

Whereas, the exercise of condign power portends punishment to the state as discussed in the previous chapter, compensatory power offers the state some form of payment or reward sufficiently beneficial or advantageous to forgo pursuit of an identified action or, indeed, to perform a certain act the state would not ordinarily undertake (Galbraith 1983: 14). Hence, in interstate relations compensatory power usually takes the form of what many would like to regard as *quid pro quo* arrangements, the value of which is clearly relative to the parties: However, when the alternative is punishment for non-compliance any form of compensation may be regarded as infinitely preferable. We look at some of these arrangements from both geopolitical and geo-economic perspectives.

The Geopolitics of Compensatory and Conditioned Powers

There are several examples in the use of compensatory power in combination with condign power; none more obvious than the US–Pakistan arrangement regarding the latter's role in the war on terror in Afghanistan. The funding of Israel as the leading edge of the Westernization process in the Middle East, ostensibly fighting terrorism in the region, is yet another example; in this case without the threat of punishment. Beyond the US–Israel relationship, the combination of condign and compensatory powers finds articulation in the Israel–Palestine and Israel–Lebanon issues, and offers a textbook lesson from which to draw. Indeed, the contrast between the relative roles of Pakistan and Israel and their relationship with the source(s) of power are particularly instructive.

The Unenviable Role of Pakistan

The transfer to Pakistan of almost US$7.0 billion in aid and military supplies to find and destroy al-Qaeda networks within and around its borders is a form of compensatory power exercised by the US. As Pakistan's President Musharraf tells it, the alternative was to feel the full force of US condign power: "You are either with us or against us" was the "ultimatum" from the then Secretary of State Colin Powell. This was allegedly followed up by the Deputy Secretary of State Armitage's meeting with Pakistan's Director General of Inter-Service Intelligence in which the message was that, if Pakistan chose to back the terrorists then it "should be prepared to be bombed back to the Stone Age"[1] (Musharraf, 2006: 201). Under these conditions and being a self-described "pragmatist" it is understandable that General Musharraf should appear with Mr. Bush at a press conference in his own country seemingly unaffected by what was perceived by many to be insulting language and posturing by the American president. Again, as Musharraf (2006: 202–3) tells it, because Pakistanis were for years "victims of terrorism by the Taliban and al-Qaeda", they welcomed the opportunity to "eliminate extremism" and "flush out terrorists" from their midst; besides, the economic benefits of "loosening the stranglehold" of Pakistan's official debts and the lifting of economic sanctions were compensation enough not to commit "suicide" over the Taliban.

Again, as General Musharraf tells it, resulting from the financial and military assistance received from the US, Pakistan captured 689 al-Qaeda members and handed over 369 to the CIA. Hence, in addition to official aid, Pakistan has "earned bounties totaling millions of dollars" (Musharraf, 2006: 237) which served to foster economic development and reduce poverty in Pakistan. In this regard, many would argue that Musharraf's choice was highly beneficial to the people of Pakistan when measured in terms of the economic growth derived from American aid. Others, on the other hand, see it as also serving to strengthen the General's hold on political governance in his country, for now. It now remains to be seen whether the kick-start to the economy arising from these financial arrangements would be built upon and be translated into tangible long term benefits for the Pakistanis; and indeed, whether there will be free and fair elections in Pakistan in January 2008.

From an American perspective, despite the apparent high costs in terms of financial aid, the US benefits from transferring the cost measured in terms of maintaining its own military operations and the potential military casualties to Pakistan who is expected to bear such costs; hence Vice President Cheney's reported "lean" on Pakistan's President Musharraf to do more to counter a resurgent Taliban and al-Qaeda.[2] In compensation and as further incentive for Pakistan to stay engaged, the US administration proposed transferring another US$800.0 million to the Musharraf government in the form of military assistance and budget support in 2008. Pakistan, it should be noted, has about 80,000 troops involved in its al-Qaeda–Taliban campaign whilst the US has less than

15,000 in Afghanistan. It is therefore not surprising that Pakistan should be hailed by Ambassador John Negroponte as: “a very committed partner in the war on terror.”[3] Hence, though fought in a distant land, the war on al-Qaeda and the Taliban is undoubtedly one of territoriality through a combination of condign and compensatory powers exercised by the US.

The exercise of this combination of power is further reinforced in the threat by the US Congress to discontinue aid to Pakistan unless it does more to seek out and destroy al-Qaeda operatives, and also does more to engage the Taliban in battle. But, behind this particular form of contracting out is the transfer of risk to others. Hence, the threat by US politicians falls under the category of rhetoric in that if the Pakistanis were to disengage from the exercise, the burden will have to be borne by Americans; and this would be disastrous for individual politicians and the Bush administration. Indeed, the consensus is that Musharraf is essential to the Bush administration’s war on terror; and General Musharraf knows it and exploits it. Moreover, the US will have no option but to treat Pakistan as siding with the Taliban and thus will be opening yet another front which is not likely to meet with approval by the American public having lost confidence in the Bush administration. Indeed, it is precisely to reduce the political risk that the Bush administration—the Pentagon and State Department in particular—outsource part of the security and other functions in Iraq to alleged mercenaries such as Blackwater Security Forces and others, as a bolster to its military presence in Iraq.

The Privileged Status of Israel

The financial and other arrangements between the US and Israel whereby Israel’s war on terror is funded by the US constitute compensatory power critical to the creation of the now well-articulated but beleaguered strategy of remaking the Middle East, arguably as the second step to ensuring US continued dominance in the twenty-first century. So, too, are the economic, strategic, and political supports unabashedly showered in consort with Europe and couched in terms of Israel’s right to exist. Indeed, for all practical purposes Israel is an extension of Western political and economic ideology beyond continental Europe, with historical religious significance for Europe as discussed in Chapter Two. It is therefore not surprising that former French president Chirac should have been as undiplomatic in his threat to “raze” Tehran should Iran ever “bomb” Tel Aviv[4]. Although Chirac backtracked from his statement, there should be no doubt about the territorial imperative of the West and, as such, exposes the thin veil of tolerance by it for others’ “right to have rights” if the exercise of such rights poses a threat to any of its members.

The willingness of Israel in July 2007 to release US$100.0 million of the almost US$1.0 billion of the taxes collected by it on behalf of the Palestinian government—which was withheld as punishment to the Palestinian people for electing Hamas in January 2006—as a reward to the Palestinian president for dismissing the Hamas government and appointing a Cabinet favorable to it, must be seen as the exercise of compensatory power by Israel. So, too, must be the restoration of US and EU foreign aid to the PLO-led Palestinian government and the lifting of sanctions by these countries.[5] The support offered by Egypt and Jordan to the PLO president and his new Cabinet is also a form of compensatory power exercised by Egypt and Jordan. But, like Pakistan, the choice for the Palestinians was either punishment—which was imposed by the West and Israel after the election of Hamas who is regarded as a terrorist organization—or compensation for compliance which Fatah led by Mr. Abbas now signals for its survival as a government in Palestine. That the choice was imposed through military support for Abbas, a moderate in the words of Mr. Bush, and therefore Fatah notwithstanding the charges of corruption leveled against its leaders, and whose splinter groups have been responsible for attacks against Israel, could signal a way out for the West and Israel in the crisis. Hamas, after all, refuses to recognize Israel, and according to Secretary Rice is bent on the destruction of Israel. Fatah's leadership, on the other hand, is not only more susceptible to Western pressure but is clearly fighting for its survival; hence its position is not dissimilar to that taken by General Musharraf of Pakistan. It is also instructive that Mr. Olmert should in July 2007 offer to take the names of 178 designated terrorists associated with Fatah off its most-wanted list and to free more than 250 Palestinian prisoners as acts of compensatory power. Fatah, of course, must recognize Israel's right to exist, renounce violence as an option, and must ratify all previously agreed terms and conditions prior to any peace negotiations. Israel, on the other hand, has yet to signal its position on borders and therefore on the status of Israeli settlements in the West Bank or, indeed, on the return of Palestinians: issues that have been contentious since 1967 and are likely to remain so in the immediate future despite Mr. Olmert's recent overtures to Abbas.

For many, getting to this point has been very difficult given the many errors in judgment, hidden agendas, and the resultant hardening of positions on both sides. The window of opportunity was, however, presented by the disagreement, between Hamas and Fatah, arguably orchestrated by the US. It is interesting to note here that the clash between Fatah and Hamas erupted in full soon after the meeting between Secretary of State Rice and the Palestinian President Abbas in December 2006. Also as observed by Sharee Makdisi of the *University of California*, both Israel and the US are providing material supplies to Fatah[6] thereby fuelling the internal conflict. Indeed, the promise to release US$100.0 million of the funds collected by Israel to the Palestinian President served as a powerful incentive to continue the conflict with Hamas which, arguably, was the expectation in the first place from withholding foreign aid and transfer of tax revenues by Israel while choking-off the flow of aid from neighboring Arab states. Whatever the politics, these acts of deprivation further evidence philosophical inconsistency: in this instance, with respect to the notion of human rights as observed by UN Human Rights envoy John Dugard.[7] Hence, rather than blame Hamas the

Palestinians are likely to continue to "blame outsiders, especially America"[8] for their woes.

Buying Arab Support

The complicity of contiguous neighbors secured by economic, military, and other support from the US and the EU, including a wink to human rights and other violations[9], also must be examined in terms of "our long-term interests and hopes for the region" as stated by Defense Secretary Designate Robert Gates in testimony to the Senate at his confirmation hearing on December 5, 2006. Many of these states operate on the basis of conditioned power derived from the instruments that created them and thus are dependent upon the goodwill of their benefactors. Others operate on the basis of compensation. As Dennis Ross pointed out in defense of US aid to Israel in a *Diane Rhem Show* in 2006 in the aftermath to John Mearsheimer and Stephen Walt's article in the *London Review of Books*, Egypt and Jordan are also recipients of US aid. What Ambassador Ross did not say was that both Egypt and Jordan are hosts to millions of Palestinian refugees whom Israel, with US support, hopes will never be returned to their pre–1948 homes. Hence, US aid to these countries is predicated on the non-return of Palestinians to their original homes. Moreover, Egypt and Jordan shared territorial responsibility for the Palestinians prior to the 1948 war with Israel and are partly responsible for the status of Arab–Palestinians.

In addition to providing sanctuary to displaced Palestinians, the roles of these so-called "moderate states" with respect to the war in Iraq have been articulated by President Bush in his new Iraq war strategy televised on January 10, 2007. In the same speech, Mr. Bush identifies Iran and Syria as responsible for the crisis in Iraq. In doing so, Mr. Bush is in effect exercising compensatory power on the one hand and condign power on the other as the leader of the Western democracies and the most powerful member in the international community. But while former British Foreign Secretary Lord Hurd agreed that Iran is fuelling the conflict in Iraq, it was in his words "a war we started." Also, according to Syria Cabinet Minister Buthaina Shaaban:

> It is easy for the American administration to try to distribute blame south and north, but the real issue is that the American occupation of Iraq has been a total disaster. They have a skill of distributing blame to the victims, and accusing the victims of being the cause of the problem.[10]

Interestingly, the US ambassador to the UN Zalmay Khalilzad has shifted some of the blame to Saudi Arabia: "We would expect and want them to help us on this strategic issue more than they are doing. And at times, some of them are not only not helping; [they] are doing things that undermine the effort to make progress." According to the *BBC NEWS*, the Ambassador made it clear to CNN that he was referring to Saudi Arabia.[11] However, according to Egyptian Foreign

Minister Ahmed Aboul Gheit, "the commitment was always to help a united Iraq to reach that point of full stability, and that we have been trying to do over the last four years."[12]

Responsibility-shifting is perceived not only in the case of Iraq but also in the war against al-Qaeda in the Pakistan–Afghanistan border. Responding to Senator Obama's threat to conduct military action without Pakistan's consent in pursuit of al-Qaeda on Pakistani soil, Pakistan's Minister of State for Information Tarsi Azeem could not have been more blunt: "This seems to be a reaction to their own failure in Afghanistan to control the US casualties and instead of addressing the situation there, they are finding scapegoats and damaging their own cause."[13]

Nuclear Weapons for Friends

With respect to the issue of nuclear proliferation, the revelation that the UK and France had secretly contributed to Israel's nuclear weapons program speaks to compensatory power premised on notions of territoriality as discussed more fully in Chapter Nine; as indeed does the nuclear cooperation agreement between the US and India secured by Mr. Bush on his visit to India in 2005. India, like Israel, is not a signatory to the Nuclear Non-proliferation Treaty (NPT) but is being compensated for its strategic location in the region from the perspective of America's territorial imperative, especially vis-à-vis China, Iran, and Pakistan who are perceived as threats to America's hegemony in the twenty-first century (see Amin 2006; Huntington, 1996). Indeed, the Chinese has openly expressed their friendship with Pakistan while seeking to build upon the window of opportunity presented through increasing trade with India.

Conditioned Power Preempted

At the other end of the NPT spectrum are the rights of North Korea and Iran under the NPT to which both are signatories. These are examples of conditioned power granted to them by the NPT and as such protected under the legal framework of that treaty. However, as witnessed, such rights are subject to change by the will of the more powerful signatories to the treaty pursuant their security interests. Indeed, as observed by John Ikenberry (2004: 326), "sovereignty has been made newly conditional: governments that fail to act like respectable, law-abiding states will lose their sovereignty," thereby providing partial answers to the issues raised by Rosemary Foot (2003: 3). It is instructive, however, that by insisting on its rights under the NPT, North Korea has managed to transform punishment to compensation for partially giving up its right to have rights.

While the US in now engaged in direct dialogue with one of the "Axis of evil" and is thinking in terms a US–North Korea bilateral working group to address the issues[14], it continues to insist that Iran should not be allowed to acquire nuclear technology other than as dictated by the West. That the West seeks to deny Iran the right to pursue nuclear energy for peaceful purposes, by way of ingeniously contrived efforts premised on perceived hostile intentions in Iran's behavior, so as to side-step the conditioned power enshrined in the NPT and other international treaties and agreements speaks to the exercise of condign power by it and to the play out of the territorial imperative. But Iran, unlike North Korea, has denied any nuclear weapons ambitions and in very many ways is being asked to prove a negative. The logic that is being applied is clearly Rumsfeld's: "Absence of evidence is not absence of weapons of mass destruction" (Ikenberry 2004: 325). Some might be tempted to counter that, perception of intention is not evidence either, with Iraq a case in point.

But Mr. Rumsfeld is not alone. It is worth noting here that while former Massachusetts governor Mario Cuomo acknowledges the inconsistency in the US policy whereby it shares nuclear weapons technology with its friends while denying the rights of others to pursue it, former Republican Speaker of the House Newt Gingrich adamantly insists that it is an inconsistency the US is morally endowed to uphold.[15] It is a position that speaks unabashedly to the imperial status of the US which Mr. Gingrich openly acknowledges.

The Geo-economics of Compensatory and Conditioned Powers

In addition to addressing reconstruction after World War II, the Bretton Woods institutions established in 1944 took state cooperation a step further. Their structures mirrored the relative power and interests of member states, with the US as the most powerful member assuming the leadership role and, of course, asymmetric advantage. As observed by Lentner (2004: 79): "Interests, especially American ones, have provided the driving force for global economic management." The decision-making process in these institutions are therefore controlled primarily by the Organization for Economic Cooperation and Development (OECD) countries, with the US providing leadership, and pursue their respective self interest as a first order requirement as evidenced by the provisions of the GATT, the forerunner to the WTO, and the changing of the roles of the IMF and World Bank, from fostering development to becoming instruments of reform in developing countries during the debt crisis of the 1980s (see Chang 2006: 5–8). These privileges accruing to the more powerful states have led Koehane to observe:

> International institutions can only be understood in terms of state power and state interests. How else could we explain the underdevelopment of development institutions as opposed to the trade and financial institutions so central to the richest, most powerful countries? (Quoted in Lentner 2004: 81).

As the Bretton Woods institutions almost exclusively served the political and economic interests of the West over the years, the lack of similar development in the Third World served to affirm the notion of a North–South divide which concerned the Under Secretary of State for Economic Affairs George Ball in the Kennedy administration. Hence, on August 23, 1961 Ball wrote to President Kennedy: "We cannot be in a position of forming a cabal of the industrialized countries against the rest of the world."[16] Ball was of the view that incorporating the Third World economies into the expanding world trading system would strengthen US power around the world; a US imperative in the face of the then growing appeal of state-centric model of development and revolutionary tendencies of newly independent states (see Peck 2006; see also Gaddis 2004: 221–246). In this regard, a China policy of containment without isolation requires that China's neighbors be fully supported in nation-building as countervailing the revolutionary rhetoric of the PRC by the process of "modernization", that is, promoting an American-centric world order through foreign aid that emphasizes the "universality of the American way" augmented by opening up the American market to products from the Third World. To this end, Japan was seen as serving the American agenda and was called upon to help combat the spread of communism in Asia. In return Japan was allowed greater access to the US market even though that meant accepting, according to George Ball, "some temporary and local injury to certain American firms, industries, and communities" (quoted in Peck 2006: 215).

It should be noted that Japan was considered a third world country during this period and was therefore excluded from GATT. Its importance to the US and thus the West was perceived more in terms of helping to maintain a balance between the communist and non-communist world (Peck, 2006: 214). Japan would eventually be accepted into GATT but its entry was conditioned on its compliance with special rules applicable exclusively to it. For example, it brought with it the restrictions on its exports of textile and clothing to the US and Europe imposed under the Multi-fiber Arrangement (MFA). The US had reinstated farm support to cotton growers in 1955 and thus restricted Japanese exports by means of voluntary export restraints (VERs). As a result of VERs, Japanese textile and clothing exports to the US declined from 63 percent in 1958 to 26 percent in 1960 (see Tussie 1987: 76). Japan continues to trade with the West by way of bilateral agreements with respect to certain of its exports notwithstanding being a member of the WTO. For example, Japan's export of automobiles to the US continues to be subject to import duties as well as quantitative restrictions and other countervailing duties (see Lentner 2004: 82; Bhagwati and Patrick 1990; Bhagwati 1988) and thus evidences erosion of the principles and rules of the GATT and its successor WTO.

Japan is not alone. China's accession to WTO membership has been similarly conditioned, with quantitative restrictions placed on imports of Chinese textile and clothing into the US and Europe. Indeed, in January 2007 both the US and EU imposed further restrictions arising from complaints from their domestic textile and cotton industries. Hence, while the demand of the US government is for a "level playing field" in international trade, its actions as observed by Lentner (2004: 81) speak to unwillingness to substantially constrain its policy options. Indeed, contrary to WTO rules the US continues to subsidize its cotton growers to the detriment of Brazilian and West African cotton growers.

Bretton Woods and Developing Countries

With respect to developing countries, while their manufactured goods are included with all others and are subject to the negotiating process of the WTO since 1995, agricultural products—their major export and hence source of foreign currency—which have been excluded since GATT are the subject of much negotiations within the WTO framework. The derogation of agriculture from the GATT has been at the insistence of the US and from which position the European Common Agricultural Policy (CAP) derived its basis in the early 1960s attendant "the embedded liberalism bargain" which allowed for "free international trade combined with welfare state protection" (Lentner 2004: 80).

Again, as observed by Lentner (2004: 79): "the stage of development of the domestic economy of the dominant power shapes the arrangements of the international regimes." Britain pushed free trade in the nineteenth century because of its dominance in manufacture; the US became isolationist in the middle of the first half of the twentieth century, again, because of the shape of its economy. Indeed, as Jagdish Bhagwati (1988) observed, free trade becomes a policy option only when one is strong, as was the case of the US in the years immediately following World War II; its recoil into protectionist rhetoric in the twenty-first century reflects a weakening economic position vis-à-vis the rest of the world.

American competitiveness, to be sure, has been eroded, albeit gradually, over the years since the 1950s, requiring a recall of many of the earlier arrangements that sheltered European economic reconstruction. Indeed, the windfall to American industries in the 1950s in consequence of the destruction of European and Japanese production capacities during the war began to dissipate in consequence of competitive products from Europe and Japan. This led to calls from the US for reconciliation of international obligations with domestic objectives; thereby clearly identifying the welfare state system as a ready candidate for reform. As such, the disagreements between the US and EU have intensified over the years and have largely centered on the reduction if not the removal of US farm subsidies—itself a manifestation of welfarism—on the one hand, and the removal of protective barriers to the European markets on the other, the latter in keeping with the well-established US strategy of opening markets for American goods and services.

The reverberations from these US–EU disagreements and rearrangements are transmitted to developing countries through the renegotiation or even abandonment of preferential arrangements that were grounded in the earlier embedded "liberalism bargain" which were extended in large measure to former European colonies. Moreover, as the larger developing countries have emerged as competitors to both US and Europe, they are expected to provide opportunities for developed countries' products to compete in their domestic markets. Hence, the US and EU both find themselves on the same page: accusing, for example, India and Brazil in 2007 of "not offering new market opportunities for manufacturing exports." At the same time, the Director General of the WTO admonishes China for not opening its markets to American exports. In sum, according to U.S. Trade Representative Susan Schwab, unless some agreement is reached in 2007, "it [the Doha Round] will go into hibernation for several years to come and most of us believe that would not be a good outcome;"[17] a possibility that was not lost on many observers on the collapse of talks in Cancun, Mexico in 2003.

These disagreements which now involve developing countries have operated to suspend the "Doha" trade talks in Geneva in 2006 as it did in October 2005 and, again, in 2003 in Cancun Mexico. As reported in 2006, the EU sees US inflexibility as responsible for the breakdown between the two sides, while the US says the EU has failed to open up its markets. EU negotiator Peter Mandelson wants the US to cut US$20.0 billion of farm subsidies whilst the US wants the EU to further reduce its tariffs. Mr. Bush's rhetoric on the other hand centers on developing countries: "The best way to help impoverished nations is to complete this Doha round to encourage the spread of wealth and opportunity through open and reasonable and fair trade."[18] Interestingly, the very countries Mr. Bush speaks of are victims of US farm subsidies.

In October 2005, negotiations for a trade accord failed because, according to the US trade negotiator, the Europeans failed to match the US offer to cut its farm subsidies by 60 percent and import duties on agricultural products by 55 percent to 90 percent.[19] The developing countries meanwhile want Western countries to "give up tens of billions of farm subsidies" which they say "unfairly encourages overproduction, and pushes down global commodity prices."[20] Three years earlier, West African developing countries helped to bring the WTO talks in Cancun, Mexico to an abrupt end by walking out over US cotton farm subsidies. The WTO is still to rule on Brazil's challenge to such subsidies.

But not all developing countries are created equal. Interestingly, while the majority of the poorer developing countries want increased access to US and European markets for their products, 19 African Caribbean and Pacific (ACP) countries led by Guyana want the EU Sugar Protocol—which not only subsidizes European beet sugar farmers but also provides for preferential treatment to these 19 member countries sugar exports to it—to either remain in place or be phased out gradually with compensation paid to them for ensuring, according to one local Guyana economist, "a reliable supply of sugar" to the EU since 1974. But as pointed out in Chang (2006), the EU had long signaled its intention to reform the sugar protocol in the light of the high cost of farm subsidies and the ruling of the WTO against such an arrangement. Moreover, by their objection to EU agricultural reform these 19 countries are essentially acting against the majority poorer developing countries that stand to benefit from the *Everything but Arms* (EBA) trade proposal of the EU. One country, Guyana, went as far as portraying dire circumstances for its economy if the planned sugar protocol reform were put into effect, while boldly expanding its sugar production facilities. Not said is that, in addition to Guyana being an inefficient and high-cost producer, the ruling political party derives its support almost entirely from the agricultural sector and that the Caribbean Sugar Association, the most fervent advocate for a protracted phase-out of subsidies, derives about 75 percent of its support from the Guyana Sugar Corporation. Moreover, Guyana is one of the countries that have pursued a development strategy predicated on the perpetual flow of foreign aid.

Greater Say for Developing Countries?

A major concern of developing countries is the inability to significantly influence decisions of the multilateral institutions. One of the major complaints of developing countries is that they are excluded from the decision-making process in trade negotiations which are conducted by the industrialized countries behind closed doors, notwithstanding they are "full members" of the WTO. In addition to having a greater say in WTO decisions, developing countries want more say in formulating policy at the IMF. Indeed, many NGOs are seen as having greater influence on WTO, IMF, and World Bank decisions than developing countries (see Woods 2003). Additionally, several Asian countries have become wary of the IMF since the Asian financial crisis in 1997–8, reducing their total borrowings from US$17.8 billion in 1997 to just over US$300.0 million in 2005, and would be less suspicious of it if they were given a greater say in policy-making. While the US and Japan appear willing to accommodate a change in the voting shares, the Europeans have been reluctant to make any changes to the voting structure of the institution.[21]

The above said, according to Musharraf (2006: 185) those who seek to blame the IMF, and presumably the World Bank, do so out of their "own inadequacies" and "use it as a scapegoat." Citing Pakistan's experience, the Pakistani president declares: "when we are not ourselves sincere in our intentions and have no appetite to fulfill our obligations and responsibilities, it is no use blaming others." Actually, many aid-dependent countries have taken a page out of Pakistan's book and are identifying "terrorists" activities or the potential there for, the expunging of which from their societies lest they become a threat to America and the West cannot be adequately carried out without the necessary financial resources. For example, the discovery of a terror-plot at J.F. Kennedy airport in New York City in May 2007 by three Guyanese has prompted the Guyana Minister of Home Affairs to allude to the need for external funding to help Guyana expunge potential terrorists from its midst.

Playing Both sides as a Strategy

Interestingly, following on the heels of the alleged terror-plot at Kennedy international airport in May 2007 the Guyana president visited Washington in June 2007, seeking additional financing from the *Inter-American Development Bank* and other official sources. Guyana, it should be noted, was one of the several countries who had their external debts written off in 2006. Now it is back, as predicted in Chang (2006), hand out-stretched and clearly playing on the vulnerability of the Bush administration. Two years earlier, the Guyana president's ruling political party proclaimed the: "usefulness of the scientific methodology of Marxism-Leninism." Moreover, its General Secretary declared Venezuelan president Hugo Chavez as: "a progressive nationalist in Venezuela and a courageous and outspoken leader of the Continent"; and that his party, and thus the government of Guyana, "is opposed to all attempts to remove Chavez's democratically elected government by undemocratic means."[22] It should be noted that in 2005 Guyana sought to step outside the CARICOM treaty to which it is a signatory so as to access discounted oil supplies from Venezuela; it is also a major trans-shipment point for illegal drugs destined for the US and Europe.

Foreign Aid

The exercise of compensatory power by way of foreign aid is also evident in the relationship between developed and developing countries. Indeed, history has witnessed a relationship that transitioned from condign power exercised by the colonial powers, to a mixture of compensatory and conditioned powers in the second half of the twentieth century. In addition to compensation for strategic or political services rendered, some countries are compensated for forgoing their right to compete with producers in donor-countries, with the assistance of insiders. The European ACP sugar protocol mentioned above evidences one such arrangement: the ACP countries forgo competition with EU sugar producers and receive a preferential price for an agreed quantity of their output. This arrangement came into effect in 1974 on the UK becoming a member of the EU.

In relying on such preferential treatment, developing countries are made vulnerable to the consequences of perverse incentives which many of them exhibit as revealed by the debate on EU's preferential treatment (Chang 2006). Because of the guaranteed price paid to ACP countries—which is the price paid to European farmers and thus well above world market price—for a specified quantity of sugar, many such producers have essentially engineered production to meet their obligations under the sugar protocol, paying very little attention to world trends or to enterprise efficiency. Indeed, Guyana, for example, took the position that the ACP sugar protocol was "enshrined" and rather than seek to diversify out of sugar as Mauritius, St. Lucia, Trinidad and Tobago, Barbados, and St Kitts have done, increased production capacity to pre–1974 levels. The

Guyana rationale being that the EU will be forced to either continue subsidizing sugar production and maintain its preferential arrangement with ACP producers or compensate the latter whom, it claims, were "misled" by EU negotiators. Either way, Guyana benefits, and so does the incumbent political party which is wholly reliant on the sugar industry for its support.

Exploiting Weaknesses in Foreign aid Frameworks

While the above example illustrates well the tendency of some developing countries to extract as much trade-related foreign aid as possible from donor countries, there is evidence to suggest that humanitarian and other forms of financial aid are equally targeted. Often, the frameworks developed by donor countries and multilateral institutions are exploited by local politicians and bureaucrats in some developing countries to serve their political and personal interests.

One such source for possible exploitation is the Poverty Reduction Strategy Paper (PRSP) which enhanced highly indebted poor countries (eHIPCs) are required to prepare for approval by the donor countries and the multilateral institutions. The loopholes in the poverty reduction program provide corrupt local politicians with opportunities to target relief to a specific community that is supportive of the incumbent political party whilst punishing residents in communities that support the political opposition. This practice is often masked by the inclusion of projects with national reach which are displayed for those bearing gifts but which often are used as a way of benefiting party supporters by way of construction and other contracts. In many cases, schools, healthcare centers and the like are constructed with little regard to the needs of the communities and to the availability of teachers and healthcare professionals to staff them or, indeed, with provision for adequate maintenance. As a result, many of the buildings, cheaply constructed in the first place, are left to decay, that is, when international aid agencies' focus is elsewhere. Meanwhile, the favored contractors get their reward for political and other support, the politicians and bureaucrats get their kickbacks, whilst the government is able to produce evidence of tangible expenditure on education and healthcare.

Another example of aid extraction is to conspire with contractors whose sub-standard work is certified acceptable, only to require substantial repairs or replacement within two or three years as a means to ensuring the flow of aid on a continuous basis. Road and sea defense projects are cases in point, as are drainage and irrigation projects. Indeed, as is well recognized in the development economics literature, large scale bureaucratic corruption is more likely to take place in the implementation of public works projects and in the awarding of major government contracts generally. The leakages that occur are usually measured to donors' tolerance and have over time made many local politicians and bureaucrats extremely rich and powerful even under the watchful eye of donors and the multilateral institutions.

Even in cases of humanitarian aid there is evidence to suggest that the seriousness of a disaster or epidemic is often overstated in an attempt to attract substantial aid or to keep its flow at a particular level. For example, in a recent report on HIV-AIDS it is suggested that the number of AIDS-related cases may be less than first estimated. Whilst a survey of cases in India will report an almost 50 percent reduction from that originally reported, others countries, Ethiopia for example, are reluctant to adjust their estimates if to do so would result in a reduction in foreign aid.[23] A discernible tendency is that, whatever the expressed concerns at the level of donor countries there always will be a number of new recipients whose affliction with whatever is in consequence of the availability of foreign aid.

Targeting Aid to Developing Countries

It is widely accepted among developing country economists and other observers that developing countries by and large were kept in a dependency relationship in consequence of colonialism and of the Bretton Woods agreements (see Amin 2006: 94; Lentner 2004; see also Gaddis 2003: 161). In this relationship, the industrialized countries compete with one another for access to raw materials. Those with former colonies seek to maintain access to their markets through preserving common bonds by creating an umbrella institution such as, for example, the British Commonwealth in the case of the UK. The French francophone grouping was a similar institution whilst Spain encouraged a looser but nonetheless cultural relationship with South America. The US relied on the Munroe Doctrine to keep direct European influences out of Latin America and over time established its hegemony in the region, with the *Organization of American States* (OAS) led by it as a semi-oversight organization. Also, as discussed in Chapter Five the US sought to establish its hegemony in the Pacific region, most notably through the exercise of condign power in the case of Korea and Vietnam but also through compensatory power in the form of bilateral trade agreements and bilateral aid.

Hence, when viewed dispassionately the primary function of official foreign aid is to serve the political, economic, and strategic interests of donor-countries who target such aid in accordance with their ideological road map that ensures continued influence over recipients' economic and political affairs (see Nicolaidsis and Lacroix 2003). In this functionality, official foreign aid necessarily supports the hegemonic ambitions of the donor no less than colonialism served the political and economic ambitions of the colonizers (see Amin 2006: 94). Indeed, the use of official foreign aid since the demise of colonialism has come to manifest most discernibly as one of the two pillars in foreign policy of states whose interests maintaining the geopolitical structures of colonialism serve, the *status quo ante* if you will; and manifest in a dependency relationship anchored in the ideology of "freedom and democracy" in the twenty-first century. Not surprisingly, then, the discourse on foreign aid, especially official foreign aid, often begs the question in support of the donor. Hence the need to clarify the unspoken if not unwritten basis of foreign aid which arguably turns on what Ardrey (1961: 12) identifies as the "innate characteristic of territoriality in man", and evidenced by the promethean will of the powerful to maintain economic and political dominance. With this in mind, humanitarian aid is distinguished from reconstruction and development aid and from surreptitious aid with regime change in mind.

Humanitarian Aid

It is not that there are no tangible benefits accruing to recipients of foreign aid, or that there is no honesty or sincerity in those promoting and pursuing aid from a humanitarian perspective. Far from it! Humanitarian foreign aid has been most beneficial to both recipient and country of origin. Indeed, humanitarian aid often operates to countervail the political proclivities of donor governments, by the display of kindness and concern, often in stark contradiction to official policy. Evidence US offer of humanitarian to its foes, and vise versa, most notably Fidel Castro's offer of assistance to the US in the wake of Hurricane Katrina in 2005. That this is so is mainly because humanitarian aid has been placed outside the political, having been rooted in religion with early manifestation in the compensatory power of the Church, albeit the reward for attending church services or religious instructions.

Given the derivation of humanitarian aid, many aid recipients make a distinction between "the American people" and "the US government" in discourse on such aid policy. The generosity of the American people is never in question nor indeed is the humanitarian response of citizens of other countries. There is therefore no denying the contribution of Habitat for Humanity to poverty reduction or the contribution of Bill and Malinda Gates Foundation to fighting the scourge of HIV/AIDS around the developing countries. There is also no denying the roles of the Red Cross, Red Crescent, and OXFAM, for example. These and other similar organizations that address themselves to specific humanitarian challenges indeed have been most effective in reversing many of the excesses of politically-derived aid; serving as a buffer to the excesses inherent in systemic individualism that has come to be expected from neo-conservative governments pursuant their respective territorial imperatives. In this latter regard, Baroness Thatcher's 1987 observation that, "there is no such thing as society. There are individual men and women, and there are families" reflects the extent to which individualism has underwritten economic and political thought, and thus policy since the 1980s. Ironically, it is often out of a common human bond, our common humanity if you will, that ordinary citizens and nongovernmental organizations (NGOs) take the lead in reaching out to others when catastrophe strikes; with race, culture, religion, and other identities relegated to the baseless political identities that they are and, but for politicians, would languish in irrelevance.

Evidence the initial response to the victims of the 2004 Tsunami, especially in Banda Ache and Thailand. It was ordinary citizens and NGOs who were the first responders in empathy and deed; the politicization of the process later followed in predicable and well-calculated hegemonic fashion.

Yet, even in times of dire humanitarian needs politics do inhibit response. Indeed, as reported by the outgoing United Nations Secretary General Kofi Annan, more than one-half of the official pledges to the victims of the 2004 Tsunami have yet to be honored at the end of 2006[24]. Similarly, Bob Geldof and many others have expressed dissatisfaction with the results of the G-8 meeting in Germany in June 2007. As pointed out, even though the group pledged US$60.0 billion of aid to combat HIV-AIDS, malaria, tuberculosis and other diseases in the developing countries, very little was new aid and no time table for its flow was established.

In addition to the politics of foreign aid as evidenced by the 2007 G-8 decision, people are inclined to be less responsive to others whom they are conditioned to regard as posing a threat to their wellbeing if not their existence. Evidence the response to the earthquake victims of Pakistan in 2005. While some would argue that Western donors were experiencing aid-fatigue in consequence of the horrendous pressure from the humanitarian and reconstruction needs of the victims of the 2004 Tsunami, the meager response to the pleadings of the earthquake victims of Pakistan had been influenced arguably by the strained US-Pakistan relations and the well-publicized al-Qaeda training camps in Pakistan. While not to deny the efforts of caring individuals around the world and, of course, the NGOs, it was in the end relatives, friends and others with cultural ties to Pakistan who formed the backbone of the relief effort in this instance. Evidence also the slow response of the Western governments to the HIV/AIDS epidemic in Africa which has been characterized in uncharitable if not radical terms by those whose civility became overwhelmed by the politics of aid. It was not until the numbers became staggering and the threat of some countries to ignore intellectual property rights as they relate to the manufacture of antiretroviral drugs that the major Western governments began to become more forthcoming; and even then, there are allegations of abuses born out of the desire for dominance and for advancing pharmacological science.

The politics of aid notwithstanding, private institutional donors such as the Gates Foundation have been at the forefront of fighting the HIV/AIDS scourge that has been inflicted upon the poor for too long. There are others whose humanitarian concerns transcend the profit motive. Brazil, for example, has established a pharmaceutical manufacturing plant in Mozambique to produce generic anti-retroviral drugs and other drugs for the suffering poor in Mozambique initially and for Africa generally.[25]

But even within states in the West, politics do get in the way of aid relief. The response to the victims of Hurricane Katrina in September 2005 is a case in point. While the government agencies dithered, the mainly black residents of New Orleans were experiencing the trauma of bureaucratic and political neglect; and this in the most advanced and powerful society in the modern world. Indeed, it took a judicial decision in December 2006 to have federal aid restored to the victims of Katrina, and even then about 80,000 are still displaced.

It should be recognized that humanitarian aid comes also in the form of military intervention in civil strife. It often requires the intervener to choose sides, relocate people away from their historical homes and the like (see Kaufmann 2004: 409). Clearly Bosnia stands out as just such intervention. While it is not beyond the realm of probability that Iraq will require humanitarian intervention, the current US involvement is seen by most observers as giving rise to such intervention as a possible lasting solution. Looking out over the horizon, similar intervention may become necessary in Lebanon, Sir Lanka, and some African countries that were put together to serve colonial interests.

Marshall Plan

The Marshall Plan followed in the wake of the defeat of Germany and Italy in Europe, and Japan in Asia. It could be regarded as the first variant of official foreign aid, although some would argue that the US and Canadian Lend-lease programs with Britain during the early years of World War II was its forerunner.

The Marshall Plan which ever so often is referred to as evidencing US generosity was not as altruistic as some would like to believe. It in fact hijacked the functions of the International Bank for Reconstruction and Development (IBRD), a Bretton Woods institution, and placed most of them firmly in the hands of the US, giving it the opportunity to promote European integration in keeping with American prescriptions on monetary and fiscal policy and domestic market liberalism (Lentner 2004: 81). While, therefore, its primary function was the rebuilding of Europe and Japan and through such process the rebuilding of lives, which it did admirably and bought international political capital for the US for decades to follow, it had as one of its objectives the creation of markets for US goods and services, and influence: imperatives of the endless accumulation of capital. In this regard, the Marshall Plan evidences the use of foreign aid as an economic and political tool. The Europeans and Japan showed their gratitude to America by tacitly acknowledging it as the new leader of Western democracy; and the Europeans, by sharing their economic reconstruction with American capitalists, contributed to US prosperity and to a false sense of economic superiority which the US has been struggling to maintain ever since.

The almost 30 glorious years of economic prosperity enjoyed by the US since coming out of the Depression was arguably in consequence of the surge in exports to Western Europe, in the absence of any productive capacity to speak of in Europe. Moreover, Western Europe became a source of investment opportunities for US firms since the rebuilding of Germany and Japan was largely conducted according to the political requirements of the victors. But even while the rebuilding of Europe was taking place, it was primarily predicated on strengthening economic and political ties of the Western democracies and, as noted above, an American-centric universal order. As a result, Japan's manufacture and exports to Europe and the US were severely restricted and reflected conditions attached to the rebuilding of its economy. It should surprise no one that Martin Tolchin should suggest an Israel Marshall Plan for the Palestinians as an aspect of any peace agreement.[26]

The Dark Side to Foreign Aid

The underlying basis for foreign aid as evolved over the decades and its ramifications have been looked at, albeit briefly in context of economic determinism—the *sine qua non* of a capitalist world economy—on the one hand, and the outstretched hands of many developing countries, on the other. We have looked at the economic benefits of foreign aid from the perspectives of donor and recipient. As shown, whilst the benefits are skewed in favor of the donor, recipients do benefit in the form of increased access to education, healthcare, and other social infrastructure to keep them engaged as partners in the accumulation of capital. We have also seen that foreign aid serves as perverse incentives to the recipients where such aid operates to negate the disciplinary mechanism of the market. It is an on-going relationship few are prepared to end because targeted aid benefits the developed countries whilst the existence of corrupt regimes and bureaucrats at the receiving end ensures the desired asymmetric relationship. The trick is to ensure that the flow-through of aid to the people is greater than a trickle, hence the unwritten criterion of acceptable leakage employed by donors. In the end, however, as evidenced by the write-off of official debts of the EHIPCs in 2006, it is a matter of cost-benefit analysis to the developed countries: the cost is measured in terms of the debts eventually written off; the benefit in terms of the trade derived not only from the aid-created markets but also from restraining the potential competitive forces latent in developing countries. While this approach to foreign has been largely left unquestioned, there is as yet a darker side to foreign aid which is fiercely resisted: when used to foment internal strife to effect regime change or to protract internal conflict in furtherance of ideology. Such aid is often supported by condign power.

Regime Change and Countervailing Responses

A cursory examination of instability around the world since the end of World War II reveals an increasing resort to foreign aid as an overt and covert tool in international relations. While one is wont to point to the West as the perpetrators of such practices in the process of universalizing democracy, and, therefore individualism, the evidence suggests that it is not exclusive to the West. Be that as it may, few would argue that regime change is not the *modus operandi* of

American foreign aid in cases where what exists is incompatible with the American notion of a world order.

With respect to the US use of foreign aid as an instrument of regime change, the role of the CIA in the removal of the democratically-elected Iranian President Mohammed Mossadegh stands in evidence. With the Iran experience behind it, the US has consistently devoted a part of its foreign aid budget to destabilizing other governments that are not compatible with the American view of the world, with Cuba, Latin America, Lebanon, the former Soviet Republics, and more recently Arab—Palestine, as prime examples. Such actions come in the form of providing technical and financial assistance to dissidents and others who are likely to effect regime change from within. It also comes in the form of creating humanitarian crisis as a necessary corollary to regime change as is fully recognized, even by the UN, with respect to Hamas-controlled Gaza. The invasion of Iraq in 2003 and the "broader war on terror" evidence the Bush administration's expansion of foreign aid combined with condign power pursuant universalizing a particular brand of ideology that requires the remaking of world order within a predetermined time span. Others are encouraged to support this process by the promise of development and humanitarian aid.

With respect to the latter, recall the then Secretary of State Colin Powell, with the US-proposed Draft Resolution in one hand and the promise of aid in the other, visiting those African countries whose votes in the UN Security Council were deemed important to legitimizing the invasion of Iraq. To paraphrase one African government official who was ready to vote in favor of the proposal to invade Iraq: it is happenstance that his country's need for aid should coincide with the needs of the US. Recall also, the promise of increase US aid to combat HIV/AIDS in Africa by President Bush at this crucial decision-making time in the Security Council. Africa became the focus of attention of US foreign policy if only briefly.

But the offer of aid could also be countervailing to the original exercise of such power. For example, it is clearly to Iran's benefit to keep American forces bogged down in Iraq by allowing the flow of technical aid if not other material aid to select Shia militias. The same could be said of Saudi Arabia whose nationals are found to be a significant part of the Sunni insurgency. With respect to the latter, it is interesting that despite reports and indeed knowledge that Saudis are to be found in the make-up of the Sunni insurgency in Iraq, the Secretaries of Defense and State are taking a US$20.0 billion arms package to Saudi Arabia and other US-friendly Arab Gulf states to entice them to support US efforts in Iraq.[27] To the extent that this visit comes on the heels of the US ambassador's accusation that Saudi Arabia is contributing to the destabilization of Iraq, it could be argued that it is to Saudi Arabia's strategic interest to portray Iran as a danger to the region for just such a response by the US, the objections of Israel to the US-aid package notwithstanding.

Likewise, the training and arming of Hezbollah, though countervailing to Israel's exercise of condign power in Lebanon, is also on the dark side; nonetheless in keeping with Ardrey's definition of the territorial imperative. Venezuela

Hugo Chavez offer of aid to his South American neighbors and cheap oil to whomever wants it is design equally to counter the expansion if not to secure the demise of American hegemony in the region. As Ardrey (1966: 236) reminds us: "We need to bear in mind that the territorial principle motivates all of the human species. Whether we approve or we disapprove, whether we like it or we do not, it is a power as much as an ally of our enemies as it is of ourselves and our friends." Interestingly, it is what makes game-theoretic models less reliable for cross-cultural application as discussed more fully in chapter eight.

NOTES

1 Mr. Armitage has publicly denied ever making such a threat.
2 Graham, S., "Chaney asks Musharraf to fight al-Qaeda", *The Associated Press*, February 26, 2007
3 US Congressional Hearing, *C-SPAN*, January 17, 2007
4 Keaten, J., "French leader backtracks on Iran comment", *Associated Press*, February 1, 2007
5 "US, EU restore Palestinian ties", *BBC News*, http://news.bbc.co.uk/go/pr/fr/-/2/hi/middle_east/6764541.stm; June 18, 2007
6 "Israel-Palestine Conflict Palestine Center", *C-SPAN2*, January 29, 2007
7 Franks, T., "UN envoy attacks Mid-East Quartet", *BBC NEWS*, http://news.bbc.co.uk/go/pr/fr/-/2/hi/middle_east/7044069.stm
8 See "Where Mr. Bush chose not to go", *The Economist*, December 2nd 2006
9 It is worth noting that 15 of the 19 terrorists responsible for 9/11 were from Saudi Arabia and that many of the insurgents in Iraq are Saudi nationals.
10 "Iraq, Four years on", *BBC World*, March 23, 2007.
11 "US envoy accuses Saudis on Iraq", *BBC NEWS*, http://news.bbc.co.uk/go/pr/fr/-/2/hi/middle_east/6921737.stm. July 30, 2007
12 Gearan, A., Baldor, L., "Rice, Gates win no new Arab help in Iraq", *Associated Press*, http://news.yahoo.com/s/ap/20070731/ap_on_re_mi_ea/us_mideast
13 "Pakistan slams 'ignorant' Obama attack warning", http://news.yahoo.com/s/afp/20070802/wl_sthasia_afp/usvote2008pakistanafghanisn
14 Hill, C., Assistant Secretary of State for East Asian and Pacific Affairs, Press Conference, June 25, 2007, *C-SPAN.*
15 "2008 Presidential Debate", American Perspective, *C-SPAN*, February 28, 2007
16 U.S. Department of State, Foreign Relations of the United States, Government Printing Office, 1961–63, 13:37–8
17 http://biz.yahoo.com/ap/070705/apec_trade.html?.v=6
18 "EU and US see fresh trade push", *BBC NEWS*, http://news.bbc.co.uk/go/pr/fr/-/2/hi/business/6240079.stm, January 8, 2007
19 Wright, T., "Global Trade Talks End Early With No Progress Made", the *New York Times*, October 20, 2005.
20 Ibid.
21 Rook, D., "Asian nations want more muscles to flex at IMF", *Associated Foreign Press*, September 10, 2006
22 "PPP welcomes Chavez Petro Caribe initiative", *Stabroek News*, Guyana, August 2, 2005

24 2006 Year-end speech, December 19, 2006.
25 Mangwiro, C., "Brazil offers drug factory to AIDS-ravaged Mozambique", http://news.yahoo.com/s/nm/20070529/hl_nm/aids_mozambique_brazil_dc,
26 Tolchin, M., Book TV, *C-SPAN2,* October 22, 2006.
27 Gray, A., and Pleming, S., "Rice, Gates offer arms, seek help on Mideast trip", http://news.yahoo.com/s/nm/20070730/pl_nm/mideast_usa_dc

Part Three

China Emerging

Chapter Five

The Dragon Awakes

("The world hustles where money beckons. The world jostles where profits thicken."
Szema Chien – 85.B.C.)[1]

Introduction

"Let China sleeps, for when she awakes the world will tremble." Just under two hundred years since the demise of Napoleon, to whom this quotation is attributed, the dragon awakes and the world has taken notice. Indeed, not since the US shed its mantle of isolationism and boldly assumed world economic and political dominance at the end of World War II has a country arrested the attention of the world as China; emerging from its long slumber, signaling as it does its intention to take an active role in world affairs, and just by being, the reordering of international political and economic relations as part of its journey in the twenty-first century.

While China in the phraseology of Gerald Segal (2004) indeed is "a middle power" and is perceived by some as deserving no more attention than Brazil in contemporary geo-economics and geopolitical discourse, the shadow cast by its history and its contribution to Western civilization are etched in the minds of contemporary man far and wide. More significantly, it is one of the ancient civilizations that has redefined itself and in so doing has learned to adapt to an essentially Western-dominated world going into the twenty-first century (see Mitter, 2003). For this reason, its presence cannot be wished away or minimized and must therefore be examined not in terms of its perception of self necessarily but rather in terms of how it is perceived by others in context of their own vulnerabilities. What these perceptions are, more specifically how they are informed is a first step to understanding the China factor in the twenty-first century and why China seemingly looms as a challenge to the Westernization imperative.

Historical Background

China's history dates back to more than 4,000 years. It became a united kingdom—the Middle Kingdom—under the Emperor Qin (Ch'in) in 221 B.C. with an imperial system that remained "remarkably" consistent for more than 2,000 years, up to the early twentieth century until it was overthrown in 1911 (See

Kesselman M., et al., 1996: 371). It is one of the very few civilizations that can point to some form of continuity dating back to B.C.E., having survived the ravages of time and, of course, conquests.

The Middle Kingdom, to be sure, has shrunk in size but it looms large in terms of history and culture, both of which continue to define the Chinese personality and relationship with non-Chinese. This continuity is credited to several interrelated factors. First, what is today's structure of government in most Western capital—a President or Prime Minister and small groups of advisers—as constituting an effective system of national government was practiced, according to Kesselman M., et al (1996: 371), "long before the strong monarchical states of Europe took form in the seventeenth century" and certainly centuries before there was a United States of America or the unification of India under British rule (Misra 1990), the oldest and the largest democracies respectively.

Second, Chinese agricultural having benefited from advanced techniques for their time, including irrigation and multi-cropping which were copied by the modern world, became the mainstay of the Chinese empire; commerce and transport were equally highly developed for the time, as was smelting. As noted by He Ping (2002: 26), studies on the development process during the Song period "have implied that imperial China was at one point economically much closer to modernity than other societies." The link between the imperial officials and the peasants was the landlord, not unlike the manorial system of England, with one discernible difference: there were over one million small villages functioning as separate entities in consort with flourishing urban centers: Hangzhou with a population of over a million people was deemed the largest and grandest city in the world in the thirteenth century. This system served to hold the empire together in relative peace and prosperity until the middle of the nineteenth century.

Third, the teachings of Confucius (c. 551–479 B.C.E) that stressed social harmony, righteous behavior, and deference to one's elders informed the official ideology and served to perpetuate the established order. Confucianism permeated Chinese psyche and became the essence of Chinese in much the same way as individualism has become the essence of American. Long before *Magna Carta*, St. Augustine, and Thomas Aquinas, the notion of removing an unjust ruler was authorized by the "Mandate of Heaven" contained in Confucianism. This mandate notwithstanding, as Kesselman M., et al. (1996: 372) observed: "Confucianism was basically a conservative orthodoxy that served to justify and maintain an autocratic state, a patriarchal culture and a stratified society." And this was at a time when the rest of the world was undergoing religious and social upheaval, as evidenced by the Inquisitions in Europe and the Christian Crusades that plagued Europe for centuries.

Finally, in addition to the factors discussed above, China was the dominant political and military power in that part of the world, imparting its cultural values to its near-abroad, with the possible exception of those south of its border who were mainly influenced by Hinduism (see Pye, 1981: 218). As a result, Japan, Korea, and Vietnam incorporated many aspects of Confucianism into their social system while the South Asian states showed a preference for Hinduism and Buddhism (see also Wang 2005). But China's influence has not always been for the good of the region: its attempts at subverting non-communists governments in the region in the early twentieth century put it at odds with its neighbors who were by this time under Western colonial influence. Hence, as observed by Shambaugh (2005: 1): "When the PRC behaves ... as a non-status quo power, it only became more marginalized from the principal actors and central dynamics of the region."

Curiously, while China had been invaded by the Mongols in 1279 and Buddhism had been introduced as a foreign influence, neither was able to dislodge Confucianism as the primary orthodoxy; rather such intrusions were absorbed by Chinese culture, such was the depth and breadth of Confucianism. As observed by Kesselman, et al., (1996: 373): "they were changed more by China than they were able to change China." Indeed, early Christianity failed to take hold in China because of the depth of Confucianism and to some extent the presence of Buddhism (see Seo and Takekawa 2006: 224). This transforming power of Confucianism led to a false sense of security which derived the belief that all non-Chinese were "barbarians" and, therefore, any challenge from the outside could be met by the Middle Kingdom—which was regarded as the center of civilization (see He Ping, 2002: 19)—without altering its basic way of life. This was largely true until around the late eighteenth century when a combination of internal and external factors began to shake the foundation of the imperial system.

Convergence of External and Internal Challenges

As noted above, throughout most of its history foreigners and foreign influences in China were "sinicized" by Chinese culture. This was no less true for the Manchu who founded the Qing (Ch'ing) dynasty in 1644, than it was for the conquering Mongolians in 1279. However, the Qing dynasty though largely successful in maintaining China's political stability during its reign was faced with the convergence of internal and external challenges not encountered since the Mongolian invasion. As turned out, both were devastating to dynastic rule and consequently to the political and social stability of the then longest surviving empire. China, like many before it, seemingly made an enemy of change itself.

With respect to external challenges, China's self-imposed isolationism served as a major contributor to its demise as an empire as did the arrogance of its imperial rulers. From having minimal contact with Europeans, China had a narrow perspective of European progress in terms of industrial development and military technology; the latter owing much to borrowed Chinese technology brought back to Europe by Marco Polo and others: While the Chinese used gun powder for celebration and reveled in their cultural power, the Europeans weaponized it and embarked on building empires of their own. As a result, China found European colonizing forces too powerful to repel and was "forced to open its borders to foreign merchants, missionaries, and diplomats on terms dictated by Britain and other Western powers" (Kesselman M., et al., 1996: 372) which it now perceives as entitling it to "special treatment in the present" (Mitter 2003: 208). Particularly humiliating to the Chinese was Britain's notion of free trade which took the form of forcing Opium on the Chinese in exchange for their tea. So humiliating was the defeat of the Chinese in the Opium War (1839–42) that modern filmic interpretations served the political propaganda machinery of the Chinese Communist Party (CCP) (see Karl 2001).

As if ordained, internal struggles added to the challenges to the Qing dynasty. Corruption, economic stagnation, and population explosion and, of course, Western influence fuelled the Tai-ping rebellion (1850–1864) in which over 20 million people were killed. The result was the beginning of the end of imperial China: China was parceled-off among the Western powers; Hong-Kong was "leased" to the British in consequence of the "unequal treaties" imposed on the Chinese; and control of trade was in the hands of foreigners.

Peoples Republic of China

The Qing dynasty and hence the Middle Kingdom, passed into history in 1911 when the Republic of China was established with Sun Yat-sen as its first president. China, for all practical purposes was knocked off its historical stability-rocker. Sun was deposed by Yuan Shikai who died in 1916. Leaderless, conflict and disintegration defined early twentieth-century China. Warlords fought for control while Western powers capitalized on the chaos.

The Chinese Communist party (CCP) was established in 1921 as an inspiration of *Bolshevik* triumph in Russia in 1917. With the advice of the Soviets, coalitions were formed between the CCP and the Nationalist Party headed by Sun who regained the leadership of the Nationalist Party after the death of Yuan. The objective of the coalition was to free the country from the domination of the warlords and to re-establish unity. However, Chiang Kai-shek who succeeded Sun in 1925 conspired with some of the remaining warlords to destroy the CCP and to consolidate power under his leadership in 1927. The result was the 'Long March' in 1934–5 by the remnants of the defeated CCP of mainly peasants led by Mao Zedong, himself a peasant, whose belief in the revolutionary potential of the peasantry became the rallying cry and thus catalyst for the establishment of the People's Republic of China (PRC) in 1949.

1949 was a turning point for many countries, not least of which was China. Mao Zedong who was elected CCP Chairman in 1943 became the first President of communist China, having defeated the US-backed Nationalist Party of Chiang Kai-shek. Prior to that, the CCP gained national support from the people by demonstrating its ability to successfully mobilize resistance to Japanese occupation (see Kesselman M., et al., 1996). It was also during this period that the peoples of Southeast Asia began to take notice of China, often in terms contrary to what Washington intended (see Peck 2006; Chung 2005; Pye 1981).

China and its Neighbors

The PRC's relationship with its neighbors for most of the latter half of the twentieth century has been one of discontent, suspicion, and curiosity at its widely perceived "dual revolutionary and peaceful coexistence image" (Pye, 1981: 221), while drawing ever so closer partly in consequence of America's aggressive unilateralism in trade in the 1980s, and partly in consequence of building economic infrastructure that fosters closer economic cooperation with its neighbors (see Garver 2005). Indeed, Wang Gungwu (2005: 187) observed: "'China fever' seems to be replacing 'China fear' and many look forward to the new "strategic partnership" and Free Trade Area being forged between ASEAN and China." However, China had to purge from its historical memory the notion that it was the hierarchical center around which the world was organized (see He Ping 2002). Indeed, serving as the final platform for other Asian countries' exports to the West has contributed greatly to instilling an understanding of cooperativeness with its neighbors (see Ohashi 2005). Moreover, many now regard economic cooperation with China as essential to their strategic interest.

The Vietnam War was particularly instructive for the PRC. Chinese paranoia vis-à-vis a potential Soviet dominated Southeast Asia motivated a less than cooperative approach with North Vietnam in its struggle with the US in South Vietnam. While the Soviet Union was the main supplier of arms to North Vietnam through China, the Chinese provided food and advice, with the latter often viewed as contrary to the interest of North Vietnam. Indeed, Pye (1981: 228) observed that: "throughout Hanoi's war the Chinese argued for strategies which the Vietnamese saw as demeaning and not what they wished to hear from a friend and ally." The invitation first of Secretary of State Henry Kissinger and later President Nixon to Beijing in 1972 was perceived by Hanoi as the ultimate betrayal.

Clearly, the PRC saw supporting US Asia policy and forging diplomatic relations with the US as being in the best interest of China even though this meant alienating Hanoi who was perceived as firmly in the camp of the Soviets and thus a bridgehead for Soviet domination in the region. The Chinese saw the Soviet challenge to the US as an opportunity to extract concessions on arms sales from the US by offering some form of security cooperation with it; which was forthcoming during the Carter administration but which ran into Reagan's distrust of, according to Talbott (1981: 89), "countries which do not share America's basic values, political philosophy, and social structure." Notwithstanding these several set backs to China's early confused policy towards its neighbors, it is significant that during this learning period the PRC, having benefited from the wisdom of India and the experiences of the Southeast Asians whose approaches to international relations were better informed in consequence of their exposure to colonialism, became less of a bully in the region and more of an influence for the betterment of its neighbors. Moreover, Chinese intellectualism began to exercise an ameliorating influence on domestic policy and international relations. As a consequence and as part of the awakening process, then, the PRC began to realize the importance of closer relationship with its neighbors to its own development and national security interest. Indeed, despite their mutual suspicion of each other and early border skirmishes, China and Russia "have cultivated a loose *entente* against the US" (Buzan, 2004: 156) which has since been strengthened in response to US invasion of Iraq and threat to Iran, and to the proposed defensive shield in Poland and Czechoslovakia, ostensibly to defend against potential attacks from North Korea and Iran but perceived clearly by the Russians as a potential threat to its security.[2]

China and the Third World

It should be noted that during this period as discussed in Chapter Four, China's policy towards the Third World was one of economic assistance predicated on the political rather than on economic development: assisting socialist governments to overcome reliance on their former colonial masters as many of them were ideologically inclined to do (see Dator 2006: 126). It was this policy that concerned the Eisenhower and Johnson administrations and determined US Asia policy for much of the period until 1971 (see Peck, 2006).

However, what started out as a generalization of its own experience as a model for other developing countries in the 1960s, morphed into advice that stressed country-specific conditions and needs and partly informed by drawing from the lessons of other countries in the 1970s (Harding, 1981: 276). This changed-approach to international relations was no doubt influenced by China's own experience of learning from the US. Recall, that President Richard Nixon in the early 1970s opened America to Chinese scholars and enterprise managers willing to learn new techniques. In addition, as the world's largest importer of copper and steel, and a significant importer of iron ore, aluminum and other raw materials, China has contributed to the increasing strength of world commodity prices which benefit developing countries exports.

The Hong Kong Paradox

As the handover of Hong Kong drew near, China began to prepare the West for a smooth process, knowing full well that the event would be used as an opportunity to highlight the difference between communism as practiced by China and capitalism as practiced by the West by emphasizing Hong Kong's unrivalled economic and financial success as a British colony. As Chow (2001: 222) tells it:

> This new narrative of global capital with its revealing ambiguities about democracy is the place where the otherwise ideologically competing—and seemingly incompatible—forces of U.S. imperialism, British colonialism, and Chinese nationalism coincide.

Indeed, Hong Kong was not only the last of the British colony of any significance; it evidences global capitalism at its very best as a result of British rule, not to mention native ingenuity and a Confucian work ethic. The continuation of its economic prosperity thus became the focus of UK and US administrations, not fully realizing that, as Chow (2001: 222) observed: "like Britain and the United States, with their considerable trade interests in the Far East, the PRC, too, in spite of its overt ideological 'difference' is now a giant investor in Hong Kong businesses"; and whose credibility is linked to the Hang Seng Index.[3] Not surprising, then, the idea of "one country, two systems" became the mantra of the PRC which, ironically, could not be disputed for the simple reason that the portrayal of Hong Kong as a democratic colony is an oxymoron. Hence the paradox in Secretary Albright's pronouncement: "We will be watching to see that the Hong Kong of tomorrow is like the Hong Kong of today" (Chow 2001: 222).

China and Economic Reform

In the West, economic reforms are first adopted as national policy, with implementation as the necessary follow through along prescribed methods, such as, for example, in welfare reform in the US where, as Weaver (2000: 258) observed: "states often adopted innovations before their efficacy in changing behavior or incomes had been demonstrated." Similarly, reforms in developing countries influenced by Western ideology tend to have processes adopted as policy only to discover their inappropriateness; aptly demonstrated by privatization (see Chang 2006). Reforms in China, on the other hand, mirrors the process in a laboratory or of a clinical trial: "gradual and incremental, without any detailed "blueprint" guiding the process" (Prasad and Rumbaugh, 2004: 2). Such an approach allows the Chinese to experiment with an approach, fine tune it, and then apply it to the country at large once efficacy has been established. While this approach is frustrating to US policymakers and practitioners whose expectations are for an American approach, it allows the Chinese to control the socio-economic disruptions that attend reforms that have not been fully thought through (see Fukuyama 1999). It also provides time to construct appropriate institutions for full and effective implementation, having benefited from the experiences of its neighbors. A good example of this approach is the experimentation with Special Economic Zones as a way of gradually introducing market concepts, borrowed technology, and foreign capital. The development effectiveness of this approach is contrasted most appropriately with the several failed privatization of state-owned enterprises in developing countries pursuant structural adjustment and carried out under the auspices of the IMF and World Bank (see Chang 2006).

Given the approach to economic reform outlined above, there are five distinct phases to China's reform program. The first phase centers on the decentralization of farming. Like the Soviet model of collectivized agriculture, China's commune system which increased access to social services and was responsible for some large-scale infrastructure projects proved to be one of the weakest links in China's command economic system in the absence of any incentive to the workers. Consequently, production levels in 1977 remained at 1957 levels. Hence in early 1980s, Deng Xiaoping supported the move of production control away from the collectivized system to a "household responsibility system" (the first phase) by contracting out farmland to individual families who took full charge of production and marketing of their crops. As a result, agricultural production grew at six percent or better in the 1980s (see Prasad and Rumbaugh 2004; Kesselman et al., 1996).

The knock-on effects of increased agricultural production manifested in improved living standards of farmers, and more significantly, in supporting Deng's efforts to expand and modernize China's industrial production. As told by Kesselman, et al (1996: 390), the Chinese countryside was transformed by a rural industrial revolution (the second phase), "that, in speed and scope, is probably unprecedented in the history of the modern world." The "township and village enterprises" (TVEs) that formed the backbone of this revolution were relatively small-scale rural factories run by local governments outside the control of the central government and accounted for more than 25 percent of the country's industrial output. Needless to say, such autonomy brought its own problems: corruption and power struggle, and at times even defiance of the central government. But the TVEs also provided competition to the state-run enterprises and drove the marketization process from 1978 to about 1996. Many of the TVEs were later privatized by way of "restructuring", with many TVE managers and employees becoming owners in joint-stock cooperatives.

Concurrent with the reforms in the rural areas, huge investments were taking place in the heavy industry sector as phases three and four. Informed primarily by ideas and knowledge brought back from the several visits to the US by Chinese leaders and enterprise managers, China's 'Big Push' industrialization strategy that signaled the demise of a purely socialist system began to take hold after 1979 on a phased-in basis as discussed above. Indeed, after 1972, investment as a share of gross domestic product (GDP) grew from just over 25 percent to about 43 percent in 1994, before falling back to just under 40 percent in 2004 (see Naughton, 2007: 57). Between 1952 and 1978, industrial output grew at an annual rate of 11.5 percent, with industrial production accounting for 44 percent by 1978. New industries were created, with some encouragement given to private-sector development, thus giving rise to a new enterprise class just about the same time British Prime Minister Margaret Thatcher was in the process of transforming the UK socioeconomic structure. Agricultural production during the same period as a share of GDP declined from 51 percent in 1952 to 28 percent in 1978 (Naughton, 2007: 56).

Phase five, of course, speaks to Deng Xiaoping's decision to integrate China into the global economic system and in particular into the Asian region (see Shambaugh 2005). This phase requires restructuring the role and function of government, gradually subjecting the economy to competition, and increasing the enterprise, social, and financial reform process as a precursor for accession to the WTO at the end of 2001. The preparation process served to expand China's economic growth further between 2002 and 2005 (see Ohashi 2005). Interestingly, while the reform experience of China shows that markets work and should be the underlying strategy of development, according to Naughton (2007: 7): "[it] provides no support for the argument that, since the market is a superior mechanism, the full panoply of market institutions should be set in place as quickly as possible in as many realms as possible."

Social Issues

As agricultural production shrank, rural labor migrated to the towns and cities, seeking non-farm occupations, thus requiring even greater investment in manufacturing industries. However, with about 50 million "transient" workers in the towns and cities, and an unemployment rate of between eight and ten percent (see Naughton, 2007: 186–7), the increasing pressures on urban housing and social services have become major concerns for the central government. Crime, prostitution, drug abuse, homelessness, and other social ills are beginning to plague city managers and the Chinese leadership. It is this concern that has forced Chinese officials to become more export oriented and to target investments to job creation. As observed by Alan Blinder of Princeton University: "China must export like mad to grow like mad to give production work to the hoards of people migrating from the country to the cities."[4] It certainly is in no position to throw open its economy as some in the West eagerly suggest.

As a result of its export drive, China's trade with the EU increased in May 2007 by 29.0 percent over May 2006 to US$129.9 billion and by 18.2 percent with the US to US$115.2 billion over the same period. It also experienced 15.1 percent increase in trade with Japan for a total of US$91.2 billion. Of concern to the US is that, whilst exports to China increased by 19.1 percent, imports increased by 28.7 percent with a trade deficit of $22.5 billion for May 2007.

China's Geo-economics and Geopolitics in the Twenty-first Century

China's economic growth and influence in the twenty-first century could be likened to a super tanker which once in open waters is propelled by its own momentum. A momentum that clearly is creating geo-economic and geopolitical challenges both in its forward motion and in its wake to the long-established international economic and political order led by the West; particularly to the US whose dominance since the end of World War II has never really been challenged. For example, China produced more cars than the US in 2006 and its economy has been growing at least three times faster than the American economy, chalking up an unprecedented 11.1 percent increase in the first quarter of 2007. At this rate, Goldman Sachs reportedly expects China's GDP at market exchange rate to surpass America's GDP by 2027 and likely to become number one on a purchasing power parity (PPP) basis within four years.[5]

But there are externality arising from China's continued economic growth. In addition to raising world commodity prices to the delight of other developing countries, Southeast Asian countries and Japan have seen their exports to China increased at unprecedented rates in consequence of a China policy that allows export-oriented foreign invested enterprises (FIEs) to import production facilities as well as parts and components for assembly, fully exempt from customs duties (see Ohashi 2005). Hence, from a total export–import perspective, China FIE Trade Ratio for 2001 shows exports at 50.1 percent and imports at 51.7 percent (Ohashi 2005, 82). In addition to exemption from customs duties, FIEs are eligible for rebate of domestic value-added taxes on their exports.

As a result of incentives offered to FIEs, China's nominal trade with the world has increased at unprecedented rates. For example Japanese exports to China increased from 3.9 percent of total exports in 1980 to 13.6 percent in 2003; Korea's from zero percent in 1980 to 20.5 percent in 2003; Singapore's from 1.6 percent in 1980 to 7.0 percent in 2003; Philippines's from 0.8 percent in 1980 to 12.0 percent in 2003; Indonesia's from zero in 1980 to 7.4 percent in 2003; and India's from 0.3 percent in 1980 to 6.4 percent in 2003 (Rumbaugh and Blancher, 2004: 11). Even exports from the EU increased from 0.8 percent in 1980 to 4.2 percent in 2003. As a consequence of the increase in imports from almost all its trading partners, China runs negative bilateral trade balances with almost all; the exceptions are, of course, the US and the EU. Indeed, for selected Asian countries and the US and EU, China's (including Hong Kong) trade deficit increased from US$4.0 billion in 1997 to US$35.0 billion in 2003 (Rumbaugh and Blancher, 2004: 11). Clearly, whilst China is serving as the final assembly platform for many of the Southeast Asian countries and runs trade deficits with them—as evidenced by the trade numbers quoted above—its trade surpluses with the US and EU are approached from a US self-serving perspective as discrete issues and as wholly accruing to the Chinese economy.

The importance of China to effective international relations is underscored by its ability to get the 'Six-party Talks' regarding North Korea's nuclear weapons program restarted when others had all but given up. While its ability to persuade the North Koreans exemplified acceptable roles from the perspective of the US to the extent that they seemingly serve America's interest at the front end, there are implications that are deemed less acceptable to the US and the West when taken in context of territoriality.

One such implication is the reaction of other Asian states to China. As remarked by Zhuang Jianshong, from Shanghai's Jiaotong University: "I don't think it would be an exaggeration to say that most Asian countries now look to China more than they look to the US."[6] This is quite a contrast to the China-Southeast Asian relationship of the 1960s and 1970s as discussed above. Zhuang Jianshong is not alone in this view. Although the US has a superior defense capability in the region and is actively seeking to strengthen strategic relations with countries such as the Philippines, South Korea, Singapore, and even Indonesia, according to Professor Ross of Boston College: "China is the shadow covering the entire region." In addition to its obvious influence in Southeast Asia, China has improved upon its relations with India, as evidenced by India's Prime Minister Vajpayee's visit to Beijing in June 2003 and the quiet diplomacy in which both are engaged to resolving the Sino-Indian boundary (see Lampton 2005). The growing cooperation in trade between China and India is also indicative of a closer tie between the two leaders in Asia. China's relationship with Pakistan also is being maintained at a cordial and respectful level (see Musharraf, 2006), without jeopardizing its improving relationship with India. As observed by Zhang, (2005: 51), China's main concern is to ensure a working relationship with the major powers in the region, "so that China will never again become isolated and encircled by great powers."

China's growing influence in the region is not entirely of its own making however. Indeed, it is being aided by the mistakes in US foreign policy not only towards Southeast Asia, as evidenced by US reaction to the 1997–8 Asian financial crisis and its neglect of ASEAN, but also by its tendency to unilateralism as evidenced by its actions in the Middle East. As remarked by the Malaysian Prime Minister, "Mr. Bush has a different agenda and the Muslims know it." In this connection, it is worth noting the little-reported agreement of the Southeast Asian countries to "pool" their foreign currency reserves in the event of a repeat of the 1997–8 speculative frenzy that befell the currencies of four of their members. Whether or not such pooling translates to a formal monetary union remains to be seen.

Challenge to Entrenched Western Dominance

But eclipsing US and the West economic dominance is not the only concern for US policymakers of an emerging China. As China's massive industrialization takes hold, its demand for raw materials, to be sure, has changed the dynamics of international trade, creating pricing pressures for certain commodities while providing increased opportunities for marginal suppliers especially in developing countries. Moreover, in addition to stimulating scale-production of raw materials and other manufacturing inputs in other developing countries, China's growing investments in their production processes have allowed it to forge new political and economic alliances, with the potential to serve as catalysts to bridging the income inequality gap between rich nations and the developing countries. It is a role that is new to China; a role it undertakes willingly however, with a level of confidence rooted in its history past and present; but it is a role fraught.

THREAT OR OPPORTUNITY?

The anxiety over China's emergence as a potential economic rival to the West is becoming increasingly manifest in academic papers and in economic and financial presentations and policy proposals. To be sure, outside of the crisis in the Middle East, there is no other contemporary issue more talked about than the perceived challenges posed by China in the twenty-first century; and for good reasons. For example, further underscoring China's momentum and perceived challenge to the West is the revelation by the WTO that China has surpassed the US in exports in the second half of 2006 and is poised to overtake Germany as the world's number one exporter in 2008.[7]

China's emergence is perceived not as benignly as the Chinese leadership hoped it would be, but rather as a significant threat to entrenched Western economic and security interests in general and to US dominance in particular. Indeed, the rhetoric of the US Congress is unmistakably anti-China, calling as it does for tariffs and other forms of protectionism against Chinese imports in response to complaints from corporate contributors and constituents affected by the increasing competition from Chinese products. Evidence, Congressman Duncan Hunter's accusation that, "China is cheating on trade."[8] Yet, as Secretary of the Treasury Henry Paulson points out in his discussion with Charlie Rose on April 23, 2007, trade helps to keep inflation rates down in America and contributes to American economic prosperity. Indeed, dispassionate analyses show that faster growth in China and other developing economies such as India and Brazil will benefit the American economy, not harm it; indeed, help to sustain it at a level that has been reached prematurely. Moreover, as pointed out above, China serves as an export platform for many countries including the EU and Japan and as such creates wealth for its trading partners while creating jobs for the millions that flock to its cities.

What Paulson and others would like to see, however, is faster liberalization of China's financial markets in addition to the steps it has already taken to reforming its economy. Indeed, the introduction of competition in the financial sector would likely raise the current interest rate on savings from two and a half percent to above five percent. Such a move not only would serve to increase access to approximately US$2.0 trillion of Chinese savings by the West but also increase the income stream to Chinese savers who would by definition and like the Japanese have more to spend on Western goods and services. But as Paulson and before him John Snow observed, the Chinese will not be pushed. Ingrained in Chinese culture is the belief that there is a time for everything and everything in its time: It has served the Chinese well for over 2,500 years.

Not surprising, then, China has yet to subscribe to the notion that promoting individualism would bring the millions in the country-side out of poverty. In fact, the American experience in the twenty-first century is far from a recommendation and indeed must give pause to countries like India and China. It is also instructive that China's commitment to job creation for its hoards is tied to its high savings rate upon which its consistently high economic growth rate is positively correlated. In this connection, it is worth noting that, foreign direct investment (FDI) as a share of GDP began to decline gradually to just under three percent in 2005 (see Naughton, 2007: 404), consistent with a greater reliance on internally-generated savings; yet the economy continues to grow at unprecedented rates. It is also worth noting further that, in 2005 Hong Kong, Taiwan, and Macau accounted for 35 percent of FDI in China whilst the US, EU and Japan combined accounted for 15 percent (see Naughton, 2007: 403).

Beyond trade issues, despite its progressive transformation to a market economy China still is being regarded as the last bastion of communism after the disintegration of the Soviet Union in 1991, such is the inflexibility in labels. As such, China in the minds of most US lawmakers replaces the Soviet Union in terms of being a target for America's democracy imperative. In this latter connection, the divergence in perspectives could not be greater. China sees democracy as country-specific in a pluralist world whose diversity must be respected as a "very important feature of the world".[9] To this end, according to the Chinese Ambassador, while recognizing the need for providing guidance to the parties in Sudan "to come to terms through peaceful negotiations" China considers the problems in Sudan as internal. President Bush, on the other hand, sees the world through the prism of idealism and has resolved to proselytize freedom and democracy: "The best hope for peace in our world is the expansion of freedom in all the world"[10] and "Iraq is only a part of a larger ideological war."[11] Clearly, *choice* as a corollary of freedom has been made for the world by Mr. Bush.

It is instructive that China considers sanctions not ends but means and, in the opinion of the Chinese Ambassador, if not used properly can be counterproductive. This said, Mr. Bush has announced new sanctions against the government of Sudan on May 28, 2007, against the backdrop of China's criticism and the possible threat of a veto at the UN Security Council.[12] It has since managed to get a peace-keeping force for Sudan approved by the Security Council.

China's possession of nuclear weapons and one of the largest standing armies in the world with a declared policy of invading Taiwan should it declare independence adds to the concerns of the US. Moreover, constant reminders of China's role in the Korean and Vietnam Wars further serve to reinforce attempts to demonize it and ever so often to reaffirm a US China policy of containment. In addition to US concerns is the announcement by the British Prime Minister in 2007 that the UK will reintroduce the use of hard power as an option to its international relations framework. Such change in policy must be seen as partly motivated by China's modernization of its military and its achievements in space. The revelation that the UK had in the past considered using nuclear weapons against China does nothing to allay historical fears nor for that matter do labels such as: "a huge challenge to the United States"; "yellow peril"; "totalitarian regime"; and "ambitious", many of which are derived from a position of waning economic competitiveness and influence in world affairs.

Specific US Concerns

US concerns appear to center not only on China's enviable economic growth rates that are more than four times that of the US—deemed unsustainable by most Western observers for over two decades—but also on its expanding political reach beyond its near abroad through the exercise of soft-power that renders existing US China policy of containment ineffective. China's no-strings attach investment policy is being widely received in Africa and South America and is seen as impacting America's influence in these regions. With respect to Latin America, for example, as observed by Representative Nita Lowey: "We are witnessing a reversal of the several political and economic gains made over the last several decades.... China is becoming a major player in the energy sector."[13] China, to be sure, has increased it presence in Latin America, concluding economic ties with Brazil, Venezuela, and others who have grown suspicious of the America that has been revealed to the world since March 2003. Many are opting for less stringently-conditioned European aid as a replacement for US aid.

This expanding reach of China is financed by its growing trade surplus and its foreign exchange reserves estimated to be US$1.2 trillion in 2007 over which the West has little or no control. While, therefore, many commentators have focused on the US trade deficit with China, from a foreign policy perspective the concern really is about China's increasing ability to exert influence in the resource-rich developing countries in Africa and South America with whom it is building solid economic relations based on a declared policy of mutual respect and non-intervention as noted above. In this latter regard, the Chinese approach predicated as it is on a *quid pro quo* relationship contrasts strikingly with a system of asymmetrics that defines a core-periphery relationship or a North/South divide (see Peck 2006: 224–5) with which developing countries are all too familiar in their transactions with the West. Moreover, as demonstrated by the reverberation of the over nine percent drop in the Shanghai stock market on February 27, 2007, the susceptibility of Western financial markets to the influence of China is a growing concern despite the rhetoric.

China's growing appetite for resources to fuel its economic growth to be sure requires that it source its needs through the international market place and where necessary through bilateral cooperative agreements. As a consequence, China's demands serve to render the long-serving Western core-periphery model of resource transfer obsolete, especially with respect to oil and other basic commodities, resulting in increased cost of raw materials to Western production centers. Evidence the increase in price for commodities from many developing countries, especially those African countries that see China's economic expansion as a boon for commodities. Evidence further, the pressure on oil prices which has taken its toll on US trade balances.

In addition to trade issues, China appears to be unresponsive to US pressure on human rights and other issues of governance, offering its own priorities constructed around its self-determined national economic and security interests. Indeed, as emphasized by the Chinese Ambassador to the United Nations (UN) in Geneva in an interview with Carrie Gracie of the BBC on *Hard Talk* in August 2006, "China does not need any advice on its internal affairs from anyone nor is it a threat to any other country." This perspective has been reiterated by Ambassador Zhou Wenzhong in 2007. With respect to the question of being a threat to its neighbors, as if to allay any fears of border disputes with them, Ambassador Zhou Wenzhong reiterated China's respect for history and for its existing borders with, for example, Russia.[14] Indeed, Russia's Ambassador to the UN Vitaly Churkin unequivocally confirmed that all border issues with China have been "completely resolved, completely settled" and that the two countries are pursuing their common economic and strategic interests bilaterally and internationally. These agreements notwithstanding, former National Security Adviser to President Carter, Zbigniew Brzezinski drawing from the well-entrenched Western perspective of China sees Russia as needing to join the West as a form of protection against China.[15] But Ambassador Churkin sees China–Russia relationship as "a very big political and cultural friendship in every way."[16]

As would be expected, the Europeans have not been far behind with their own concerns which for now center mainly on trade issues but which have not risen to a level to prevent them from seeking investment opportunities in China. Indeed, US companies have been playing catch-up in the 'gold rush' of the East. Some US companies, *Google*, for example, have even rebutted attempts by US politicians to impose their political agenda upon it.

While Western investments are welcomed in China, they are received cautiously. To the extent investments are "foot-loose", they are perceived as fuelling a speculative bubble not unlike that witnessed in the East Asian countries in the years just before the 1997–8 financial crisis. As noted in Chang (2006), that crisis had its roots in an over-dependence on short-term investment flows to finance economic growth. It is thus a credit to the Chinese government to have recognized the consequence of speculative capital inflows and to seek to control their impact on the Chinese economy despite protestations to the contrary. Indeed, it is to Western long-term economic interests that the Chinese economy be not subjected to the disruption that attended the South-East Asian financial crisis of 1997–8.

The Strain on US Foreign Policy

Curiously, President Bush was one of the first to betray a link, albeit obliquely, between China's emergence and the crisis in the Middle East. Recall his unscripted remark that China's energy demands are putting a strain on US foreign policy. Recall further, in his meeting with President Lula da Silva of Brazil on March 8, 2007, where he again pronounced on the energy demands of China; only on this occasion adding India to the equation and stressing the need for developing alternative energy sources—not for export to the US however, but for Brazil's domestic consumption—so as to reduce the pricing pressure on the US.[17]

The strain on US foreign policy as we have witnessed manifest most blatantly in the invasion of Iraq and in the propping-up of despotic regimes friendly to the US and the West in contradiction to the expressed policy of "spreading democracy and freedom." In addition, the looming self-fulfilling prophesies of confrontation with Iran designed arguably to preempt any alliance between it and China—the Confucius–Islamic connection, if you will—are all too revealing. Moreover, when considered in context of the long-term objective, the well-publicized arguments for Israel's right to exist or to defend itself is arguably no more than an over-played geopolitical card, albeit an important card in context of Middle East politics, in the presumed overarching grand strategy of containing China. Any lingering doubts as to the role of Israel in this broader strategy should be dispelled by the revelation that Israel's invasion of Lebanon was a necessary first step to a preemptive strike on Iran.[18] Also, Israeli Prime Minister Olmert's oblique reference in December 2006 to Israel's possession of nuclear weapons and declaring that it is "more than able to defend against all enemies" is equally telling, as are its incursions in Syria's airspace.

Given the above, as with its Middle East policy since 2003 the Bush Administration's China policy must be seen necessarily in context of its declared policy of "preventive" actions and arguably rooted in Huntington's notion of a clash between the US and China. Indeed, the inevitability of such a clash is cast in terms of China's emerging challenge as discussed above and its resolve to defend its national sovereignty and historical heritage while the US, initially buoyed by the exercise of its "moral authority" under George Bush, though locked in an ideological war of its choosing, is propelled necessarily by the territorial imperative. This is an unavoidable conclusion made more immediate when considered in context of the Bush narrative which when taken as a whole curiously exposes an almost discernible neoconservative grand strategy for containing China. It is, therefore, no accident that the BBC in a commentary on the crisis in the Middle East should refer to China's emerging hegemony in Africa and its increasing energy demands and rhetorically asked whether the real conflict is still to come.

Jaw-boning Visits

This heightened and growing anxiety of the US over China is further reflected in the visit to China in 2005 by the then Treasury Secretary John Snow, with follow-up visits by his successor and by the Chairman of the Federal Reserve System in 2006 and 2007. These visits are design principally to express US concerns over the growing US-China trade imbalance, perceived as it were to be the consequence of an undervalued Chinese currency, and to jaw-bone corrective actions by the Chinese. They were also intended according to Secretary Henry Paulson to persuade the Chinese to speed up their reforms and to liberalize their financial sector. There are, however, contradicting signals from the administration and the Congress which are likely to keep China cautious of US overtures.

Fear-mongering as a Tactic

While the Treasury Secretary and the Federal Reserve Bank Chairman seek to gain concessions from the Chinese, Secretary of State Rice unabashedly engages in promoting the US administration's take on China's hegemony as an imminent danger to the region, while former Secretary of Defense Rumsfeld's contribution takes the form of direct questions and pronouncements on China's increase in military spending: both are reflective of attempts to contain China by stimulating fears in its neighbors and are reminiscent of the Eisenhower policy of containment without isolation in the 1950s.

President Bush's visit to India and engaging in what is perceived as inconsistent with the international nuclear non-proliferation treaty (NPT) by entering into a nuclear cooperation agreement—approved by the US Congress in 2006—as part of a broader strategic agreement with a country that is not a party to the NPT is also indicative of reviving Eisenhower's China policy. Equally telling is the silence of the US administration and indeed the US news media in general on the failed test launch of an intercontinental ballistic missile by India just days after North Korea's failed attempt to test its long-range missile on July 4, 2006 was roundly condemned.

Clearly, up until the failure of Israel to dislodge Hezbollah from its strategic position from an Iranian defense perspective, US policy towards China was less than accommodating or warming. Indeed, despite the rhetoric the Bush administration policy could be perceived as indirectly aggressive to the extent that it openly seeks to encircle China through strategic alliances in the region in hopes of completing the containment by gaining control of Middle East oil and strengthening Israel's position in the region. But, as is being played-out, rather than contain China, the Bush administration's Middle East policy of "aggressive unilateralism", now widely perceived as a failure has served to strengthen ties between Russia and China, and to place Iran out of military reach by Israel and the West without consequences.

The Huntington Factor

One of the first to express concern over China's emergence is Samuel Huntington (1996: 313). His perception of an emerging China as, "the biggest player in the history of man" whose "assertiveness" in the region "would be contrary to American interests as they have been historically constructed" cannot be ignored and arguably has served to inform the presumptive neoconservative grand strategy designed to contain China. Indeed, Huntington's perspectives undoubtedly resonate with an essentially neoconservative US administration in a world that has been largely constructed on dominance and economic determinism (see Dator 2006; Adem 2004). But it is a world now in turmoil in consequence of an America that has been taken down the path of militarism by an intelligentsia that has been seduced by notions of absolute power on the one hand, and finding support in those who dream of re-establishing the Kingdom of Israel, on the other.

The blind and not so blind seduction to the cause of neoconservatives and dreamers alike of "think-tanks" which heretofore had been a reliable source of dispassionate analyses in the construction of US foreign policy could not have been more complete. Consider, for example, labels and comments such as: "Axis of evil"; "Islamo-fascists"; and "a bunch of men in cave" which serve to rally Americans around their cause. But while such shallow expressions have crowd appeal and serve to prop up egocentrism, they do call into question the rationality and quality of analyses in the US post-9/11, and clearly speak to the dangerous gap in the understanding of the wider world outside the US and the extent to which the exercise of power calls forth countervailing power.

Not unexpectedly, then, when viewed through the lens of *The Clash of Civilizations* and resultant polemics that have come to inform twenty-first century discourse, China's growing influence in regional and world affairs necessarily conjure up fear and distrust by the West. Adding to the China-phobia in the US are the unavoidable trade deficits with China which in 2005 stood at US$202 billion; its growing foreign currency reserves, estimated to be over US$1.2 trillion in 2007, and its use of such reserves to either acquire energy properties around the world or invest in energy production facilities in other countries; and its refusal to side with the US and the West in their bid to impose punitive sanctions on North Korea and Iran. China's condemnation of Israel at the Special Meeting of the Security Council in August 2006 for killing four UN peacekeepers in Lebanon in July 2006 did nothing to ease the tensions between it and the supporters of Israel who were intent on absolving the Jewish state from any responsibility. Indeed, conspicuously absent from Secretary of State Rice's address to the Security Council was any reference to Lebanese civilian casualties or to the destruction inflicted upon Lebanon by Israel's relentless aerial attacks.

China and the Middle East Crisis

Given the heightened anxiety over China's emergence, then, there is the nagging suspicion the invasion of Iraq and consequential play-out of self-fulfilling prophesies there and elsewhere in the region are largely the results of the initial stage of a grand strategy to contain China gone awry as discussed in Chapter Seven; a strategy that arguably has as its ultimate objective the containment of China's economic growth and growing influence through controlling its access to Middle East oil. Indeed, when viewed through the prism of the clash of civilizations, China's increasing energy demands to fuel its rapidly-growing economy, according to Huntington (1996: 240) "are likely to impel it to expand its relations with Iran, Iraq, and Saudi Arabia as well as Kazakhstan and Azerbaijan"; and must be of concern to the West in general and the US in particular. Since this observation was first made, Iraq was invaded by the "coalition of the willing" in March 2003 on the basis of a perceived threat to world peace by the Saddam Hussein regime purportedly in possession of WMD, and thereby coincidentally eliminating one of the potential China alliances identified by Huntington. At the same time, Kazakhstan and Azerbaijan are being openly courted by the US—much to the displeasure of Russia's President Putin—while schemes to control Central Asia are proffered by others.

With respect to a China–Iran alliance envisaged by Huntington, Iran's pursuit of nuclear energy for domestic use is yet another opportunity to thwart such an alliance. Indeed, despite denials to the contrary by the Iranian government and, as with the invasion of Iraq, no supporting evidence—just suspicions of intent—of a nuclear weapons program, the Bush administration supported by the UK, France, and Germany have labeled Iran's uranium enrichment program as a precursory to the production of nuclear weapons, and through a UN resolution have effectively issued an ultimatum to Iran to stop such enrichment by August 31, 2006 or face sanctions. As expected, Iran refusal to comply "to the will of the international community" brought forth sanctions against it—expanded and made more immediate by the results of the Israel–Hezbollah war in July–August 2006—but was initially rebuffed by the Russian Foreign Minister, Sergei Lavrov: "We take into account the experience of the past and we cannot ally ourselves with ultimatums, which all lead to a dead end.'[19] China meanwhile has made investments in Iran gas industry in excess of the US$20.0 million annual limit arbitrarily and unilaterally set by the US in 1996, and further invited the Iranian President to the 2006 Shanghai Corporation Conference, much to the displeasure of the US.

As to other alliances, in January 2006 the Chinese government secured co-operation agreements on energy with the King of Saudi Arabia on his historic visit to China; and in August 2006, similar agreement for the supply of oil were entered into with Venezuela. China is tapping into Cuban gas reserves which must be of further concern to the US. These agreements follow on the heels of the decision of the US Congress to prevent China from acquiring any interest in US energy properties and the apparent closing of the doors to Chinese investments in Canadian energy properties on the replacement of Paul Martin as Prime Minister of Canada with someone more sympathetic to a conservative agenda.

NOTES

1 Translated by Lin Yutang.
2 Heintz, J., "Russia test-launches new ICBM", http://news.yahoo.com/s/ap/20070529/ap_on_re_eu/russia_missile_test
3 Friedman, T.L., "Hang Seng salvation", *The New York Times*, July 3, 1997
4 "Charlie Rose", *PBS.org*, 26 April, 2007
5 "Come in number one, your time is up", *The Economist*, April 14, 2007, p. 12
6 Geown, K., "China challenges US at apec forum", *BBC NEWS*, http://news.bbc.co.uk/go/pr/fr/-/2/hi/asia-pacific/6150406.stm ; November 15, 2006
7 Klapper, B.S., "WTO: 'China overtakes U.S. in exports", http://news.yahoo.com/s/ap/20070412/ap_on_bi_ge/wto_china
8 "Iowa Republican Fundraiser and Straw Poll", *C-SPAN*,, 11 August, 2007
9 Zhou Wenzhong, China's Ambassador to the US, "Chinese Developing International Relations", *Watson's Institute for International Relations*, Brown University, *C-SPAN2,* March 22, 2007
10 Excerpt from the President's Inaugural Address in January 2005.
11 Interview with Jim Lehrer, 'News Hour', PBS.org, January 16, 2007
12 Knox, O., "Bush slaps new sanctions on Sudan, seeks UN action", http://news.yahoo.com/s/afp/20070529/wl_africa_afp/sudandarfurus;_ylt=At0sm18y5MSGqlqcjDSIphRvaA8F
13 2008 State Department & foreign Operations Spending' House Budget Committee, www.appropriations.org , *C-SPAN*, March 21, 2007
14 Zhou Wenzhong, China's Ambassador to the US, "Chinese Developing International Relations", *Watson's Institute for International Relations*, Brown University, *C-SPAN2*, March 22, 2007
15 Brzezinski's interview, "Charlie Rose", *PBS.org*, June 15, 2007
16 Interview with Charlie Rose, "Charlie Rose", PBS.org, July 7, 2007.
17 NPR News, *National Public Radio*, March 8, 2007
18 "US involved in planning Israel's operations in Lebanon", *Associated Press*, August 13, 2006
19 Interfax

Part Four

America's Territorial Imperative

Chapter Six

The American Experience: "It's the Economy Stupid"

Introduction

According to the *Economist* magazine: "slowly but surely, team American is being overtaken in all sorts of economic rankings."[1] It lost its position as the world's number one exporter to Germany and now is at risk of being pushed out of the number two position by China whose exports in the second half of 2006 exceeded those of American exporters. In addition, Toyota is poised to eclipse General Motors in 2007. But the Asian economies are not the only source of concern for the US. Putin's Russia is forging ahead on many fronts: In 2006, its stock market grew by 51.0 percent—second only to China's 107.0 percent—while the US eked out 13.9 percent, putting it at fourth from the bottom of a list of 14 countries.[2] Also, Russia as one of the largest producer of crude oil continues to benefit from high oil prices, using its windfall revenues to increase state investment in infrastructure and other employment-producing projects and social safety net, especially for the elderly.[3] On a comparative basis, then, the US is losing ground in several key indicators. However, as the *Economist* consolingly reminds us, "the goal of policy should be to maximize a country's absolute rate of growth, not its relative rate."

Furthermore, in 2004, according to Martin Mühleisen (2004: 5): "The United States is on course to increase its net external liabilities to around 40 percent of GDP within the next few years." Similarly, Martin Wolf of the *Financial Times* advanced the argument that, "the US is being driven along a road of ever rising deficits and debt that risk destroying the country's credit and the global role of its currency."[4] Both Mühleisen and Wolf have been proven correct with respect to US external liabilities and currency valuation. Indeed, both underestimated the impact of a Bush administration on the national debt which in 2007 is over 100 percent of GDP. At the same time the US Dollar is on a steep slide, depreciating against the major currencies to lows not seen in over 25 years. It has, for example, depreciated by about 28 percent against the Canadian Dollar (C$), with the C$ on par with the US Dollar for the first time in decades. In Europe, the dollar has depreciated by about 40 percent against the Pound Sterling since 2002, while setting record lows against the Euro which is fast becoming the currency of choice in a global financial market. At the same time, there is a marked decline in the inward flows of foreign investment, compelling reassurances to foreign investors from both President Bush and Secretary Paulson.[5] Meanwhile, factory orders again fell by 3.3 percent in August 2007 and the country is experiencing the worst housing slump in 16 years. Be that as it may, to Americans who have come to bask in the glory of being the most powerful nation on earth, accepting second place to China would not be easy.

Confluence of Factors

Whether Americans like it or not, there are many factors at play, all combining to exert pressures hitherto unknown in a post-World War II America that has expended the benefits derived from European post-war reconstruction to further the unrealistic notion of an American empire; all impacting its way of life and its foreign policy in 2003 in consequence. Indeed, seven years earlier, former Harvard University President Derek Bok (1996: 90) observed that, despite being the wealthiest industrial nation on earth, America's traditional formula for achieving national prosperity that emphasizes individualism and minimum government "has not been wholly successful." Of the highly industrialized countries, America's gross national product (GNP) average annual growth rate of 1.6 percent for the period 1965–89 was below the average of 2.5 percent for the *Organization for Economic Cooperation and Development* (OECD) countries[6] and well below the growth rates of the Southeast Asian economies (see Chang 2006: 33; Huntington 1996: 104). Besides relatively slower growth rates, "incomes for half of all American families have barely risen during the past twenty years." As Bok further observed: "Our practice of maximizing incentives by allowing high rewards for the successful has not managed to lift all Americans to levels of prosperity above those of citizens in other countries." Indeed, on a comparative basis, especially in healthcare and education, the US lags the major OECD countries.

Bok's critique was validated most strikingly nine years later by Hurricane Katrina in 2005. The false prosperity claimed by the Bush administration, indeed by a Republican Congress dedicated to the reduction of entitlement programs, was exposed; not just to those traumatized by the hurricane but to all Americans who were shocked into reality. Despite efforts to accommodate the hundreds of thousands displaced by Hurricane Katrina, as of May 2007 there were still 80,000 Americans living in "FEMA trailers"; many contracting upper respiratory diseases; many suffering from depression. Nationally, at the end of 2006, there were over 47 million Americans without health insurance and 33.0 million, or 11.0 percent of the population, deemed living in poverty. Percentage wise, this is equal to the percentage of Chinese living on less than US$1.00 per day (the UN criterion); in terms of purchasing power parity (PPP), the number of poor in America is two times as much as China, whose poor is estimated by the Chinese Premier at 16 million. The comparison does not end there.

Declining Economic Indicators

Compared with other developed countries, the average American lags his European counterpart despite the advances in technology and wealth generated in the US, often in consequence of not wanting to be part of a welfare-state system or to be led by a Europe it helped rebuild. One example that speaks to the latter observation is its slowness to recognize the consequence of carbon emissions and the need to take immediate corrective actions. While the US, influenced by special interest groups has not signed on to the Kyoto Protocol, the UK and Europe have and are able to create more jobs by addressing the issue of global warming; and in the process are able to keep the income inequality gap from getting wider. On the other hand, the inherent contradiction of free market economics and social equality could hardly be missed in an America that is steadily losing ground in exports; whose budget deficits are beginning to matter—contrary to Mr. Cheney's pronouncement that "Reagan proved budget deficits don't matter"—and whose poor is increasing while the poor in China and Russia are being lifted out of poverty through social programs targeted at poverty reduction.

With respect to exports as a percentage of GDP, as depicted by the World Bank, the high-income countries, including the US, have lost ground to low–and middle–income countries since the early 1990s. They similarly have fallen behind in attracting foreign direct investments (FDI) for the same period (World Bank, 2004: 65). Arising from the shift in exports away from high–income countries to low–and middle–income countries, relative growth in productivity is implicitly being shifted away from the high–income countries to the low–and middle–income countries (World Bank, 2004: 65); in other words, the low–and middle–income countries are narrowing the competitive gap, a trend that has been in motion since the 1960s.

For the US, then, it is reasonable to assume that the incremental capital–output ratio (ICOR) is increasing for the manufacturing and industrial sectors and decreasing for the low–and middle–income economies which, as stated elsewhere in this book are benefiting from rapid technology transfer while maintaining low labor costs. At the same time, an increasing proportion of GDP of the US and the Western European countries is derived from financial market activity and ownership of financial assets world wide. In the case of the US, for example, such income as a percentage of GDP increased from 22.47 percent in the 1970s to 33.49 percent in the 1990s (Sum, 2005: 107). This structural shift in the American national income stream is arguably one of the major contributors to the widening income inequality gap in the US and one that portends social problems in the future. Indeed, when one-third of the GDP is concentrated in the hands of the high-income group, it follows that mean and median income statistics have lost meaning as indicators of overall prosperity in an America whose population growth is concentrated in the lower income groups.

Despite evidence of a changing economic order, there are those who are in denial of the changing economic reality of a global economy. For example, CATO's Brink Lindsey seemingly in denial of the unchallenged data tells his audience that the US is in every respect ahead of every other country in the world.[7] Curiously, having exalted the American economic and social model, he acknowledges that 21.6 percent of Americans are below the poverty line; more curiously, he places responsibility for this disparity in income levels to an inability or unwillingness of the lower income earners to take advantage of the offerings of the American economy. At the same program, however, David Brooks of the *New York Times* suggested that the declining social mobility in America is evidence of a growing income inequality gap.

With respect to budget deficits, bluntly put by David Walker, Comptroller General of the United States:

> The most serious threat to the United States is not someone hiding in a cave in Afghanistan or Pakistan but our own fiscal irresponsibility....We suffer from a fiscal cancer; it is growing within us and if we do not treat it, it could have catastrophic consequences for our country.[8]

Since the publication of the Comptroller General's dire warning, Treasury Secretary Paulson has expressed optimism that by 2012 the budget will be in surplus. Secretary Paulson is not alone. Federal Reserve Chairman Bernanke confidently predicts that the budget will be in surplus by 2012. This view is supported by the Democratic Party-led House of Representatives. But such optimistic forecasts are predicated on an economic growth rate of over three and one-half percent and a reduction in government expenditure. For Mr. Paulson and the Chairman of the Federal Reserve System, the required reduction in expenditure must come from entitlement programs; for the Democrats, on the other hand, bringing an end to US participation in the civil war in Iraq is seen as central. With respect to the economic growth rate, actual first quarter 2007 growth was 0.6 percent[9]; more than 50 percent less than the 1.3 percent that was estimated by the administration and needed to validate the Treasury Secretary's optimistic predictions for the US economy.

"Our Way of Life"

With respect to America's foreign policy, in the phraseology of President Clinton, "it's the economy stupid"[10] or as articulated by House Republican Minority Leader Representative John Boehner, defending "our way of life"[11]. Of course, no US politician has yet offered a definition of "our way of life", although the minority leader of the House in an unprecedented display of raw emotionalism sees "killing" the terrorists in Iraq as absolutely essential and thus speaks volumes to the territorial imperative. That a definition is proving illusive is perhaps because the phrase is a catch-all for much more than just, in yet another variation on a theme of politicians, "our love of freedom and democracy" or perhaps because, as concluded by David Walker, the current standard of living in the US is unsustainable unless some drastic action is taken.

Explored below, then, are some of the factors that are impacting on "our way of life"—other than the embrace of freedom and democracy—in context of the grave concerns of the US Comptroller General, fully cognizant that, as T.S. Eliot observed: "We humans can't stand too much reality".

The National Debt

According to the Chairman of the Senate Budget Committee Senator Kent Conrad in his presentation to the US Senate,[12] the national debt has increased from US$5.8 trillion in 2000 to $9.0 trillion in 2006, making the US the world's biggest debtor nation, a fact not lost on the *Economist* magazine or indeed on dispassionate analysts. The proposed extension of the existing tax cut in the President's 2008 Budget proposal that allocates 71 percent of the benefits to those earning over $400,000 a year would propel the debt to over 100 percent of GDP in the absence of any off-setting revenues; thus making Mühleisen's (2004) estimate of 40 percent an extremely low estimate.

One of the acknowledged leakages in revenue collection is the "tax gap", that is, the difference between what is actually collected and what should be collected. This difference as reported by the *Internal Revenue Service* was US$345.0 billion for 2001; hence narrowing the gap would go a long way to reducing the national debt, provided, of course, it is not squandered in pursuit of neoconservative idealism. Another source of revenue leakage is the use of offshore tax havens, as claimed by Senator Conrad. Many US corporations are located in these tax havens in the Caribbean and elsewhere. One of the latest to announce such a move is Halliburton, notwithstanding that there may be other reasons for relocating its operating headquarters in the Persian Gulf.

The Reagan Effect

The national debt came into focus during the Reagan era. Prior to Ronald Reagan, US national debt was non-existent or insignificant. Even though the US was experiencing a recession in the late 1970s and early 1980s, it was doing so from a position of relative fiscal strength; every other economy was experiencing similar setbacks in economic growth. However, because the Reagan administration decided to meet head on the challenge of communism, it embarked on a policy of out-spending the Soviets with its "Star Wars" program and became the biggest spender of any US administration in history, the present

Bush administration excepted, despite the rhetoric of reducing the size of government. As a result, the national debt has become a constant in US economic analysis and discourse ever since.

Rebalancing the Books

During the Clinton administration, budget deficits turned into budget surpluses which went to reduce the national debt. The federal budget, including the social security surplus, changed from a deficit of four and one-half percent of GDP in Fiscal Year 1992 to two and one-half percent of GDP in fiscal year 2000 (Mühleisen, 2004:1). This favorable fiscal budget environment allowed the Bush administration that followed in 2001 to embark on a policy of stimulating investment by way of tax incentives to corporations and investors. It also embarked on a policy of reducing entitlement programs as a way of partially offsetting the impact of the tax cuts. However, any idea of further reducing the national debt gave way to prosecuting the war on al-Qaeda in Afghanistan and in the invasion and occupation of Iraq at a cost of over US$10.0 billion per month. With respect to the latter, the gross miscalculations in terms of costs have dealt a severe blow to any idea of sustaining the US economy on its merits. The expected benefits to the US economy from the control of Iraqi oil production and reserves as poffered by Deputy Secretary of Defence Wolfowitz have been replaced by a burgeoning national debt and an increasing dependency on foreigners to finance the national debt and US ecnomy at current levels.

Negative Savings Rate

Another significant factor, is the negative or relatively low savings rate of Americans. As observed by Mühleisen (2004: 5): "the current account deficit increasingly reflects low saving rather than high investment." While the US continues to experience steady economic growth in comparison with the ups and down of Western Europe, Japan, and some of the Southeast Asian countries, such growth increasingly manifest in domestic consumption and investment in excess of domestic savings which are unsustainable in the longer term as noted by the US Comptroller General.

Economic theory tells us that when a country runs a budget deficit it has to be financed by someone. As an individual or a single state, you cannot consume more than you produce or spend more than you earn; it a mathematical fact. One therefore must either beg, or borrow or steal. Hence, if consumption, investment, and government spending together exceed national production, the difference must come in the form of imports of goods or capital inflows from foreigners. Therefore, US economic growth and budget deficits are increasingly being financed by foreigners in consequence of the low national savings rate which was negative in 2005 in comparison with the savings rate of about 50 percent in China and double-digits in Japan. As a result of the excess of expenditure over income at the end of 2006, the national debt as noted above stood at US$9.0 trillion, 40 percent of which is owed to foreigners; five percent to China.

The concern of many in Congress, then, centers on the consequences of a reversal in the willingness of foreigners, especially the Chinese, to hold US dollar assets and a possible conversion out of dollar-denominated financial instruments. But, in seeking to allay the fears of a "China pull-out", Treasury Secretary Henry Paulson equates Chinese holdings of US treasuries to about one day's trade in the US Bond market.[13] Nonetheless, the impact of such a move would not be in America's best interest. The assumption by Mr. Paulson is that the void will be filled by others. Indeed, for most US politicians would that such were the case; the US Congress still bristles at the thought that a communist country—the Chinese to boot—should be seen as financing the free-spending of the bastion of Western capitalism. Evidence Republican Presidential Candidate Ron Paul: "The US is borrowing US$2.5 billion a day, most of which is is coming, unbelievably, from the Chinese."[14] Given this psychological vulnerability, America's anxiety soon or late will translate to irrational policies, if it has not already done so. Hence, the potential for a shift in foreign-investor sentiment now must be factored into the equation in a liberalized global financial market. The risk premium attached to investing in the US will have to be factored into investment decisions as well; and it is not zero.

But in addition to exposing the US to the fickleness of foreigners to hold dollar-denominated assets, there are two other negative effects of fiscal budget deficits. The first is the effect of crowding-out on private investment which occurs in consequence of an increase in interest rates and which will be exacerbated should there be a reduction in inflows of foreign investment. The second is that the higher fiscal deficit and public debt in the US is likely to absorb the savings of its traditional lenders, thereby causing higher world interest rates (see Cardarelli and Kose 2004). It is partly for this reason as discussed below that Secretary Paulson is trying to get China to liberalize its financial sector so that the accumulated US$2.0 trillion of Chinese savings can be accessed by the US and other OECD countries, either as payment for goods and services or as a source of investment capital.

A Softer Approach?

An interesting twist to the US Treasury Secretary's approach to Chinese stubbornness is to assume the role of adviser and seek to convince them that it would be in their best interest if they were to open their financial sector to foreign competition. As told to Jim Lehrer of *News Hour* by the Secretary,[15] Chinese savers are receiving two and one-half percent on their US$2.0 trillion savings. As former head of one of the largest investment banking firms in the US, he believes they could do much better, about double the current interest rate, through liberalization of their financial markets. According to Paulson, the increase in income would operate to reduce the need to save at such a high rate. The rationale, of course, is that the US could then tap into this increase in the income stream—presumably considered "discretionary"—through increase exports of American-produced goods and services. As the logic goes, both sides benefit: the Chinese by receiving higher interest income on their savings, and the US by exporting more to them. At the same time, any action that increases economic growth in the US should help to reduce the fiscal budget deficit and hence the cost of servicing the national debt. The idea, of course, is to keep real interest rates in the industrialized countries from increasing since higher borrowing costs to the US would have adverse effects on global investment and output (see Mühleisen, 2004: 5). But, the focus of China's high economic growth rates as told by Chinese officials is principally to broaden the income opportunity for all Chinese through job creation which, for now, is concentrated in the traded-goods sector, an imperative of development not lost on Alan Blinder of Princeton University who, as noted in Chapter Five, recognized that China's export drive is motivated by its need to: "give production work to the hoards of people migrating from the country to the cities."[16] While, therefore, there is much to commend Mr. Paulson's prescription in terms of his bid to reduce the pressure on global interest rates arising from the low savings rate in America, the Chinese are not quite ready to abandon 2,500 years of Confucianism for the Western ideology of individualism that is barely over 225 years old and, therefore, in terms of their sense of time is still at the proving-in stage. China, to be sure, for all its outward appearances is still influenced by Confucius ideology. Hence the continued belief that: "The people must have sufficient food and good dress before they can talk honor. The good customs and social amenities come from wealth and disappear when the country is poor" (Lin Yutang 1960: 208–9). Indeed, this has been the refrain of Chinese officials to issues on human rights and other issues of individual rights raised by the West.

A Culture of Consumerism

It is instructive that, rather than suggest that Americans as individuals need to save more, the Federal Reserve Chairman Ben Bernanke seeks to be politically correct: "the most direct way to address savings is to try and improve savings in the government sector" so as to reduce reliance on foreign capital flows into the US because "there is the risk sometime in the future there will be less demand for dollar assets.[17] For many observers, this is clearly playing to a conservative agenda that advocates smaller government and support for the capitalist class; it is telling the administration what it wants to hear. But somewhat confusingly, it is also acknowledging the precarious condition of the American economy for those who would listen: America cannot afford to restrain consumer spending without alternative means of increasing income; nor can it afford the degree of oversight and inspection necessary to ensure food safety or national security or indeed, to realistically stem the flow of illeagal workers, despite the rhetoric.

America is locked into a culture of consumerism. At the same time, it is seeking to build an intellectual capitalist class on the backs of cheap immigrant labor whose basic needs must be satisfied through cheap imports from China and other low-cost producing countries. The Starbucks coffee-drinking class is not America as the averages would lead one to presume. They do, however, control over 70 percent of the wealth as alluded to by Derek Bok. They are also the investor-class of America whose proportion of GDP from investment is increasing, as discussed above. It is for this reason that *Wal-Mart*, and *McDonald's* have become symbols of Americanism at the other end of the income divide, with cheap imports contributing to the equation. In this connection, it is noteworthy that the *Center for Strategic and International Studies* estimates the benefits to US consumers from cheap imports to be around US$70.0 billion a year.[18] Yet, there are many who stand ready to blame the Chinese for America's economic woes. For example, according to Congressman Duncan Hunter: "Communist China is cheating on trade."[19] The Congressman, of course, is seeking the Republican nomination for the 2008 Presidental election.

Despite the rhetoric, according to Charles Conkey of the *Wall Street Journal*, "economic growth has hit its slowest pace in four years, and only brisk consumer spending has kept it from falling more."[20] But, as shown by Martin Wolf, between 1996 and 2003 real domestic demand has grown faster than real GDP in every year. Moreover, when demand slows, it is reflected in an even slower growth in GDP as in 2001.[21] This is a little different from the optimistic view expressed by the administration and more recently by Anne Krueger who attributes the slowdown primarily to the slow growth rate experienced by the OECD countries.[22] Clearly, then, building on Krueger's theory that, as economic growth in the OECD countries picks up, as they are showing signs of doing, the expectation is for the US economy to benefit. But this is 1950s reality. Moreover, Professor Krueger is not disposed to supporting the blame game of the Washington establishment either. Thus, while it is understandable that Secretary Paulson sees the low savings rates of Americans as an indication of confidence in the US economy thereby reinforcing Federal Reserve Chairman Bernanke's notion of increased consumer spending, the argument is not persuasive; neither is the prediction of a reversal of the budget deficit by 2012.

Clearly, both Chairman Bernanke and Secretary Paulson are basing their optimism on future growth of the US economy and a successful outcome to the conflicts in the Middle East and the ability of the US to successfully orchestrate the direction of competitive forces around the world. They are also placing a great deal of reliance on the administration's perceived ability to control the growth of the Chinese economy through the classic American approach of external pressure and intervention as needed: Super 301 is still on the table as an option, albeit a dangerous one given the precarious condition of the American economy. Indeed, the US of today is not the US of the Reagan era; neither is

China in 2007 the Japan of the 1980s. Despite the spin to which Secretary Paulson appears wedded, this understanding is not lost on him who every now and again offers flashes of reality (see interview with Charlie Rose and with Jim Lehrer[23]). Hence, for the Bush administration the imponderables are increasing and are looming more ominous the longer Iraq continues to be a drain on American resources. This has been reinforced by the fall-out of the "Sub-prime" mortgage crisis.

Based on the observations of Mr Bernanke and Mr Paulson, rather than encourage savings by individuals, Americans are encouraged to spend more in support of an essentially consumer-driven economic model built arguably on the presumption of America's unrivalled productivity rates and access to resources, including Middle Eastern oil. Moreover, according to Mr Bernanke, consumer spending needs to be increased further to cover the increase in the minimum wage authorized by the Congress in 2007. But given that the savings rate in America with the exception of the Depression years is at its lowest point in US history, it follows logically that the suggested increase in consumer spending has to be financed by foreigners or by a depreciation of the US Dollar both of which add to the image of a diminished giant; a status clearly rejected as unacceptable to the Bush administration and its supporters as evidenced by current events in the Middle East and its push to have China revalue its currency.

Revaluation of the Yuan: a US Imperative

According to Mr Paulson, there are significant benefits to be had from persuading the Chinese to revalue their currency. One benefit that is likely to accrue to the US is the theoretical increase in US exports to China attendant a shift in relative prices. According to the theory, American products would be made less expensive to Chinese consumers by virtue of the revaluation. The second theoretical benefit from a revaluation of the Yuan is that Chinese exports would be made relatively more expensive and thus less competitive, not only in the US but also in third markets, thereby narrowing the US overall trade gap. The third potential benefit is, of course, slowing the growth of the Chinese economy and its accumulation of foreign exchange reserves as a knock-on effect of the first two. The fourth potential benefit is that it will likely force the Chinese to rely on foreign capital if they want to continue to grow beyond what their domestic savings rate allows, thereby passing some control of the Chinese economy over to foreign investors. Needless to say these are very self-interested perspectives despite Desmond Lachman and Kenneth Rogoff[24] attempts to cast a reduction in Chinese savings rate and foreign exchange reserves as being in the interest of the Chinese people.

Lessons from the Asian Financial Crisis, 1997–8

Economic theory notwithstanding, the lessons from the Asian financial crisis of 1997–8 are still fresh in the minds of the Asians. Briefly, according to ex-post analyses the economic growth rates of the affected economies which had reached a stage of diminishing marginal returns—that is, more and more investment dollars were needed to produce one additional dollar of real GDP as measured by the incremental capital-output ratio (ICOR)—could not be sustained without huge inflows of foreign capital, which were largely protected by a regime of fixed exchange rates. The problem arises when the flow of investment dollars dries up and a reversal of largely speculative capital ensues, facilitating further speculation on their respective currencies (see Chang 2006; Sundaram 2004). Indeed, the World Bank has concluded ex-post that: "Portfolio flows can change direction very quickly, putting pressure on exchange rates and fragile banking sectors and sometimes causing currency or banking crisis" (World Bank, 2004, 113); an understanding of foot-loose capitalism that had been articulated as far back as 1994, however. Equally significant, it vindicated those who held out the 1997 Asian financial crisis as arising primarily from private borrowing. With such lesson still fresh in the minds of the Asians, it is unlikely that China would allow itself to be pushed beyond what it considers to be in its own best interest. This was made abundantly clear in the 2-day high-level talks between China's Deputy Premier Wu Yi and US Treasury Secretary Henry Paulson that ended on Wednesday, May 23, 2007. Apart from raising China's interest rates and increasing the daily trading band of the Yuan[25] the Chinese have not made the concessions sought by Paulson whose parting comments were that the Chinese Delegation would likely hear "some strong views" from the Democratic-controlled Congress.[26] Despite these parting words from Mr Paulson, the Chinese, as noted in the previous chapter, will continue to take an incremental approach to reform.

Wrongheaded Policy?

To a neoconservative-led administration enamored with power, then, controlling competitors' access to resources appears still to be first best choice. While the Treasury Secretary continues to hammer away at Chinese stubbornness with respect to Western concerns over the value of the Yuan, intellectual property rights, financial market liberalization, and any other ideas that can be thrown at them, American hard power is employed at seeking to control their access to the resource most needed to fuel their economy: oil. Hence, still informing the Bush administration foreign policy—at least up to the time of writing—is the idea of dissuading America's up and coming competitor(s) from engaging in "asymmetrical challenges" by way of the "demonstrative value of a preemptive attack" on Iraq, and possibly Iran, "matched with plans for how the world's second largest oil reserve might be divided among the world's contractors" as attributed to the former Secretary of Defense Donald Rumsfeld (Suskind 2004: 96). But for many observers and certainly for the Democratic Party leadership, such a policy is deemed "wrongheaded" at this stage of the game. The drain on American resources is too great a price; they prefer to have America "moderate its ventures" as Huntington (1996: 311) counseled, especially in the Middle East five years into what many are characterizing as a quagmire in Iraq. From the perspective of the wider world, however, it is a policy that offers a valuable lesson on the territorial imperative, manifesting in the botched attempt at Westernization of the Middle East as a first-order requirement.

Misplaced Emphasis

A more realistic and ironically orthodox approach, one that long would have been recommended by the IMF and World Bank to developing countries, would be to curb the profligacy and reduce the fiscal budget deficit. One would have thought that if the high savings rate of the Chinese is responsible for generating economic growth rates of 10.0 per cent per annum, and a low savings rate in the US is generating economic growth rates of less than 2.0 percent—as indicated by the 0.6 percent growth in the first quarter in 2007—the logical policy prescription would be to encourage Americans to curb their spending habits and save more. This is not novel. High savings rates have contributed to the extraordinary growth rates of the Asian economies in the second half of the twentieth century (see Krugman 1999; Amsden 1989). Instead, both Bernanke and Paulson appear committed to the school of thought that says as long as the US can export the ideology of consumerism, it is okay for Americans to be free-spenders. The contradiction is inescapable and evidences policy inconsistency as a means to offsetting vulnerability. It also evidences the predicament of the American economy and attendant irrationality in a world that is no longer mesmerized by the awesome military might of a superpower. Hence, both the Federal Reserve Chairman and the Treasury Secretary must continue with "spin" while employing gentle persuasion with the Chinese.

Rising Current Account Deficits

There are two aspects to the current account deficits which reflect upon the health of the US economy. The first is arising from the trade imbalance with American trading partners while the second arises from the inflow of foreign capital not only to help finance the government budget deficit but also to bridge the saving-investment gap that has become an integral aspect of the American political economic framework. With respect to the inflow of foreign capital, it is the cost of servicing the growing national debt coupled with the payment of dividends and interest to foreigners that add to the deficit on current account.

Trade Deficit

For politicians seeking to make quick points with their constituents, the trade deficit provides a ready means. According to the rhetoric, American trading partners are engaging in unfair trading practices; there are subsidizing their manufacturers to maintain a competitive edge over US manufacturers; they are employing child labor and are not complying with international standards, and so on.. This is a replay of the old familiar tune. We witnessed it in connection with Japanese imports in the 1980s; we witnessed it in connection with Mexico in the lead-up to the North America Free Trade Agreement (NAFTA); and we are witnessing it in the twenty-first century. In the case of Japan, voluntary exports restraints (VERs) were the answer combined with currency management despite denial to the contrary. In case of Mexico, NAFTA was conceived as the answer, with the US as the senior partner.

With respect to the NAFTA, before the ink was dry on the agreement US trade union representatives went south of the border to lend support to Mexican workers whom they determined needed higher wages and better working conditions. US manufacturers also got what they wanted: the requirement of a high percentage of local content in Mexican exports to the US, thereby preventing the Japanese from using Mexico as an export platform. As a result, the loss of American jobs to Mexico was temporally arrested; that problem was transferred to the Canadians who unwittingly traded the bilateral free trade agreement with the US for becoming a partner of NAFTA. Americans once again can continue to spend, assured in the strength of the US economy and its ability to prevail in international trade agreements. In addition, the Japanese threat was removed by a combination of currency management and unilateral sanctions under Super 301of the amended Trade and Tariff Act, 1974 (see Bhagwati and Patrick 1990).

With such successes behind it, the question for the US then becomes: why not employ the same tactics with China? The answer is not as simple as politicians seem to make out. Indeed, it is bound up with "our way of life". According to Chairman Bernanke, "consumer spending is the mainstay of the US economy"[27]: it accounts for about 70 percent. American prosperity is also tied to maintaining a low inflation rate. The two are contradictory in a condition of full employment, which is also a goal of every US administration. Meanwhile, America is gradually losing its competitive edge in many areas of basic manufacture in consequence of higher wage and other labor-related costs and must therefore rely upon a steady flow of imports from low-cost producing countries while it seeks to expand its intellectual capital and services sectors. In the mean time the expectation is that it will be able to pry open the Chinese and other rapidly-growing economies; but it is a well-worn and fimilar path.

Without such cheap imports to meet the demands of its burgeoning immigrant working class, the inflation rate would be much higher than it is currently, leading to demands for even higher wages. And without an equivalent in high-end exports, the trade imbalance will continue to pose a problem for the US administration. Moreover, an oft overlooked fact is that the trade deficit with the EU is greater than the trade deficit with China. Indeed, the trade deficit with China is about 25 percent of the total US deficit on current account.

On the export side of the trade coin, there are domestic restrictions on American exports notwithstanding the export requirement to counterbalance its reliance on import of consumer goods. It is not that China and other similar developing countries do not want American products; they just do not want to buy what America wants them to buy. Highly protective of its hegemony, US export of advanced technology—its comparative and competitive advantage—is restricted to friends and allies; but it is what the Chinese and others want, not first or second generation technology or specialized equipment the maintenance of which is tied to accepting US hegemony and thus could be held hostage. The US on the other hand continues to hold firm to a policy that is rooted in capital accumulation, which is, to export services and ideology that serve not only to breakdown cultural and ideological barriers but also to generate financial rewards to American investors in the process. But as noted earlier, China is not Japan: it does not feel beholden to any Western country, least of all to America, and, as told to Carrie Gracie of the BBC by the Chinese Ambassador to the UN in Geneva, will vigorously oppose attempts by any Western country to interfere with its way of life. To this end, the Chinese vigorously filters imports of both goods and services from the West. Even the flow of capital is controlled lest it should facilitate the pass through of propaganda aimed at derailing the Chinese economy: China, to be sure, is not without its version of paranoia.

As a result of this contradictory approach to trade, the US trade deficit has moved from positive to negative over the last 50 years. In other words, despite being the most productive, innovative, and efficient economy in the world, America must rely on cheap imports to fuel its insatiable appetite for consumption goods while relying on friends and allies, indeed its military industrial complex, to support its technological sector. Hence, at the end of 2006 the trade deficit stood at US$856.7 billion, representing 6.5 percent of gross domestic product (GDP) of which US$232.55 billion was with China and US$88.44 billion with Japan. But the analysis should not end there.

As pointed out in Chapter Five, China serves as a processing and assembly platform for the Southeast Asian countries and as such runs substantial trade deficits with them. For example, for 2003 China had trade deficits with the following countries: Japan (-US$30.0 billion); Korea (-US$30.0 billion); Taiwan (-US$51.0 billion); ASEAN (US$30.0 billion); and others (-US$11.0 billion). While therefore on a purely bilateral basis China runs a trade surplus with the

US, it arguably does so partly on behalf of those countries using it as an export platform.

Eroding Influence

Clearly, the advantage the US enjoyed in rebuilding Europe after World War II, and the competitive advantage enjoyed from innovations, especially in consumer technology, have been eroded over the years primarily because of the inevitable diffusion of technology at an ever-shortening time span. Moreover, the narrowing of asymmetries in trade agreements which the US enjoyed over its competitors during this period has been a major factor. In addition to the tangible, there is the intangible. The halo-effect as savior of the world has lost its shine over the passage of time, especially in a Europe that sees itself as standing up to America's dominance: the refusal of France and Germany to join the American-led "coalition of the willing" in the invasion of Iraq speaks to this observation. The European Union's refusal to give way to US pressure to open its markets and on subsidies is equally telling. But despite the shift in the pattern of international trade and a steady erosion of US competitiveness and influence, US consumption pattern remains largely unchanged from the 1950s, making it difficult for it to find acceptable solutions to disagreements on trade. Other countries on the other hand have been adjusting to the changing reality of a new world economic and likely political order, although not in all areas. Equally significant is the steady stream of immigrants to the US whose consumption pattern serves to reinforce a culture of consumerism as noted above but whose labor is essential to "our way of life."

Universalizing Consumerism

Given this propensity to high consumption relative to other countries, then, the US finds itself at an increasingly competitive disadvantage which is reflected in its growing trade deficits, especially with China. One way out of the relative economic slide, the easy way, as offered by the Federal Reserve Chairman, is to create more markets for US goods and services, that is, to universalize consumerism. For this reason the pressure on the Europeans to open their market to US products has been relentless. At the same time the EU is also bent on staying competitive at home and abroad and have resorted to trading accusations with the US: the EU accusing the US of being "inflexible" while the US accuses the EU of closed markets, with Mr Bush playing the concern for third world development card as noted in Chapter Four.

The second approach which is by no means a stand alone approach, is to have foreign countries, especially China, reduce their savings rate, that is, adopt "our way of life" as a consumer-oriented society and to buy what is made available to them. This was, after all, the tacit agreement of new entrants to the WTO. As charter members of the WTO club, both the US and the EU are in full agreement with this approach, although the EU has proven to be less ideological.

Chairman Bernanke's proposal is nothing new; exporting "our way of life" is the hallmark of America's hegemony. This the US can do by exercising its hard power when jaw-boning fails. As observed by Sklair (1995: 47–8): "Those cultural practices that cannot be incorporated into the culture-ideology of consumerism become oppositional counter-hegemonic forces to be harnessed or marginalized, and if that fails, destroyed physically." Sklair is not alone in this assessment. Donaldson (1989: 31) expressed concern for, "the legitimate rights of a nation, large or small, to economic self-determinism." But to many observers, freedom and democracy when proselytized by way of the sword convey a sense of desperation, especially when the unspoken objective is to forcefully create markets in foreign countries, and as emphasized in this book, to have unrestricted access to and control over vital resources. Recall Mr. Rumsfeld's plans for Iraqi oil reserves as told by Paul O'Neill, the former Secretary of the Treasury.

The Illusion of Competitiveness

In addition to the need to expand its market share by whatever means, despite the free-trade rhetoric and reverence for the "invisible hand" the US must continue to subsidize agriculture and impose quantitative and other restrictions on many foreign imports such as automobiles from Japan, cotton and textile goods from China, lamb from New Zealand, steel from Europe and Brazil, and ethanol from Brazil. Without such trade restrictions, neither the US automobile industry nor the textile and cotton industry would survive; indeed, neither would US agriculture or the steel industry survive without the heavy subsidies and protection from foreign competition. The billions of dollars in subsidies to many sectors of the economy help to maintain the illusion of competitiveness and "our way of life" both of which are partly supported ironically by the very people with whom the US is in competition. Such subsidies further serve to keep poor countries in a dependent relationship as discussed in Chapter Four. Hence, the need for a level playing field cuts both ways if ever Americans would allow themselves to be less self-absorbed. Indeed, the subsidies paid to American farmers are greater that the GNP of several developing countries put together; yet the clamor is for a level playing field. Ethopian coffee growers, for example, get less than a dollar per pould for their coffee; the same coffee cost US$8.00 per cup on the *Rive Gouche* in Paris or at *Starbucks*.

Inflow of Foreign Capital

But trade is not the only contributing factor to the US current account deficit. Despite the Bush tax cut to the wealthy and other incentives to key industries, such as the pharmaceutical and petroleum industries, savings for investment fall short of what is required to sustain economic growth at a healthy rate. Prior to 2000, this shortfall in the saving-investment ratio has been made up readily by foreigners seeking a safe haven for their capital. Indeed, the strength of the US economy and the strength of the US Dollar have been supported in part by the bullish sentiment of foreign investors. Like a good growth stock, its present market value is a function of its perceived future worth. But as the savings-investment gap began to widen and the government began to run fiscal deficits again, the deficit on current account began to reflect the discrepancies at an alarmingly increasing rate. As noted above, according to Anne Krueger of Johns Hopkins University, the high rate of return in the US vis-à-vis other OECD countries has been a factor to the Current Account deficit, in addition to, of course, "fiscal structural deficit."[28] Sound economic management has truly given way to, in the phraseology of the former president George Herbert Walker Bush, "voodoo economics." Hence the clamor for curbing the trade deficit while seeking to shore up the inflow of foreign capital from a position of extreme vulnerability and spin.

But despite the optimistic view of Harvard University's Kenneth Rogoff, and *American Enterprise Institute's* Desmond Lachman[29] and others, America's ability to attract foreign investment has begun to wane in recent years. Since 9/11 and the invasion of Iraq, foreigners have become wary of investing in the US given the heightened resort to scrutiny of things foreign and increased regulatory oversight. Moreover, countries that are not directly affected by the Iraq war provide good opportunities for investment. Their stock markets have outperformed the American stock market in 2006 in terms of percentage increase and their economies are better managed. As a consequence of the decline in foreign investment in the US, the number of Americans employed by foreign firms in the private sector, according to the numbers released by the US treasury, declined from 5.7 million in 2000 to 5.1 million in 2005. This decline in foreign investment in the US has prompted the President to seek to reassure foreign investors:

> As both the world's largest investor and the world's largest recipient of investment, the United States has a key stake in promoting an open investment regime.... My administration is committed to ensuring that the United States continues to be the most attractive place in the world to invest.[30]

This was followed up by Treasury Secretary Paulson: "We just want to make it very clear that we welcome foreign investment and it's vital to our economic strength going forward." However, as recognized by California Governor Arnold Schwarzenegger: "The marketplace is now the whole world, and that offers tremendous growth potential for our companies, but our competition is also worldwide."[31] And this is not only for goods and services but also for investment capital.

An Over-valued Dollar

It is the argument of the US and certain members of the EU that their trade deficits where exist are partly due to the undervaluation of their trading partners' currencies. If this were true, then it is also true that the affected economies are operating with overvalued currencies. Indeed, a refrain in the US and Europe is that the Chinese Yuan is undervalued[32], but as observed in Chang (2006), the currency-valuation argument is a double-edged sword: it was wielded by Chairman Greenspan in one direction during the Southeast Asian financial crisis in 1997–8, that is, insisting that the affected countries maintain their fixed exchange rates even though their currencies were clearly overvalued; and now it is being wielded in the other direction by Chairman Bernanke with respect to the perceived undervaluation of the Chinese currency. The question then is: what is preventing the US from devaluing the US Dollar?

The simple but truthful answer is, of course, the US is in a catch-22 with respect to the valuation of the Dollar. An unstable and eroding currency does not for investor confidence make. It needs to maintain a stable if not high valuation first, because of the high foreign component of its debt-holders and secondly, because of its dependency on the inward flow of foreign investment to finance future economic growth at affordable rates. Tax incentives to the rich while helpful is not enough to stimulate the level of domestic savings needed to maintain the current growth rate, and any cut back on consumer spending would likely lead to a recession. Moreover, the idea that the US will grow itself out of the downdraft appears to many as wishful thinking in light of the rapid growth of the Chinese and Indian economies which are clearly enjoying the benefits of lower costs, especially labor-related costs. At the same time, US traditional manufacture increasingly are becoming uncompetitive in the global market place, and more to the point, in the home market by maintaining the US dollar at an artificially high valuation. Its depreciation in 2007 vis-à-vis the Pound Sterling and the Euro should help; but would it be enough to reverse the trend?

Rising Cost of Production

An oft overlooked point is that America's productivity growth is slowing. The benefits of technological innovations of the 1980s and 1990s are close to being maximized. What this means is that, like the Southeast Asian countries of the 1990s, there is evidence of diminishing marginal returns on investment, that is, more and more investment is needed to produce an additional dollar of GDP.

And this is notwithstanding the contribution from lower labor cost attendant a growing reliance on cheap immigrant labor. For the US, then, given its reliance on consumer spending this means a greater dependency on the inward flow of foreign investment. It is also one of the reasons for outsourcing to Asia and elsewhere and for having a porous border.

Absent the illegal or migrant workers, the productivity rate would arguably be lower than it is currently. For example, the productivity rate for the first quarter of 2007 rose by one percent compared to the projected 1.7 percent by the government.[33] These facts are largely kept from the American people for political reasons: it serves the political agenda to blame someone else for the eroding prosperity of Americans as does question-begging in Congressional hearings and debates serves the agendas of politicians and their special-interest groups. No politician sees the issues in holistic terms; and Americans are accustomed to not hearing the truth. This said, there are a few Republican Senators, Chuck Hagel for example, who have emerged from the state of denial in March 2007 and have openly criticized the administration for misleading the public, not just about the war in Iraq but in general.

The glowing picture of prosperity of the US economy as protrayed by politicians, then, is but a reflection of their denial. US manufacturing costs of production are increasing at an alarming rate. Such cost pressures are coming from several sources, with cost of healthcare, entitlement programs, and energy as the main contributors. It is no accident that at the end on 2006 over 47 million Americans are without healthcare insurance coverage—an increase of two million from 2003—and that the Bush administration's 2008 Budget Proposal includes drastic cuts to entitlement programs. As observed by the US Comptroller General, "we are spending more money than we make, we are charging it to a credit card and expecting our grandchildren to pay for it."[34]

Healthcare Costs

As further recognized by Mr.Bernanke in his testimony to the US Senate, healthcare costs are one of the fastest growing costs to US businesses. Also, according to Congressional Budget Office Director Peter Orszag, healthcare costs account for six percent of GDP.[35] This point has been made by Senator Kent Conrad the Chairman of the Senate Budget Committee in an earlier presentation on the 2008 Budget proposal. The US spends more per capita in comparison with other developed countries and must seek to control costs in other areas if it is to maintain its competitiveness. This view has been reiterated in less diplomatic terms by the US Comptroller General: "If there is one thing that could bankrupt America, it is healthcare. Its not just eating up the federal budget, it is eating up state budgets, it's eating up the budgets of the private sector enterprises."[36] On the other hand, Americans as a rule are accustomed to seeking medical attention for almost every ailment in comparison with citizens in other countries; hence, any attempt to limit access to healthcare would be politically costly to any politician who should dare suggest limiting such access. Because of this mindset of Americans and the influence of politics, health insurance costs have been steadily rising and have become a significant cost burden on American businesses, especially small and medium size firms. Many such firms cannot afford to offer health insurance at such high cost and remain competitive in the global market.

In addition to the American mindset with respect to access to healthcare, the impact of the lobbies of pharmaceutical and healthcare industries is to keep healthcare costs high. Americans pay more for prescription drugs than any other nation; they also pay more at primary care institutions and for dental and other ambulatory medical services. It is the only developed country without a universal health insurance plan. These costs find their way into the cost structure of businesses either directly as benefits or indirectly through higher wages. But politicians dependent on financial support from special interest groups are often forced to find ways to transfer the burden onto foreign competitors by imposing health and safety standards at the production level of goods entering the US.

Entitlement Programs

According to Chairman Bernanke, entitlement programs account for about ten percent of GDP. At this rate, he argues, tax revenues will have to be increased from 18 percent of GDP to 25 percent of GDP by 2030. Therefore, the Bush administration's 2008 Budget Proposal to Congress as noted above is proposing drastic cuts in many such programs, including education and healthcare. But as observed eleven years ago by Bok (1996: 90):

> Levels of productivity throughout the industrialized world will come to depend more and more on the basic ingredients of investment, education, and training. It is here that the United States lags behind in ways that our traditional approach cannot readily overcome.

Indeed, a well recognized fact of the Asian economic miracle is the role played by education and to providing a safety net (see Krugman 1999: 35; Amsden, 1989). However, despite this understanding of the importance of education, surveys in the US reveal that, 43 percent of Hispanic Americans are without a high school diploma compared with 25 percent of Black Americans and 15 percent of whites. With minorities accounting for one-third of the population at the end of 2006, and expected to comprise over 50 percent of the population by 2050, if not sooner, cut-backs in the funding of education and library services portend even greater erosion of US competitiveness. Moreover, as is well recognized, low productivity manifest in poverty. At the same time, with five times as many black Americans and two times as many Hispanic Americans than whites in prison, the US spends more per capita to incarcerate members of these groups than to educate them; yet, the argument is for greater expenditure on the prison system.

While the US is forced to cut back on basics such as healthcare and education, other countries are narrowing the productivity gap as their access to advanced technology is facilitated by globalization, accompanied by an unmatched emphasis on an educated workforce. This is an observable phenomenon in India and China despite attempts to slow the transfer of advanced technology to them, especially to China. But China and India are not alone. The UK, for example, is seeking to remain competitive in the field of science and technology by promoting interest in higher mathematics.[37] Yet, cost pressures, budget deficits, and a less than committed approach to pluralism and diversity—rhetoric notwithstanding—are forcing the US to skimp on these all-important determinants of future growth. Indeed, the emphasis is to transfer the burden onto the individual by seeking to privatize education, social security, and healthcare, further disadvantaging the poor which is largely made up of minorities.

But the US is not alone with respect to the rising cost of entitlement programs. Whilst the issue in the US arises from its diversity, in Europe it is a function of changing demographics: the greater the inflow of non-European immigrants, the greater the concern over rising costs of social safety-nets and of integrating peoples from disparate cultures. The election of Nicolas Sarkozy as President of a multi-ethnic France in May 2007 speaks to the concern of the French middle class over the increasing burden of France's social welfare programs. However, while good-intentioned in his promise to lift France out of the economic doldrums, the newly-elected French President runs the risk of adding to the disaffected with his proposal to make overtime income tax-exempt. Such a policy speaks of elitism or exclusion and unless there are job-creating programs for the burgeoning unemployed will add to the income inequality divide in France. At the other end of the demographic spectrum, for societies that are fairly homogenous, as in the case of Sweden, for example, the concern is somewhat muted, although it too is beginning to express some concern over the rising cost of its welfare state.

While the US and to some extent Western Europe are grappling with the increasing cost of their social welfare programs, Russia is increasing its expenditure for care of the elderly. As remarked by President Putin in his final address on the state of the state, a country that does not take care of its elderly is a country that is doomed to failure. The Chinese government is also concerned about China's poor and, as discussed more fully in Chapter Five, has geared its economic policies to bring them out of poverty. The US, at the other extreme is "dumping" the medically-indigent in skid row where, in the City of Los Angeles, for example, over 80,000 homeless congregate.

Rising Energy Costs

The spike in the price of oil to over US$70.00 per barrel is a major contributor to the economic woes of the US as reflected in the trade deficit numbers. A contributing factor to the spike in the price of oil is the loss of two million barrels a day in consequence of the Iraq war. Also, as recognized by the Chairman Bernanke, US short-term demand for oil is inelastic, that is, almost the same quantity of oil will be imported even though the price of oil is increasing. Indeed, there is a greater correlation between the trade deficit and the price of oil than with trade with China. For example, while the trade deficit with China receded in the first quarter of 2007, the overall US trade deficit set yet another record in consequence of the high cost of oil imports. This observation is supported by the relationships in the previous quarter: In the fourth quarter of 2006, the previous quarter, although the trade deficit with China increased, the overall deficit was 14.6 percent less than the third quarter of 2006 and has been attributed to the drop in the relative price of oil during the fourth quarter in 2006.

Another statistic of note is that, whereas in the 1980s the US imported about 42 percent of its oil, in 2006 it is importing about 61 percent of its usage at prices that have increased over five-fold. Reinforcing this evidence is the finding by Sheldon Johnson and Laura McLay of the University of Illinois that the US consumes 938 million gallons of gasoline more per year in 2006 than it did in 1960. These statistics notwithstanding, Ford Motor, General Motors, Toyota, and the United Auto Workers Unions testified jointly to Congress in March 2007 against setting higher mileage standards for automobiles.

Clearly, Americans have not adjusted their life style to reflect the reality of high oil prices. Rather, they find justification for continuing their demand for oil on the false logic that Europeans are paying more than two times the price for gas. Not considered in this rationalization is the fact that gas prices in Europe reflect higher taxes imposed on usage and that Europeans have reliable public transport systems which serve their everyday transport needs. For many concerned about the rising demand for gas in the US and for the environment, the number of single passenger SUVs on the roads is grossly irresponsible. Moreover, it conveys the message to the world that what America wants America will take. But energy conversavation is but a small part of the solution. Hence, as conjectured earlier, the increase in the price of oil arguably is driving the US foreign policy in the Middle East, simply because the Middle East holds a large percentage of the known oil reserves in the world. Therefore, from a cost–benefit perspective, it is here suggested that the neoconservative grand strategy considered the control of Middle East oil reserves to be the most cost-effective approach. Why? As well recognized by Republican Representative John Peterson, "the country cannot compete without affordable energy." More pointedly, accordinging to the Congressman: "we have to have affordable, available energy or Americans will be out of Jobs."[38] As evidence, consider that, according to Representative Peterson, the cost of natural gas to Dow Chemicals has increased from US$8.0 billion to US$ 22.0 billion over the last five years.

Hence, as a high-energy dependent economy, the US needs to find alternative sources of energy for its long run sustainability. In the short–to medium–term, it needs to keep oil prices from escalating and this, as argued, is to seek control over access to oil. In this regard, recall Mr Bush's continuing reference to the demand for energy by China and India and his exhortation to the Brazilian President to produce more ethanol, not necessarily for export to the US however, since reduction or elimination of the approximately US$0.54 per gallon tariff placed on US import of ethanol from Brazil, according to Mr Bush, "is not going to happen".

Organized Labor

Whereas labor unions were needed as countervailing the power of the employer as discussed in Chapter Three, their impact in the latter part of the twentieth century has been to add to the cost burden of the American manufacturing and industrial sectors. That they brought collective bargaining to bear on securing a living wage, retirement, healthcare, and other benefits is not to be discounted. Without their activism, American workers unarguably would be less well off today, if the widening income inequality gap in America is a reliable indicator. But, as exemplified by the crisis in the American auto industry, the inability to adjust to the reality of globalization is a significant contributor to the loss of American industrial competitiveness. Labor and labor related costs account for a substantial proportion of the cost of manufacture in American traditional industries compared with similar industries in Asia and other developing regions.

While many analysts have attributed the problems of the American auto industry to inappropriate business models, labor related costs have become unsustainable even after taking account of tariff and non-tariff barriers erected to protect it from foreign competition. The industry has become reliant on their lobby in Washington to exact concessions from foreign governments in trade agreements or to find other ways of protecting American jobs. But as is well documented, the exporting of economic and social regulations has only served to provide a false sense of security to many of America's traditional industries and to reinforce the inertia typical of them. Indeed, these industries appear not to have drawn any lessons from the British experience of the 1970s and 1980s. Equally disquieting, is that American politicians dependant on campaign financing from special interest groups are beholden to industry lobbies and are therefore reluctant to put their jobs on the line. Hence they equivocate on issues hoping that by ignoring them they will right themselves or will be passed on to the next batch in Congress.

Exporting Economic and Social Regulations

In the 1960s and 1970s, the West began to pay more attention to social and environmental issues. Scrubbers were installed on smoke stacks to reduce pollution from coal-burning factories. "Pea soup" fog became a rarity in London. Workers rights were legislated into law throughout Western Europe and the US. International labor standards were set and the OECD countries adopted aspects of social regulations for its members, such was the propserity of the 30 glorious years after the Great Depression. European and American manufacturers were able to pass on the additional costs of caring for workers and the environment onto consumers, that is, until competition from Asia began to erode their bottom lines. This gave rise to the notion of generalizing some of these regulations to developing countries. Evidence President Bush's position that China and India as major contributors to carbon emissions now must be included in any plan on climate change.[39]

Not able to retreat from its commitment to human rights and the cleaning up of the environment which up to the 1980s was entirely the consequence of Western industrialization, the US began to impose standards on imports, first with respect to labelling and thereafter to production processes. Notions of human rights began to creep into trade agreements; child labor became an issue. American competitiveness was once again rescued not by American manufacturers becoming more efficient but by getting their government to impose costly production requirements and first world standards on Third World production processes.

The pattern is an all too familiar one. For example, the US Congress and the Bush administration agreed in May 2007 to incorporate the following in bilateral trade agreements: The ban of child labor and forced labor; guaranteed rights of organized labor; and enforcing existing national and international law.[40] The first of these pending bilateral trade agreements are with Panama, Peru, South Korea, and Columbia. However, some see this agreement to "fast-track"[41] by the Congress as a means to laying the foundations for corporate financial support in the 2008 general elections. Agreements under "fast-track", as told to Bill Moyers by John R. MacArthur, author of *The Selling of Free Trade*, allows American corporations to transfer their manufacturing operations overseas with an aim to exploiting cheap labor and less stringent environmental and other standards.[42] Moreover, while over 140 countries, including the US, have ratified International Labor Organization (ILO) Convention 182 which prohibits child labor of any kind, child labor remains a human rights violation by many of the signatories. In this regard it is instructive that, while the US criticizes developing countries for employing child labor, it does so from a less than morally upright position. As Iowa Senator Tom Harkin tells it in *Stolen Childhoods*: "we have tens of thousands of children every year working in agriculture in America, that are not subject to our *Fair Labor Standards Act*.... Children ten years old are subject to insecticides, pesticides; working ten hours a day seven days a week."[43]

Conclusion

Clearly, despite the spin from the Treasury Secretary and the tight-rope walk by Federal Reserve Chairman Bernanke, the status of the American economy in 2007 cannot help but serve to heighten US anxieties over China's growing economic strength and its political influence arising there from. Attempts to push China into effecting reforms at a pace acceptable to the US have largely come up against a brick wall. As recognized by Mr Paulson and the former Secretary of the Treasury John Snow, China will do what it considers to be in the best interest of China. The leverage the US had over the Japanese in the 1980s is not present in its relationship with China. Indeed, America's influence in Southeast Asia has diminished substantially as evidenced by the Singapore's Prime Minister's warning to Mr Bush at their bilateral talks in Washington: "Good relations between America and the major countries are critical because the south-east Asian countries want to be friends with both, and do not want to have to choose sides with either."[44] Interestingly, the Bush administration has not attended the last three meeting of ASEAN.

What is significant about this lecture from the Signporean prime minister is that the Southeast Asian countries historically have been distrustful of China (see Pye 1981: 216–7) but have now come to depend on it as the final stage in the processing and assembling of their consumer technology products (Prasad and Rumbaugh 2004) and hence their prosperity. In addition, the Southeast Asian countries—Brunei, Burma, Cambodia, Indonesia, Laos, Malaysia, Philippines, Singapore, Thailand, and Vietnam—have agreed to establish even closer ties with one another to include greater political unity and to establish a free trade zone by 2015.[45] At the same time, many South America countries have either joined the Hugo Chavez camp or have taken a step back from closer ties with the US: In almost every Latin American country Mr Bush visited in 2007, the people protested his foreign policy.

Beyond trade issues, the international liquidity amassed by China is an obvious concern for the OECD countries, specifically the US who sees it as a threat to its ability to influence third countries. Recall, the Chinese have a no-string attached policy to investment in other developing countries. What is curious in most discourse on China's international liquidity, however, is that its foreign exchange reserves are perceived as arising from sterilization and thus are analyzed in context of currency management by the government. This analytical framework leads to the conclusion that China must reduce its "restrictions" and allow the consumers to benefit from increased imports. This, however, is contrary to what Chinese officials see as in the best interest of China. Indeed, as Anne Krueger argues, China's export-led growth is a strategy no less different from that of Korea, Taiwan, and others of the 1960s and 1970s (see also World Bank 1993; Amsden, 1989), and that if the risk to the Chinese economy is inflation, as many have argued, then they, the Chinese, will deal with it as it arises. Oxford University Brad Setser argues that China's foreign exchange reserves are the direct result of policy by the Chinese. What is not considered however is that, as a predominantly state-centric economic system China's foreign reserves are not entirely the result of sterilization but rather include the foreign exchange earnings of the public-sector. When viewed in this way, there is very little difference between its foreign exchange reserves and the capital reserves of a profitable Western corporation such as, for example, Microsoft.

Like well-run corporations that use some of their capital reserves to diversify, the Chinese foreign exchange reserves allow China to diversify out of traditional Chinese properties—as evidenced in its failed bid to acquire UNOCOL and its proposed almost US$4.0 billion investment in Blackstone, a US private equity investment company—which, as one analyst observed, "could help restore some equilibrium to China's account with the U.S."[46]

The problem is that, used in such a way China's foreign exchange reserves are seen as a geopolitically empowering tool which is perceived as being contrary to American interest as it is presently constructed (see Huntington, 1996). Indeed, the rather shaky foundation of the American sense of economic prosperity is only just beginning to become unavoidably clear. Unfortunately, the failure to fully recognize the contribution of World War II European reconstruction to American prosperity in the first instance, and secondly, predicating US growth on the continued economic growth of OECD countries on a going forward basis—a relationship not lost on Anne Kreuger—is beginning to manifest in irrational policies in the twenty-first century. Indeed, when approached from this vantage point, the relatively lower economic growth rates in OECD countries since the 1960s when taken in conjunction with the American interests as they are presently constructed—at least since the 1950s—demand that the US either partake in the economic growth of those developing countries whose growth rates are greater than the OECD countries—just as it did in the Europe of the 1950s—or, alternatively, slow their economic progress to below OECD countries' performance.

This imperative attendant America's interests has been made immediate in consequence of the widening income inequality gap in the US. In other words, the widening income inequality gap which is approaching crittical mass in the US is partly a function of the transfer of wealth from the middle and working classes to the intellectual capital class in consequence of free-market economics since the 1980s. Moreover, an increasing proportion of GNP is from foreign investment and not from domestic economic activity. Hence, absent additional domestic sources of income for the working and middle classes the US will be forced to resort to condign power, as it has, to control other economic actors.

Given the above, Mr Bush's dire predictions for failure in Iraq must be seen not in terms of America's vulnerability to terrorism as the president would like all Americans to believe, but rather in terms of the economic consequences of failure to gain control over the world's second largest oil reserve. A virtually debt-free China growing at 11.0 percent per annum with foreign exchange reserves of about US$1.2 trillion according to the Peoples Bank of China; a Southeast Asia that is asserting itself having learned a very valuable lesson from the financial crisis of 1997–8; an alienated Russia equally debt-free with few if any levers of control available to the West and growing at an impressive rate as well, when combined with the burden of servicing a national debt of US$10.0 trillion with no revenues to be had from Iraq as planned, do not in the phraseology of Donald Rumsfeld make "for an irresistible combination." The prospects indeed do appear daunting for an America that considers winning as the only thing and whose continued hegemony depends crucially on the Westernization of the Middle East and, therefore, significant influence over the development of its oil reserves as a first step. It is therefore instructive that, one of the conditions for US pull-out from Iraq is agreement among the three factions—Kurds, Sunnis and Shiite-Arabs—to a framework that enshrines first, the equitable sharing of oil revenues among themselves and second, the establishment of a stable legal environment that ensures opportunities for Western investment in the oil industry as second-best to actual control as earlier envisaged by the neoconservatives.

NOTES

1 "Come in number one, your time is up", *The Economist*, April 14, 2007, p. 12
2 Barker, B., "Today's Strong Buys: International Edition", *Wall Street Journal*, April 17, 2007, http://www.fool.com/investing/international/2007/04/17/todays-strong-buys-international-edition.aspx
3 President Putin's state of the nation address, *C-SPAN2*, April 26, 2007; see also "Putin looks ahead in final address", *BBC News*, April 26, 2007
4 Wolf, M., "America is now on the comfortable path to ruin", *The Financial Times*, August 18, 2004, p.17
5 "US launches campaign for more foreign investment", http://news.yahoo.com/s/afp/20070510/bs_afp/useconomytrade_070510164110
6 *World Development Report*, 1991, 204–5
7 Lindsey, B., CATO Institute, 'Book TV', *C-SPAN2*, May 30, 2007
8 Walker, D. '60 Minutes', *CBS*, March 4, 2007
9 Aversa, J., "Economy has worst showing since 2002", http://biz.yahoo.com/ap/070531/economy.html?.v=11
10 Some observers would prefer to credit President Clinton's Chief of Staff Carver for coining this phrase.
11 "Iraq War Debate", U.S. House of Representative, *C-SPAN*, February 16, 2007
12 "2008 Budget Plan" *C-SPAN2*, March 22, 2007
13 "Charlie Rose", *PBS*, April 23, 2007
14 "Campaign 2008", Iowa Republican Fundraiser and straw Poll, *C-SPAN*, August 11, 2007
15 Henry Paulson interview with Jim Lehrer, 'News Hour', PBS.org, May 17, 2007
16 "Charlie Rose", *PBS.org*, April 26, 2007

17 "U.S. Economic Outlook", House Financial Services Committee, *C-SPAN*, February 16, 2007
18 "The China Trade", *The Wall Street Journal*, May 21, 2007, A16.
19 "Campaign 2008", Iowa Republican Fundraiser and straw Poll, *C-SPAN*, August 11, 2007
20 Conkey, C., "As Sleepy Sector Stir, Economy may Wake Up Without Consumers' Prodding", *The Wall Street Journal*, May 21, 2007, A2
21 Wolf, M., "America is now on the comfortable path to ruin", *The Financial Times*, August 18, 2004, p.17
22 Krueger, A.O., "Impact of the Dollar on the Global Economy", *C-SPAN*, May 31, 2007
23 Interview with Jim Lehrer, 'News Hour', *PBS.org*, May 17, 2007
24 "Impact of the Dollar on the Global Economy", *C-SPAN*, May 31, 2007
25 See *Wall Street Journal* report by Baston, A., Areddy, J., and Phillips, M., May 19–20, 2007
26 Klug, W., "U.S., China Reach Minor Agreement", http:/biz.yahoo.com/ap/070523/us_china_trade.html?.v=17
27 Ibid.
28 Krueger, A.O., "Impact of the Dollar on the Global Economy", *C-SPAN*, May 31, 2007
29 See "Impact of the Dollar on the Global Economy", *C-SPAN*, May 31, 2007
30 "US launches campaign for more foreign investment, http://news.yahoo.com/s/afp/20070510/bs_afp/useconomytrade_070510164110
31 Liedtke, M. "China begins U.S. buying mission", *Associated Press*, May 10, 2007
32 Wilson, S., "U.S.-China gap widening", *Los Angeles Times*, May 10, 2007
33 Crutsinger, M., "Productivity Down in First quarter", *Associated Press*, http://biz.yahoo.com/ap/070606/economy.html?.v=14
34 Walker, D. '60 Minutes', *CBS*, March 4, 2007
35 Orszag, P., Senate Budget Committee Hearing, *C-SPAN2*, June 21, 2007
36 Walker, D., "Role of the National Guard and Reserves", Commission on the National Guard and Reserves, *C-SPAN*, June 20, 2007.
37 "Mathematicians set Chinese test", *BBC NEWS*, April 24, 2007, http://news.bbc.co.uk/go/pr/fr/-/2/hi/uk_news/education/6589301.stm
38 Rep. Peterson, J., U.S. House of Representative, *C-SPAN*, September 6, 2007
39 Mason, J., "Europeans cool to Bush plan on Climate change", http://news.yahoo.com/s/nm/20070601/ts_nm/climate_bush_dc_4
40 NEWS HOUR, *PBS.org*, May 11, 2007
41 "Fast track" gives the administration authority to negotiate trade agreements and treaties which may then be submitted to Congress for an up or down vote, with no opportunity for amendments.
42 "Bill Moyers Journal", *PBS.org*; May 18, 2007
43 "Stolen Childhoods" *etvstore.org*
44 "Singapore PM warns US over China", Story from *BBC NEWS*, http://news.bbc.co.uk/go/pr/fr/-/2/hi/asia-pacific/6627361.stm; May 5, 2007
45 "Asian nations pledge closer ties", Story from *BBC NEWS*, http://news.bbc.co.uk/go/pr/fr/-/2/hi/asia-pacific/6256351.stm
46 Linebaugh, K., et al., "China Puts Cash to Work in Deal With Blackstone", *The Wall Street Journal*, May 21, 2007, p.A1.

Chapter Seven

Is an Emerging China America's Dilemma?

("Where is the wisdom we have lost in knowledge?
Where is the knowledge we have lost in information?" – T.S. Eliot)

Introduction

As told by the former Central Intelligence Agency (CIA) Director George Tenet: "When you write an estimate, you are writing what you don't know. Intelligence is not always about the truth; it's about peoples' best judgment; it is about what the truth may be." As it is with the National Intelligence Estimate (NIE), so it is with the proposition advanced in this chapter: that the crisis in the Middle East is but a manifestation of a game-theoretic model contrived as part of a grand strategy to contain China gone awry. It is a proposition premised on Samuel Huntington's contention—adopted by the neoconservatives—that an emerging China motivated by a desire for regional dominance and beyond portends a "Confucian–Islamic connection" which is anathema to American interests.

Why China and not Japan?

In addition to the disparities in economic growth and international trade between China and the US as discussed in Chapters Five and Six, China in the eyes of most Americans is not an ally. It is also still a third world country and clearly lags the US in technological development, both militarily and commercially. As argued by Gerald Segal (1999), its economy is a fraction of the US in absolute terms and its GDP per capita has a long way to go to catch up with the US, with its culture not worth the attention given to it. Given these perceived disparities, the burning question then is: Why China? Why not Japan, the second largest economy in the world with a people predisposed to perfection? Moreover, Japanese–American relations has been waning for sometime, more specifically since the late 1980s attendant America's resort to Super 301 as a means to curbing increasing Japanese exports to the US, on the presumption of an undervalued Yen vis-à-vis the Dollar: Japan's share of world exports increased from 1.4 percent in 1950 to 6.4 percent in 1980 (see Bhagwati, 1988) while US share of global exports has been declining ever since. Indeed, Japanese-bashing was rife during the G.H.W. Bush administration, manifesting in the smashing of Japanese cars in Detroit and elsewhere; and Japan's attitude towards the First Gulf

War did nothing to endear it to the then Bush Administration. Moreover, whereas 87 percent of Americans in 1985 were deemed friendly toward Japan, by 1993 this had dropped to 50 percent (Huntington, 1996: 222), reflecting a successful propaganda campaign against all things Japanese.

Despite the decline in Japanese popularity with Americans, in the eyes of succeeding US administrations, Japan is still less of a threat than China: it harbors neither military ambitions nor indeed any desire for geopolitical influence, and it is the only reliable US link to East Asia. Moreover, the Japanese economy arguably was successfully maneuvered into recession and remained in the doldrums for the remainder of the 1990s and the early years in the twenty-first century. As a consequence, the US began to moderate its criticisms of Japan. Also, the Japanese economy is fast becoming to look much like the American economy. For example, its GDP growth rate is almost a carbon copy of the US growth rate for 2007 and projected 2008, having trailed the US for most of the mid1990s through to 2006[1]. Japan, for all practical purposes, then, has learned to follow the leader.

China on the other hand was and still is a communist country, and like the former Soviet Union is viewed through a different ideological prism by the West, often suspiciously so in consequence of its growing influence or potential influence in Asia (see Dillon 2007: Ikenberry 2004). Moreover, US concerns, to be sure, are informed by its immediate post-World War II interaction with the ruling CCP. Not only had the CCP successfully defeated the US-backed Nationalist Party of Chiang Kai-shek who found a safe haven on Taiwan, but the PRC also intervened in the Korean War: initially with the intention to preserve at least part of North Korea as a buffer but in actuality thwarted President Truman's objective of the "unification of Korea" (see Halprein 2004: 183). In addition to which, in negotiations with the US on Korea and Indochina the PRC disarmingly stressed as policy the peaceful coexistence with its neighbors in Asia; the American expectation was for a display of, according to James Peck (2006: 180), "inherent hostility to the requirements of the global order" upon which Washington's Asia policy turned.

US hostility towards China was hardly contained during the 1950s and 1960s. As James Peck (2006: 179) tells it: "The intensity with which Eisenhower sought to isolate China dominated his strategic, ideological, and economic policies in Asia from the very beginning." Moreover, Secretary Dulles in pursuing a policy of deterrence threatened to "use nuclear weapons to discourage aggression at all levels." (Gaddis 2004: 226). This overt threat did not end with the armistice in Korea in 1953 but rather became a permanent feature in language emanating from Eisenhower and Dulles and directed primarily at China. As Bundy (2004: 88) observed:

> In two later crisis [following the Korean War], over the offshore islands of Quemoy and Matsu in 1955 and 1958, Eisenhower used both open references to nuclear weapons and visible deployments of nuclear-armed forces to underline the risks Mao was running.

Given this antagonistic policy approach to China, Secretary of State John Foster Dulles allegedly refused to shake hands with Zhou (Cho) Enlai in Geneva in 1954 (see Talbott, 1981) as part of the scripted "tactics" for the Geneva meeting which were: "The US should ... endeavor to stimulate the communists to the adoption of harsh negotiating tactics and inflexible positions" (Peck, 2006: 181) so as not to reach an agreement with them and to make them appear hostile in the eyes of the world. But as Peck tells it: "The Chinese seemed peaceful; the United States, warlike. Zhou Enlai seemed flexible, willing to negotiate; Dulles, rigid and hard-line."

Eisenhower's China policy found support in the Johnson administration despite President Johnson's insistence that he would not heed "those who urge us to use our great power in a reckless or casual manner" (quoted in Gaddis 2004: 226). Evidence a March I, 1966 memorandum from James C. Thompson Jr. "*Some Propositions on a China Strategy*" quoted by Peck, (2006: 180):

> If Communist behavior is such that tensions in the Far East are substantially reduced, most Asian countries, except Nationalist China [Taiwan], Korea, and Vietnam, would probably cautiously relax their present suspicions of Peiping and move gradually toward broader contacts and normal diplomatic relations with Communist China. This, in time, would enlarge Peiping's ability to influence these countries.... Any softening on the part of the U.S. would have extremely serious consequences.

Ebb and Flow in US–China Relations

It was not until President Nixon visited China in 1972 that US-China relationship began to warm, culminating in formal diplomatic relations in 1979. Evidently Panda diplomacy—Ling-Ling and Sing-Sing—proved to be a workable approach for the Chinese, not to mention their desire to block what appeared to them to be the threat of Soviet hegemony in the region on the one hand, and the lure of China as a potential market for American-made products, on the other. Even then, the two countries continued to view each other with suspicion fuelled by extremists on both sides. Indeed, prior to turning his attention to the Soviet Union, presidential candidate Ronald Reagan was critical of the Carter administration for normalizing relations with the PRC and held out the possibility of reestablishing relations with Taiwan which, of course, roiled the Chinese. The Chinese accused Reagan of wanting to turn back the clock (Salomon 1981: 4). Moreover, the inscrutable nature of the Chinese was perceived as too costly and time consuming for those who thrive on instant gratification. Hence, US attention was directed at societies that were more in keeping with its own or to countries falling within its sphere of influence such as Japan, Taiwan, and South Korea, for example.

US–China relations reached its lowest point in 1995. Indeed, America's relentless criticisms of China's human rights record and its alleged influence in staging the Tiananmen Square protest in 1989[2] served to prompt President Deng Xiaoping to declare in September 1991 that the conflicts between the two countries rose to the level of "a new cold war." These sentiments were articulated by President Jiang Zemin in August 1995: "Western hostile forces have not for a moment abandoned their plot to Westernize and divide our country" (quoted in Huntington, 1996: 223).

For its own strategic reasons, the US did nothing to allay the increasing animosity expressed by China's leaders and scholars, and more importantly, military. Indeed, it openly sought to assert its own influence by permitting the Taiwanese President to come to America and hosting him; selling Taiwan 150 F-16s fighters; opposing China's entry into the WTO and accusing it of exporting weapons-technology and military components to Iran. The Clinton administration also dispatched Secretary Warren Christopher to tell the Chinese what was expected of them by a Democratic President and Congress; the Secretary returned a much enlightened diplomat.

The Hong Kong Handover

The handover of Hong Kong in 1997 also added to the tensions between China and the UK and, of course, the US (see Chow 2001). Both the US and Britain, with substantial investment in the financial–based economy whose success has been largely held out as the result of British stewardship, find themselves obliged to hold the island-economy out as a bastion of democracy, even though it was a colony of the UK. The paradox, as Chow (2001: 222) tells it, is in the declaration of US Secretary Albright: "We will be watching to see that the Hong Kong of tomorrow is like the Hong Kong of today." Chow rhetorically asked: "Since Albright's words mean that even though it is officially no longer a colony, it need not advance any further politically so that it can remain the "same" as it was in 1997?"

The UK, of course, played its swan song with much pomp and bravado. The Chinese, on the other hand, heard it as the last call and played down the lecture from outgoing Governor General Chris Patten, emphasizing its "one country, two systems" formula for incorporating the island economy into China in seeming appeasement to an emotional UK. To the Chinese, however, the sun will never again rise on the British Empire in East Asia and that was all that mattered. The doom and gloom predicted by China watchers did not occur if only because in the years preceding the handover China began to lay the ground work for a smooth transition, fully realizing that Hong Kong was its gateway to Western capital and markets.

Hong Kong continues to be an important entry point into China for Western capitalism. Westerners cannot get enough of China in the twenty-first century. Indeed, most dispassionate analyses portray China as the basis for continued growth in Western economies and counsel navigating the shallows and moderating expectations[3] in the early years. But for most Americans and others with the fever of empire still in their blood, it is a bitter pill to swallow. Hence, Gerald Segal's provocative question, "Does China matter?" is itself an acknowledgement that, for policymakers in the West it seemingly does and, therefore, is a reality of territoriality, even though it would be better for an enlightened world that it should not (See Buzan and Foot, 2004: xi). Put another way, does being number one matter?

On the other side of the coin, in terms of historical time lines the memory of China's humiliation attendant the Opium War, the carving up of the Middle Kingdom by Western powers, and the betrayal by the Nationalist Party led by Chaing Kai-shek still burn in the belly of CCP-led China, and arguably are kept alive partly by informing the PRC's relationship with the West and partly by the attitude of the West to a culture it never fully understood nor was able to subdue. And a twenty-first century West knows it, despite attempts to portray nineteenth- and twentieth-century Chinese development history in terms of "insufficient modernization, incomplete modernity, and or aborted modernism" (Karl, 2001: 238). Also, contrary to Western expectation, the "liberal rhetoric of resistance" of the liberal intellectuals has yet to impinge on the admitted "oppressiveness" of the CCP which, it is argued, "comes from its [CCP's] determination to ensure social stability as a necessary precondition for economic modernization" (Zhang, 2001: 338). Evidently, liberal intellectuals in China still find compelling the argument that the whole is greater than the sum of its individual parts. Not what the West in general and the US in particular want to hear in a post 9/11 world however. As we are reminded by the events in the Middle East, the US has neither the patience nor the time to be accommodating of Confucian ideology, or any other for that matter, in its quest for continued hegemony.

US impatience and the influence of Western capitalism notwithstanding, Confucianism still exerts an overwhelming influence in socio-economic and political thought in China, and manifest most forcefully in its modernization narrative and supported, confusingly to Western observers, by the liberal intelligentsia, (see Zhang, 2001: 338). Not to be unkind, the Japanese on the other hand lost their essential Japanese identity partly at Hiroshima and Nagasaki but mainly in the process of reaching its "true potential" as defined in Western ideological terms. This is not to say that the next generation of Chinese would not go the way of their Japanese counterpart.

China matters then, not as a direct economic rival to America or the West which informs Western intellectual discourse and thus policy. Rather, China matters because Confucianism is perceived in the West as a challenge to Western ideology; a challenge to those who continue to hold to the view that China needs to be "transformed ... to follow the path of reform towards marketization, plurality and even democracy" (Yahuda, 2004: 10); but it is a challenge that remains unmet since the nineteenth century.

Comparative Foreign Investment

As is now well recognized, China is using its vast foreign exchange reserves to invest in energy producing countries in Latin America, Africa and beyond. Indeed, its investment in the energy sector in Iran is in defiance of US declared restrictions imposed on third countries. But much like US restrictions on third country investments in and trade with Cuba, its restrictions on Chinese foreign investment is largely ineffective. Moreover, many countries have come to the realization that short of its military power, America is in the phraseology of Bhagwati manifesting evidence of the "diminished giant syndrome." In addition to its declining share of world trade, its share of world GDP declined from 40.3 percent in 1950 to 21.8 percent in 1980 and further still in the 1990s despite attempts to stem the decline through bilateral and regional trade agreements, and, of course, quantitative restrictions. The US also is now the world's biggest debtor nation with a national debt of US$9.0 trillion (see Chapter Six).

China on the other hand is growing at the phenomenal rate of over ten percent per annum—11.1 percent in the first quarter of 2007—and there is no letting up in its export drive. As recognized by Alan Blinder of Princeton University, "China must export like mad to grow like mad." In this connection, it is on the treadmill of economic growth which, unfortunately, is regarded by many Americans and not just the neoconservatives as eclipsing America's hegemony. And, notwithstanding that China's export drive is America's continued low-inflation rate, many would rather just have it all by seeking to contain China through the exercise of condign power. Evidently, there is more to territoriality than just things material. Recall, Richard Perle's expressed desire for flexing America's hard power. Indeed, as observed by Ikenberry (2004: 324):

> The United States will not seek security through the more modest realist strategy of operating within a global system of power balancing, nor will it pursue a liberal strategy in which institutions, democracy, and integrated markets reduce the importance of power politics altogether.

Recall further Mr. Blair's announcement that the UK intends to incorporate hard power as an aspect of its foreign policy which is in lock step with the grand strategy of the US.

China Modernization of its Military

As is becoming clear in 2007, there is increasing concern over China's modernization of its military notwithstanding that the US, Russia, and indeed the UK are also upgrading their weapon systems. As former President Clinton remarked, the change over by the Chinese navy to diesel-powered submarines allows them to run deeper and become less tractable. The shooting down of one of its own satellites by laser in early 2007 has also raised concern at the Pentagon. Joint military exercises between Russian and Chinese forces are also raising red flags at the Pentagon, even though they are in keeping with what is considered normal defensive exercises, not unlike those of the US battle groups in the Persian Gulf.

Clearly, the Chinese unlike the Japanese are not intimidated by US or Western fire power despite being no more than a "middle power." As one Chinese leader reportedly remarked in the 1950s, China can afford to lose 500 million people in any nuclear confrontation with the West. A frightening thought, to be sure, when you consider that the US population reached 300 million at the end of 2006, and the combined population of the expanded EU and US is still 500 million less than China's. Mutual destruction therefore is not assured unless America and the West can hit China from all corners of the globe and from above. It is for this reason that there is concern over China's developing capability in space. It is also for this reason and the perceived potential for a "Confucian–Islamic connection" that the West led by the US is seemingly deeply committed to preventing Middle-East Arab countries and more especially Iran from acquiring nuclear weapons. When examined in context of the Eisenhower China policy these actions suggest a continuation of the policy of containing China by way of subversion. Indeed, the opportunity for a "showdown" with China, as debated and summarized in the June 1966 *Long Range Study* by the US State Department, has passed with China's acquisition of advanced technology and the modernization of its military well on its way. Hence, containment must come through squeezing it economically.

Game–theoretic Model

It has been said in many quarters that the Bush administration's foreign policy is aggressive, unilateral and is doomed to failure in the Middle East. But it is here contended that if it failed, it is because the policy although conceived by the brightest minds the neoconservatives could muster is fundamentally flawed. To understand this we need to accept the proposition that the primary objective of the neoconservative grand strategy is to circuitously contain China in a post Cold-war environment by way of a phased multifaceted foreign policy strategy—referred to as the grand strategy for purposes of this exercise—that is opaque to all but its architects, at least in the critical stages of its application. This contention as noted in the introduction is premised partly on Huntington's perception of the implications for the US attendant the emergence of China and partly on embedded animosity towards it which arguably arises from previous administrations' inability to fully contain it through other means as discussed above and in Chapter Five. Therefore, when viewed in context of the grand strategy, President Bush's assertion that "Iraq is only part of a larger ideological war" and wants it to be, "an ally in the war on terror"[4] betrays the hidden agenda of the neoconservatives with respect to China. Recall Jon Stewart's "lemon" theory: to sell more lemons, you push for stronger lemon-scented detergents.

The systematic attempts of the Bush administration to keep the attention of Americans and the world focused on the war on terror and not on the invasion and occupation of Iraq; the aggressive verbal exchanges with Iran; and the Arab–Israel conflict, are all designed to keep Americans and indeed the rest of the world engaged without divulging the true motivation for the Middle East conflict: to prevent a Confucian–Islamic connection. While the period is the twenty-first century, the strategy comes out of the playbook of the Eisenhower administration of the 1950s.

The Evidence

Lending credence to the supposition of a grand strategy designed to contain China through control of its access to energy is the revelation by Paul O'Neill former US Treasury Secretary, that:

> Rumsfeld, Cheney, and Wolfowitz [and a cadre of neoconservatives as Pentagon advisers that included Richard Perle] who were already planning the next war in Iraq and the shape of a post-Saddam country ... were mapping Iraq's oil fields and exploration areas and listing companies that might be interested in leveraging the precious asset (Suskind, 2004: 96).

Indeed, Secretary Rumsfeld is quoted as saying: "Imagine what the region would look like without Saddam and with a regime that's *aligned with U.S. interests*. It would change everything in the region and beyond it. It would demonstrate what U.S. policy is all about [emphasis added]" (Suskind, 2004: 85). Moreover, that the Secretary of Defense should entertain "the desire to 'dissuade' countries from engaging in 'asymmetrical challenges' to the United States" by way of a preemptive attack on Iraq contemplated even before the events of 9/11, "matched with plans for how the world's second largest oil reserve might be divided among the world's contractors" (Suskind, 2004: 96) adds support to the notion of a grand strategy of which the invasion of Iraq was but only the beginning.

The assertion made above becomes credible when it is realized that China's demand for oil has outgrown its domestic supply. As revealed by Naughton, (2007: 340-1), China became a net importer of oil in 1993, with imports increasing steadily since then. Thus by 2004, China was importing 2.5 million barrels a day and is expected to surpass Japan's imports of five million barrels a day by 2015. The US in contrast imports 13 million barrels a day or about 25 percent of the oil transacted on the world oil markets. At the same time, *Robert L. Hirsch's Peaking of World Oil Production: Impact, Mitigation, and Risk Management* report concludes that world oil peaking is inevitable and presents a unique challenge to the world. The majority of the major oil companies agree that oil production is at or near peak. This perspective finds support in a September 2005 report by the U.S. Army Corp of Engineers which quoted a study that claims the price of oil will reach US$180.00 per barrel in a few years.[5] In this connection, it should be noted that the US derives 85 percent of its energy from fossil fuel.

In addition to the above, and further supporting the contention of a grand strategy are items number I and 4 in Secretary Rumsfeld's memorandum to the then Treasury Secretary O'Neill titled *Talking points, FY01 and FY02–07 Budget Issues*:

> 1. The collapse of the Soviet Union has produced centrifugal forces in the world that have created new regional powers. Several of these are intensely hostile to the United States and are *arming to deter us from bringing our conventional or nuclear power to bear in a regional crisis* [emphasis added]. 4. China, Russia, Iran, Iraq, North Korea and others are investing in these capabilities.... Liberalized international trade will propagate these capabilities to others (Suskind, 2004: 76–7).

Analyzing the two talking points, it is clear that the focus is really on China. It is China who is perceived as fast becoming the major challenge to US economic and geopolitical dominance; not Iran, not Iraq, and certainly not North Korea. Moreover, given that these "talking points" were conceived before 9/11, they had to have been informed by long-held perceptions of the team of neoconservatives re-constituted in the Bush administration. Indeed, according to John Ikenberry (2004: 324), a new strategy that has as its goal the "fundamental commitment to maintaining a unipolar world in which the United States has no peer competitor" was contained in a leaked Pentagon memorandum written by the then Assistant Secretary of Defense in the G.H.W. Bush administration, Paul Wolfowitz. Also noteworthy is the characterization of China by the late President Reagan as: "a country whose government subscribes to an ideology based on the belief in destroying governments like ours" (Salomon, 1981, 4). Given these perceptions at the highest level in the US administration of US power, on the one hand, and of China, on the other, it would be illogical to assume that they do not now influence US foreign policy. Moreover, with regard to Russia's role in the new world order, the prevailing wisdom of the Bush team is that it can be persuaded to join the West through economic and strategic cooperation, albeit as a junior partner. Moreover, the former Russian Republics incorporated into the EU would serve as launching pads for any missile defense system; closer to the Kremlin and further away from Washington or London.

Despite the evidence, there always will be those who would either deny such a grand strategy or dispute the interpretation of the evidence in keeping with Nietzsche's notion that, there are no facts only interpretations. But such denial would find limited support outside the US. No foreign government reading the comments of the Secretary of Defense or assessing the actions of the Bush administration in the Middle East would honestly buy into the rhetoric that the US is acting out of concern for others. The Russians clearly have not. Referring to the US proposal to install a nuclear weapons shield in the Czech Republic and Poland, President Putin remarked: "This is not just a defense system; this is part of the US nuclear weapons system."[6]

While the Secretary of State and Secretary of Defense are obliged to counter Putin's accusations, it is clear that Russia's refusal to join the West in disarming Iran—instead, arming Iran with defensive missiles so "it does not feel it is all alone"—is the trigger for such a strategic move. Moreover, resulting from the aggressive posturing and rhetoric of the Bush team in Russia's backyard, the Russians have become distrustful of the Bush administration's foreign policy and are gradually but surely deepening their relations with China through energy supply and other cooperative agreements, including strategic. This is clearly not what the West wants; but, to be sure, it is what they have gotten through costly blunders rooted in a blind commitment to stay with a failed grand strategy.

The Grand Strategy

The grand strategy as conjectured is one premised on containment and subversion not unlike that of the Eisenhower/Johnson era. Indeed, there are discernible elements in the Bush foreign policy model that are out of the Eisenhower/Johnson foreign policy playbooks. For example, to construct a policy of containment and subversion it is necessary, according to a 1966 Department of State document quoted by James Peck (2006: 226), to: (1), cast China as an advocate of "wars of national liberation" against "bourgeois" states, and (2) the restoration of China to its past position of grandeur and influence in Asia, and the extension of this influence onto a worldwide stage." The visits of the Secretary of State and Secretary of Defense in 2006 to several Southeast Asian countries reminding them of China's "ambitions" are undoubtedly in keeping with this aspect of the grand strategy. Similarly, Israeli Prime Minister Olmert's visit to India speaks to reaffirming the strategy and at the same time sending an unambiguous message to Pakistan at a time when President Musharraf appeared to be wavering in his support for the US war on terror. In this latter connection, recall Musharraf's (2006: 202) concern that "India would have loved to assist the United States to the hilt" in any military action against Pakistan.

The second piece of the grand strategy, subversion, is to control China's access to raw materials, more specifically its access to energy supplies from the Middle East. To do this, Chinese investment in Iran's energy sector has to be restricted if not stopped in its tracks; so also must be the potential for Chinese investments in an Iraq that would have been freed of the more constraining UN sanctions if the UN weapons inspectors had been allowed to finish their work and, as is now well established, found no WMD. Recall, Huntington's point on possible China–Iraq and China–Iran alliances as ways for China to source its energy needs. Recall also, Donald Rumsfeld's points for discussion noted above.

With respect to WMD in Iraq, recall the flurry of diplomatic efforts by the US and the UK to set time constrains on the UN weapons inspectors and to closely direct their efforts. The rush to war by the Bush–Blair team would most likely be revealed in the fullness of time as a coordinated effort to put into effect the grand strategy to contain China, with Israel a strategic and thus an equal partner whose reward for its role is its greatest dream: return of the Promised Land. This strategy is best explained in terms of three phases in the Middle East.

The Three Phases

Under this hypothesized overarching grand strategy—the conception of which is necessarily attributed to the neoconservatives who first came together as a team during the Reagan and Bush years (see Greg Grandin, 2006)—Iraq would be invaded as the first of three game-theoretic models, with its own discrete inputs and objectives; not because "we just want to buy their oil", as *American Enterprise Institute* Dinesh D'Souza patronizingly claims[7], but rather, and more fundamentally, to control the flow of oil from one of the major sources outside of Saudi Arabia. Paul O'Neill's account of meetings with Rumsfeld and his staff stands in evidence, as do the myriad of statements emanating from a Democratic-controlled Congress. Moreover, the US Congress did not intervene to scuttle China's attempt to acquire an American energy company just because it wanted to ensure the supply of refined petroleum products to US industries; rather, it intervened because it does not want China to own properties of strategic importance to the US. That the US has expressed concern about Chinese investments in Canada's energy sector reinforces the perception that the US intends to contain China through limiting its access to energy resources.

Phase two of the strategy requires Israel to put into play yet another discrete game-theoretic model by finding cause to invade Lebanon. Such action assumes that Israel will have secured agreement to a two-state solution acceptable to the Arab League and to the Palestinians led by Fatah, and that Syria will have been driven out of Lebanon—which it was in 2005—leaving Hezbollah as an easy target for Israeli military action. Lending credence to this assumption is the revelation by Seymour Hersh of the *New Yorker magazine* that the invasion of Lebanon was on the drawing board and had the Bush administration's blessings. Indeed, destroying Hezbollah and bringing Lebanon under Israeli control arguably is a critical component to the sub-strategy for remaking the Middle East to the specifications of the neoconservatives in America, and concurrently taking the dream of a revived kingdom of Israel a step further. Recall, Secretary Rice's "birth pangs of a new Middle East." Recall also, Lebanon is an artificial state whose sovereignty is kept open to dispute.

With Iraq and Lebanon firmly under Western and Israeli control respectively, phase three requires that Iran be invaded by a coalition probably led by Israel; the rhetoric from Tel Aviv matched that emanating from the White House, with Ahmadinejad having taken the bait. With Hezbollah destroyed, the argument goes, Israel would then be more than able to target Iran at will without putting its own cities and population at risk. Indeed, such attacks could be launched from southern Lebanon. Interestingly, as if unable to pull back from the dress rehearsal, Israel's Ambassador to the UN Dan Gillerman followed through with the offer of help to rebuild Lebanon even as the bombing of southern Lebanon continues. Clearly, Ambassador Gillerman was already thinking in terms of, indeed articulating, Israel's expanded role in the region.

Acceptance by the Arab League and the Wider World

Yet another imputed assumption for remaking the Middle East is that the Arab League, satisfied with bringing an end to the Israel–Arab conflict, would welcome the destruction of any potential Shia revival in the region given the historical animosity between the two (see Nasr 2006). Indeed, that the major Arab countries initially condemned Hezbollah for capturing the two Israeli soldiers was clearly out of the game-theoretic playbook and not unexpectedly underscored the rhetoric of the Secretary of State with respect to Hezbollah.

The model further assumes that by the end of the second term of the Bush administration the world would be fully supportive of the interventions in the Middle East, even over the objection of China and Russia as permanent members of the UN Security Council. Indeed, China also by this time will have been contained without being isolated, surrounded by bilateral strategic alliances in the region engineered by the US, with its access to oil subject to the de facto control of the West, and unable to use its large foreign exchange reserves to gain influence in other developing countries. Recall, in Chapter Five China's imports of raw materials to feed its industrial expansion serve to forge closer economic links with other developing countries. Such economic links which translate to higher commodity prices to producers in developing countries are also reflected in US manufacturing cost of production (see Chapter Six). Hence, putting the brakes on Chinese exports and pushing the Chinese economy to breaking point would arguably ensure a drain on its foreign exchange reserves not dissimilar to that orchestrated against the Japanese economy in the late 1980s and early 1990s. At the same time, the containment of Russia also will have been secured through incorporating former Soviet Republics into the EU, thus isolating it from the rest of Europe. With respect to the latter, the dismissive approach to Russia by the Bush team, especially evidenced by Vice President Cheney's visit to the former Russian Republics and invoking distrust for Russia, is staying to the script, not unlike the Secretary of State's visit to Southeast Asia seeking to sow seeds of suspicion over "China's regional ambitions" as perceived by the Bush administration. The problem with such tactics is that they are in support of a strategy that has proven to be fundamentally flawed and, therefore, are themselves ineffective.

Theory–Practice Problematic

While many dispassionate discrete analyses offer sound expert technical explanations for the apparent failure in Iraq and Lebanon, it is doubtful any thus far approached the issues holistically in terms of territoriality; and more significantly in terms of a hidden over-arching grand strategy to contain China. The reason for the narrow if preconditioned focus arguably lies partly in the embrace of modeling for specific results which treats each model as discrete, the *sine qua non* of modern Western intellectualism and, as noted in Chapter One, partly because of effective management of the evaluative process and information flow by the Bush team. Any doubt about this would be readily dispelled by watching Robert McNeil's series *America at a Crossroads*, in particular part three that featured Richard Perle attempts at justifying the doctrine of preemption. At the same time, many dispassionate analyses have revealed the limitations of the game-theoretic models and have thus provided the basis for an overarching evaluation by offering credible pieces of information which when put together reveal a grand strategy that is kept hidden from public view.

The Limitations of Models

According to Honi Haber (1994): "Creation is only possible given the tools of our vocabulary and since vocabularies are always already social, cultural and historical products, they always speak for an interested viewpoint", as "Shock and Awe" well illustrates. Hence, it is not that models in of themselves are ineffective; rather they function effectively within the confines of the cultural, political, and historical environment within which they were hatched. Within such environment, theory-practice problematic tend to be either unrecognized or at best understated if only because opposing models constructed within a shared cultural-political-historical environment necessarily exhibit recognizable common errors—ego, prejudices, competition, and the like—and thus tend to cancel one another.

The successful cross-cultural model is one that not only out-thinks the opponent but conceals its vulnerabilities while minimizing the "unknown unknowns." But you can out-think the opponent only if you are operating in an environment in which the unknown unknowns are few and the "known unknowns" are capable of reasonably accurate assessment. Moreover, reasonable assessment is itself a subjective process. Hence, unless the model is subjected to critical examination—which no hidden agenda is in practice—and is not identifiable with a particular mindset, it becomes exposed, indeed ineffective, just by examining the emotional and intellectual make up of its architects.

Given the above as crucial to success, the game-theoretic model(s) of the Bush team were doomed from inception as discussed in greater detail below. Indeed, the readiness of some to be identified with the program or plan, which is inevitable in a highly competitive, individualistic, and narcissistic society, is one of the basic weaknesses of modeling for cross-cultural application.

Intellectual Rigidity

Given the inherent constraints of models outlined above, the architects of the Bush foreign policy steeped in Western ideology and methodologies are shown to be prisoners of their own intellectualism. Bent on their quest to "deterritorialize" societies everywhere and to universalize liberal democracy or the "Enlightenment", they either could not or did not think outside the Western ideological box. Forgotten, or discounted, is the simple fact that the Enlightenment was an exclusively Western European experience (see Huntington 1996; Thatcher, 1995) whereas, as correctly observed by Argusto with respect to the Iraq crisis, "Arabs lands were not tamed by the Enlightenment."[8] The Lockean perspective of virtue in selfishness (see McClelland 1996; Bloom 1987: 175), popularized by Ayn Rand and upon which modern Western society turns, to be sure, has had very little influence in the Middle East despite numerous attempts to penetrate the barriers of Islam. Indeed, if one were to categorize Muslims in Western philosophical terms, they more likely would be classified as Hobbesian, where "feel" not "reason" determines behavior. As Alan Bloom (1987: 174) observed:

> Man gets his bearings by his most powerful passions.... You should imagine how you feel when another man holds a gun to your temple and threatens to shoot you.... At that moment one is a real self, not a false consciousness, not alienated by opinions of the church, the state or the public.

Strangely enough, this necessity to stand in another man's shoes, of self-examination if you will, as a means to policy determination was posed by Senator Richard Durbin in a Senate hearing on July 24, 2007 to the Attorney General Alberto Gonzalez with respect to denying the detainees at *Guantanamo* their perceived rights under the Genève Convention. Clearly, the notion of feeling is not an input in the Bush administration's game-theoretic models.

Given the emphasis on rationality, the tendency in the West is to draw a distinction between cultures in terms of rationality, with non-Western peoples deemed irrational in the differential logic of language games. But, as Lin Yutang reminds us, to be logical is not always to be right. Moreover, as the notion of individualism reaches for new heights in America—the neo-liberal mandate—its perceived benefits become suspect in the West, causing many instinctively to ponder the consequences of disconnection from the larger collective, from "feeling", if you will, the all-consuming cost associated with the ideology of selfishness.

In the citadel of Western intellectual achievements, as indicated by the number of Nobel prizes for example, modeling is the name of the game: Everyone has a model for something or the other. Modeling is a way of life in the corridors of power as it is of street gangs. In the late1990s we witnessed the collapse of Long-term Capital Management (LTCM) as a model for hedging risk. In 2007, the unraveling of the "Sub-prime" mortgage model devised to keep the American housing boom at unsustainable levels while enriching a few, what former Treasury Secretary Lawrence Summers characterized as "predatory lending"[9] offers yet another example of the dangers of models that are essentially reflective of American "intellectual capitalism": self-interested and short-term in their outlook. However, as would have been gathered from the preceding paragraphs, one of the major problems of models, modeling in general, is that they necessarily reflect the strengths and weaknesses of their architects: psychosis and ideology become inseparable and manifest in models that often prove dangerous for good or evil. Many dispassionate observers have characterized the models for the invasion of Iraq and Lebanon in similar terms.

Fixation with Power

Given the superpower-fixation of the Bush team and its proclivity to unilateralism premised on America's economic and military dominance, it would not be unreasonable to assume that its foreign-policy model reflects an exaggerated perception of "our strengths" and "their weaknesses" in keeping with the perception of self. In such models, one necessarily finds a less than realistic assessment of the strengths of the opposition and "our weaknesses" if only because arrogance rooted in a sense of superiority finds its way into the equation. That is, their "A" is not equal to our "A" and, therefore, the objective becomes a "slam dunk" to those who hold the view that there has to be some advantage to being a superpower. Needless to say, such models necessarily beg successful outcomes.

This overwhelming reliance on strength with an equally overwhelming disregard for inherent weaknesses can be discerned from the personality of the architects of the strategy for a new Middle East. In addition to the parade of "experts" drawn from the pool of fundamentalists and intellectuals—the neoconservatives, if you will—the fixation with power by the former Deputy Secretary of Defense Paul Wolfowitz stands out as rising to the same level of Richard Perle's who, as then Chairman of the National Defense Board at the Pentagon, had an overwhelming influence in bringing to policy ideas that were hatched in the 1980s and early 1990s and arguably refined in secret during the Clinton presidency. For example, Secretary Wolfowitz's testimony to Congress in which he grossly underestimated the cost of the Iraq war and the number of military personnel needed to secure the country after invasion speak to an approach that betrays an exaggerated projection of the outcome from "Shock and Awe." Indeed, this mindset with respect to the strength and rights of a superpower is further evidenced by Mr. Wolfowitz's alleged disregard for established code of ethics and for the perspectives of others at the World Bank; a behavior many observers regarded as a carryover from this tenure as Deputy Secretary of Defense.

In addition to Perle and Wolfowitz, the Vice President, the Secretary of Defense, and the Secretary of State are principal players and thus contributors to the theory-practice problematic. Evidence, Mr. Cheney's assertions that US troops will be greeted with garlands of flowers, a variation on Perle's "liberators" theme; that the insurgency is its last throes, notwithstanding that the number of attacks by the insurgency increased from 26,000 in 2005 to 42,000 in 2006. Evidence further the Pentagon's assessment that only 6,000 US troops would be needed in Iraq at the end of 2006; and Secretary of State Rice's characterization of Lebanese civilian deaths in consequence of the Israeli bombardment in July 2006 as "the birth pangs of a New Middle East" on the modeled assumption that Hezbollah would be crushed in short order by the Israeli military. Seemingly ignored or minimized in all the models are the countervailing actions of the opposition, the primal instinct to survive if you will. But as Ardrey (1966: 236) reminds us, the territorial principle that drives us, "is not something the American thought up, like the skyscraper or the Chevrolet.... Whether we like it or we do not, it is a power as much an ally to our enemies as it is of ourselves and our friends."

Examined below, then, are some of the perceived false assumptions of the Bush administration's grand strategy and the attendant consequences of a game-theoretic models which arguably has its roots in Cold War politics—given that its architects were almost all involved in orchestrating the demise of the Soviet Union—and, therefore, inappropriately applied to a poorly understood and indeed discounted culture and region.

The Unraveling

Apparently largely constructed by way of recycled cold-war logic that was responsible for the demise of the Soviet Union, the grand strategy as stated earlier is designed to contain China's economic progress and hence its geopolitical influence. Also as stated earlier, the strategy requires that China's access to energy supplies be under the control of the West if not the US. But since the world's oil reserves are mainly located in the Middle East with Iraq considered home of the second largest, and Iran accounting for a significant portion of the remainder, the strategy requires constructing three game-theoretic models: one for the invasion of Iraq, the second for Israel to invade Lebanon after it has successfully partitioned the Palestinians, and the third for the invasion of Iran as discussed earlier. These discrete models essentially reflect the basic inputs drawn from the Cold War model, with a few adjustments as deemed necessary for implementation in the Middle East.

With respect to the second model, that is, the invasion of Lebanon, based on the evidence, Israel was left to devise its own methodology, with timing to be coordinated with the Bush administration just before implementation. Evidence the Israeli Prime Minister visits to the White House just before implementing his plan for unilateral withdrawal from the Gaza and the West Bank, for constructing the wall, and for invading Lebanon. They all speak to consultation and coordination; indeed, they can be linked to the several "leaks" of intelligence activities around the time and to Mr. Bush's clockwork pronouncements on Israel's right to defend itself.

As is being played out currently in the Middle East, then, the game-theoretic model(s), to be sure, evidences theory-practice problematic arising from fundamentally-flawed assumptions inherent in intellectual rigidity that has been fostered by the ever-narrowing focus of game-theoretic models pursued by influential academic institutions and think-tanks and manifest increasingly in questionable basis for policies and methodologies. In such constructs, especially those with a particularly strong bias for American military power, the assumptions are tailored to support the desired outcome; but with disastrous results as the invasion and occupation of Iraq evidence. Such miscalculations compel rationalization, for example, by the former Secretary of Defense Rumsfeld: "The enemy is smart, it is always adjusting to changes in tactics; there are things that we known and things that we don't known etc, etc." Those familiar with game-theoretic modeling would readily recognize the language. To be sure, these attempts at rationalizing the consequences of the war to a skeptical American public betray not only the nature of the model but also its construct and indeed weaknesses. Evidence further, the development of a counterinsurgency as an added tactic four years into the war. Its absence as an input to the original model betrays yet another example of intellectual rigidity discussed above.

The First Theory-Practice Problem

As implied above, crucial to the success of the neoconservative grand strategy is that the three phases in the Middle East had to be successfully implemented within a given time frame, that is, before the adversaries worked them out and certainly before the end of a two-term Bush presidency. As a result, the first theory-practice problem is that, like everything else in America, the theory comes with a short attention span and essentially is time sensitive. As such, it relies upon two basic facts: one, the US is the unchallenged power in the world, and two, it has the resources and wherewithal to demolish any resistance within a short time frame and at a minimal cost in resources and lives: ergo Wolfowitz's confident assertions to Congress. Indeed, according to Compton (2005: 44), "Shock and Awe" was predicated on a spectacular, and overwhelming display of military might aimed at destroying an opponent's will to fight. It centers on the psychological intimidation of the enemy and downplays the need for traditional military ground forces. This idea is clearly evident in the attack on Iraq by the US and in Israel's bombardment of Lebanon in July 2006.

Evidencing the convergence of military operations and information warfare, the apparent success of "Shock and Awe" was quickly followed up with the President's pronouncement of "mission accomplished" just under two months after the invasion and when US casualty was below 400. In the case of the Israeli operation, the world was being prepared psychologically for a new Middle East under Israel's control. Recall the narrative of the Israeli government: it was consistent with conquest backed as it were by the US. Even the UN Secretary General Kofi Anan was unable to avoid the influence of the US–UK–Israel alliance as was clearly discernible in St Petersburg, Russia in July 2006.

The world was indeed captivated by the awesome display of American fire power while the President's declaration of success was in accordance with the time table. Moreover, the hunt for Osama bin Laden and al-Qaeda, having been rationalized to the American people and outsourced to Pakistan in the run-up to the invasion of Iraq, could now be incorporated into the mopping-up process in Iraq as part of the original strategy.

Not unexpectedly, then, Al-Qaeda was invited to join the party in Iraq by the President with his "bring it on" challenge. Moreover, having gone to war on what has been proven to be an exaggeration of the risks posed to the US and the supporting evidence, Mr. Bush needed to link the war in Iraq to the war on terror as a way of minimizing criticisms for his unilateral actions; a "slam dunk" in the words of Vice President Cheney, if you will, but for the absence of WMD in Iraq.

The resultant unraveling of the contrived basis for the war underscores the beginning of the undoing of the grand strategy. More than that, with the passage of time "Shock and Awe" proved to be a fundamentally flawed concept for twenty-first century sensitivities: It was not and could not have been entirely Machiavellian where total destruction is the primary objective. The American people and the world would not stand for such a proposition; and, strangely enough, neither would the subconscious of its architects: Total destruction is too nihilist in the first place and, in the second and equally important, the cause was not in keeping with the definition of a just war as defined by St. Augustine (see chapter two). As a result, even as the architects of the war celebrated "Shock and Awe" self-doubt was an ever-present factor, albeit subconsciously so. More importantly, the model arguably did not fully consider the reaction of the people under siege, the territorial imperative which impelled the primal instinct of survival. Rather, it reflected the perceptions of conquests past; and most certainly the narcissism, the baggage if you will, of its architects.

The model further assumes that American troops would be welcome as liberators, with garland, and dancing Iraqis marking the occasion, an often-made representation by Vice President Cheney in the run up to the invasion. However, the reality in 2007—now into the second half of George Bush's second term as president—is that American and coalition forces are viewed as invaders and occupiers, fuelling resentment and a growing insurgency by their presence, despite Mr. Cheney's pronouncement that "the insurgency is in its last throes" two years ago. Clearly, "Shock and Awe" as the methodology of choice while successful in destroying Iraq's infrastructure and its formal military failed to prevent grass-root opposition to occupation. In this regard, the model failed to adequately assess the role of oppositional politics, and more fundamentally, the role of the primal instinct in man to survive as dictated not by someone else's perception of life but rather by his own notion of survival.

The Second Theory-Practice Problem

The notion of "freedom" as obtained in the West and upon which the Bush narrative turns, increasingly requires Islam as a way of life be rejected by those whose very existence is inseparable from it. This expectation clearly betrays a void in the understanding of the depth and importance of Islam to Muslims and thus evidences the second theory-practice problem of the model. Yet this problem could have been avoided had the planners paid attention to the lessons of history and the wisdom that are derived from such teachings. Indeed, many of the problems faced in Iraq were brought to the attention of President Bush by several detractors to the war, most forcefully by Senators Edward Kennedy and Ike Skelton whose prediction of the chaos in Iraq now reads like a script.

More importantly, the aggressive if not inflammatory rhetoric of the Bush team hardly disguises inherent prejudices if not contempt, and through articulation fears; fears that are easily betrayed to the highly instinctive. It happened in Vietnam but seemingly discounted in the Middle East models out of belief in superior military training and assets. However, then as now, the survival instinct remains unquantifiable; one of the "unknowns" which, as so often happened in the past, determine outcome.

The Third Theory-Practice Problem

The third theory-practice problem for the Iraq model is the assumptions with respect to acceptance of the invasion in terms of casualties and financial cost, not only by the international community but also by the American people. From the perspective of the international community, the cold-war model that says Iraq poses a threat to world peace was seen as quite a reach when contrasted with the real threat posed by militarily engaging the then Soviet Union with equal capability; hence few countries subscribed to the hype as evidenced by the refusal of France and Germany to join the US-led collation. Additionally, the promise of aid to certain African and South American countries on the UN Security Council proved futile. Few were willing to subscribe to the US narrative; not even when British intelligence—faulty, as it turned out —was being presented as evidence by the Secretary of State Colin Powell, with the British Prime Minister staking his impeccable career on it.

The South Americans did not fall for the false premise; for that matter neither did the Chinese nor the Russians, both permanent members of the UN Security Council. Nonetheless, the idea that Iraq was a threat to Western civilization was still being advanced by both Bush and Blair as the reason for invasion, despite increasing and persistent questions as to the credibility of the intelligence which increasingly was being revealed as unreliable, if not fabricated, but which both Mr. Bush and Mr. Blair felt compelled to publicize as accurate at home and to the world at large on the mistaken belief that WMD would be found to exonerate them.

The assumptions clearly were flawed and in consequence turned out to be yet another theory-practice problem for the Bush–Blair alliance. Nonetheless, the British Prime Minister continues to insist that WMD will be found notwithstanding the search has been abandoned by the US. These unsubstantiated and costly claims have resulted in tremendous loss of credibility for both the US and the UK. Moreover, they exposed their respective publics to terror attacks as evidenced by the 2005 London bombing and the many others that were foiled. The enormous moral authority with which the Bush administration was endowed in persecuting the perpetrators of 9/11 was squandered in the invasion of Iraq. This was well articulated by the Malaysia Prime Minister who accused Mr. Bush of pursuing a different agenda.

With respect to US casualties and financial costs, while the model contemplated some resistance from the over-rated Iraqi Republican Guard, "Shock and Awe", as theorized, would ensure conquest with minimal US casualty and financial cost; at least acceptable to the American people who would see them as a reasonable price to pay for destroying Saddam Hussein's alleged arsenal of nuclear weapons. Indeed, conscious of this risk of losing support at home for the war the administration as part of the information warfare was quick to draw attention to the low US casualty—which was under 400 at the time "mission accomplished" was declared—in comparison with the casualty suffered in the First Gulf War a decade earlier.

With respect to costs, as asserted by Paul Wolfowitz, the then Deputy Secretary of Defense, revenues from the sale of Iraqi oil would be more than enough to compensate for war damage, reconstruction, and possible reimbursement to members of the coalition who took part in the invasion. Secretary Rumsfeld advanced "a number that's something under $50bn as the cost of the war."[10] Moreover, according to Secretary Rumsfeld's Pentagon, "only 5,000 US troops would be required in Iraq by the end of 2006."[11] The reality in 2007 is that, in terms of manpower, the President sent another 8,000 troops to the surge of 21,000 he announced in January 2007, thus bringing the total closer to 160,000. In addition, Mr. Bush requested an additional US$100 billion as supplemental funding in 2007.

In terms of casualties, as of September 2007, US casualties stood at over 3,800 with at least another 50,000 severely injured as reported by the Department of Veteran Affairs (VA) in February 2007, that is, until that number was changed on intervention by the White House.[12] The widely-reported scandal on the treatment of returning injured soldiers lends some support to claims that the government had been managing the numbers. In terms of cost, while the cost of the war is placed by the Inspector General at over US$500.0 billion, according to estimates by Blimes and Joseph Stiglitz, the true cost is closer to US$2.5 trillion which includes:

> the cash costs of running the combat operations, the long-term costs of replenishing military equipment and taking care of the veterans, and [increased costs] at the Pentagon.... The economic cost, which is the differential between reservists' pay in their civilian jobs and what they're paid in the military and the macroeconomic costs, such as the percentage of the oil-price increase.[13]

Whether or not the macroeconomic costs should be included is debatable. It attributes the spike in oil prices to the Iraq war which has not been established, although one could argue that the loss of 2 million barrels a day is a contributing factor. No matter, from all accounts it appears that the actual cost of the war has been grossly underrepresented by the administration.

The Fourth Theory-Practice Problem

As noted above, the US-led invasion of Iraq in March 2003 is cited by critics of the war as one of the prime examples of a change in US foreign policy. Whilst the invasion of Iraq was predetermined (see Clarke 2004; see also *Frontline*) its success was partly marred by the fiendish events of 9/11 as indicated by Mr. Cheney's attempt link it to Iraq. Not only did the administration not contemplate the events of 9/11 despite indications that the terrorists were planning "something big" for the summer as claimed by Clarke (2004) and by former CIA Director Tenet, but also failed to think through fully the basis for the invasion and occupation of Iraq, hence Mr. Cheney's scribbled notation[14] seeking to make a link between al-Qaeda and Iraq.

The hunt for Bin Laden, to be sure, took away from the strategy in terms of physical assets, funding, and manpower which arguably had intended for invading Iraq. It was for this reason that outsourcing the hunt for Bin Laden and al-Qaeda to Pakistan was seen as the way out in terms of both cost and military assets and personnel. Beyond the cost, however, 9/11 had a psychological impact on the American notion of invulnerability. More importantly, it changed the dynamic of the planned invasion, indeed of the three game-theoretic models by introducing vulnerability. Moreover, what resulted was derived not from reasonable contemplation of the inputs to the models prior to 9/11 but rather from knee-jerk reaction to 9/11; and thus incorporates notions of retribution that are perceived as indiscriminately targeting Muslims and their fundamental beliefs. So, invasion was met with insurgency, not garlands of flowers and dancing Iraqis.

Conclusion

As seen through the eyes of many, especially the Muslims, then, the Bush foreign policy was exposed as nestled in the presumed unassailable "global war on terror" proselytized most effectively on the basis of fear and intimidation. More disturbingly, as is currently being played out in the Middle East where the notion of creating "a new Middle East" was revealed by the Secretary of State Condoleezza Rice, it is a foreign policy that is unconditionally perceived as portending US geopolitical and economic dominance over the Middle East, irrespective of cost in terms of human lives, as the administration's rationalization of casualties reveals.

These errors in judgment and construction permeate all three models: Iraq, Lebanon, and Iran and call forth countervailing responses. Evidence the inflammatory rhetoric of the Iran's President, Mahmoud Ahmadinejad: "the U.S. intends to cause insecurity and dispute and weaken independent governments in the region to continue with its dominance over the Middle East."[15] Evidence also Russia's President Putin's charge that the US militaristic approach to foreign policy was "nourishing an arms race"[16], and the arming of Iran with Russian-made defensive missiles. For all practical purposes, then, the neoconservative grand strategy unraveled at the seams.

By changing the original reason which was to disarm Saddam Hussein of WMD, to one premised on invoking the atrocities of 9/11 as the justification for preemptive military strikes against any country or group supporting terrorism notwithstanding established international laws and procedures (see Ikenberry 2004: 324), proved too great a stretch for the Bush administration. Not only is the US bogged down in Iraq, but as noted above, Russia has armed Iran and a strategic alliance has been negotiated between Russia and China. Such an alliance signals the demise of the neoconservative ambitions for prolonging US hegemony beyond its natural course. Moreover, the failure of Israel to settle the Palestinian issue peacefully prior to the attack on Lebanon and its failure to destroy Hezbollah in July 2006 have struck another blow to the grand strategy. But even then, as this manuscript goes to print the Bush narrative is once again morphing: this time to link Iran to the failure of the mission in Iraq, thereby paving the way for an assault on Iran under existing Congressional authorization.

NOTES

1 See "Economic and financial indicators"', *The Economist*, April 14, 2007, p.109

2 Buchanan, P.,

3 See "Come in number one, your time is up", *The Economist*, April 14, 2007, p. 12

4 "Interview with Jim Lehrer", News Hour, *PBS.org*, January 16, 2007

5 See Rep. Roscoe Bartlett presentation to US House of Representative on June 25, 2007, *C-SPAN*, June 25, 2007.

6 "Putin steps up missiles warning", *BBC NEWS*: April 27, 2007, http://news.bbc.co.uk/go/pr/fr/-/2/hi/europe/6599647.stm
7 "In Depth" Book TV, *C-SPAN2*, February 4, 2007
8 *C-SPAN*, January 27, 2007
9 "This Week", ABC Television, August 26, 2007
10 Stephen, A., "Iraq: the hidden cost of the war", http://www.newstateman.com/200703120024
11 Ibid.
12 Ibid
13 Ibid.
14 "The dark side", *Frontline*, PBS.org
15 Krane, J. "US warns Iran to back down", *Associated Press*, January 23, 2007
16 Weir, F. "Russia intensifies efforts to rebuild its military machine", *The Christian Science Monitor*, February 12, 2007

Chapter Eight

The Bush Foreign Policy: From Preemption to Transformation?

Introduction

In testifying to the House Budget Committee on Wednesday 21 March 2007[1] to the administration's 2008 *State Department & Foreign Operations Spending* budget proposal, Secretary of State Condoleezza Rice advised the Committee that the administration's foreign policy is "a transformation policy" requiring a state department budget of US$18.6 billion for 2008 (an increase of 21 percent over 2006) reflective of a proposed increase in foreign aid. This revelation contrasts strikingly with the administration's earlier rejection of deterrence, containment, and diplomacy as the foundation of US foreign policy for one that is predicated on preemption and prevention, effecting regime change around the world starting with the invasion of Iraq in March 2003: "Our security requires all Americans to be forward-looking and resolute, to be ready for preemptive action when necessary to defend our liberty and to defend our lives"[2] [and] "We cannot wait for the final proof. It could come in the form of a mushroom cloud."

For the four years following this June 2002 pronouncement, preemption defined the Bush foreign policy, that is, until the full implications of Israel's misadventure in the summer of 2006 began to take hold, and the realization that by most indicators the administration's grand strategy which includes remaking the Middle East was a resounding failure. Indeed, failure in Iraq has been made inescapably clear by the mass protest against US occupation in the city of Najaf and elsewhere—ironically by the very people who were supposed to be grateful to the US and its allies—on the fourth anniversary of the removal of the statute of Saddam Hussein. In an *ABC* and *USA Today* poll conducted in early April 2007, 97 percent of Sunni–Iraqi and 83 percent of Shia–Iraqi were against the presence of US troops.

In addition, as the carnage in Iraq continues unabated and the prospect for peace in Palestine ebbs and flows with the perception of success or failure of Bush's war on terror, the Bush administration is finding itself increasingly isolated both at home and abroad: the change in the composition of the Congress in 2007 brought the message of the American people home to the Bush White House while members of the coalition of the willing began peeling-off one after the other.

While many are wont to question the difference between "transformation" and "change", in context of international relations the former is encouraged by "carrots", patience and time—diplomacy, some would say—whilst the latter speaks to a short-order requirement and relies almost exclusively on "sticks"—the exercise of condign power, if you will—that has come to be associated with the Bush administration's impatience with a perceived deviant world. The danger of the latter approach is, of course, prolonged resistance: you can kill a man but as history tells us killing the spirit is not inevitable. As observed by US intelligence officer in Iraq, children are now populating the insurgency.[3] Moreover, as has been well illustrated by the reaction to the invasion of Iraq, the world has come to regard the use of condign power by a superpower as a last resort and then only when it is justified before hand—as opposed to being made justifiable *ex-post*—on the basis of credible and verifiable evidence.

In stark contrast to her July 2006 pronouncement on the death and destruction resulting from the Israeli bombardment of Lebanon as, "the birth pangs of a new Middle East", Secretary Rice was at great pains to be agreeable and to portray a foreign policy approach that now speaks to alleviating poverty and promoting development in the Third World. According to the Secretary:

> For many of the issues we are dealing with in the world today there is no military solution.... The development of well-governed states that can deliver for the people is really the answer to America's security in the long-term [hence], helping foreign citizens and their governments to literarily transform their countries, to move them toward peace, freedom, prosperity, and social justice [is] the national security mission of the State Department today.[4]

A Costly Learning Curve

While this indicates a positive change in policy for the remaining tenure of the Bush administration, assuming it is believable, the damage has been done. In the minds of many, the Bush experiment with preemption has been a very costly learning curve. Indeed, in the opinion of countless world leaders, academics, and ordinary people around the world, the consequences of one of the greatest abuse of power ever perpetrated in modern history in the name of freedom and democracy is to leave the world distrustful of US foreign policy and less secure for generations to come. Several US Senators and Representatives, even Bush insiders, have come to the view that the administration by its aggressive unilateralism has elicited untold animosity and distrust around the world that would take generations to reverse. According to US Army Brigadier General John Johns (Ret):

> Not only has our effort in Iraq have been misplaced in inappropriate use of US forces but it has resulted in alienating most of the world, specifically in the Middle East.... The major damage it has done to the United States and our national security is that it has eroded our moral standing throughout the world.[5]

General Johns is not alone. Retired Marine Corps General, John Sheehan holds a similar opinion: "The Iraq invasion has created a real and existential crisis for nearly all Middle Eastern countries and created divisions among our traditional European allies, making cooperation on other issues more difficult."[6] Four years earlier, Senators Ike Skelton and Edward Kennedy forewarned of the consequence of invading Iraq; and on the eve of unleashing "Shock and Awe" upon Iraq, Senator Robert Bird marked the occasion poignantly: "Today, I cry for my country"; arguably, not only because of the inevitable death and destruction from "Shock and Awe", but also because of the apparent reckless squander of America's credibility and moral authority. Despite the evidence of growing distrust around the world, however, Richard Perle, the neoconservative and one of the architects of the Bush doctrine of preemption continues to believe it was the right thing to do.[7] So too does the Chairman of the Joint Chiefs, General Peter Pace.

Rejecting the Bush Narrative of Universality

As articulated by President Bush, his administration's foreign policy is premised on the utopian idea that, "the best hope for peace in our world is the expansion of freedom in all the world"[8] which has been described by the conservative Republican Patrick Buchanan as "Rousseauistic" and which, ironically, has been described increasingly around the world as dangerous for world peace, not because freedom is inherently bad but because the Bush narrative and methodology—open resort to condign power as first best choice—are perceived as philosophically inconsistent, unaccommodating of "Other" and evidence universality by the sword. Indeed, according to Huntington (1966: 310), "the belief that non-Western peoples should adopt Western values, institutions, and culture is immoral because of what would be necessary to bring it about." Moreover, any effort by the West to impose its will on other societies as Huntington further observes: "is contrary to the Western values of self-determination and democracy"; it forecloses on difference, on pluralism, which, ironically, is the essence of Americanism but for the aberration that heralded in the twenty-first century.

Supporting this observation of philosophical inconsistency is the perception that the Bush doctrine derives not from reasoned contemplation of the geopolitical issues but rather from the exploitation of the fiendish events of 9/11 as a perverse opportunity to effect a concocted grand strategy contemplated prior to 9/11. It is a doctrine that not only incorporates notions of retribution which are perceived as indiscriminately targeting Muslims and their fundamental beliefs but also one which takes advantage of the situation to put into play a policy of creating a Middle East receptive to US and thus Western dominance.

To many observers, then, especially the Muslims who believe they are being targeted despite White House denials to the contrary, it is a foreign policy premised on condign power supported by a campaign of information management, fear, and intimidation having found anchor in the administration's war on terror. Americans will recall the rush at the behest of Secretary of Homeland Security Tom Ridge to acquire duct tape to seal windows and doors in fear of a biological attack from Saddam Hussein.

More disturbingly, as is being played out in the Middle East where the notion of creating a new Middle East had been prematurely celebrated by the Secretary of State Rice, the Bush foreign policy speaks to territoriality, widely perceived by non-Western peoples as imposing universality of Americanism: "one ring to rule them all" in the vocabulary of J.R.R. Tolkien. Indeed, as Huntington (1966: 310) observed: "Imperialism is the necessary logical consequence of universalism", hence Rosemary Foot's rhetorical question. It is thus significant that General Sheehan should choose to use the term "existential" in describing the crisis in the Middle East. Curiously, many see nothing wrong with American imperialism. Dinesh D'Souza, for example, proclaimed: "If this be the workings of empire, let us have more of it."[9]

Only those in denial would fail to recognize the territorial imperative at play in the Middle East and the causal relationship between the Madrid train bombing in 2004 and the London bombing in 2005, and the Iraq invasion and occupation. Both Spain and the UK took part in the invasion and occupation of Iraq. Moreover, according to Robert Pape (2006) of the University of Chicago, documents obtained from the Norwegian government revealed that the war in Iraq and its occupation by coalition forces, and the well-publicized excesses at *Abu Ghraib* and *Guantanamo*, were the *ex-ante* stated reasons for the two suicide bombings. In addition, Pape (2006) showed a direct correlation between the increase in suicide bombings with the invasion of Iraq and attendant alleged atrocities at *Abu Ghraib* and *Guantanamo*. While Spain has tacitly acknowledged this causal relationship and has since withdrawn it troops from Iraq, the British government under Prime Minister Blair continues to downplay if not deny any link between the growing terror threats in the UK and its support for US foreign policy and the occupation of Iraq.

In terms of Muslim reaction to Western intervention in the Middle East, the narrative of the Iran's President Mahmoud Ahmadinejad could not be more direct and inflammatory: "The U.S. intends to cause insecurity and dispute and weaken independent governments in the region to continue with its dominance over the Middle East."[10] While many in the West have taken exception to Ahmadinejad's rhetoric, it is no more than recognition of Huntington's prescription for the preservation of Western civilization which is:

> To restrain the development of the conventional and unconventional military power of Islamic and Sinic countries ... to maintain Western technological and military superiority over other civilizations (1996: 312).

And because the US is the most powerful Western country, and therefore *de facto* guardian of Western civilization, President Bush has insisted on exercising a declared right of preemption to any perceived threat to the shared security and strategic interests of the West. In doing so, the US actions in the Middle East could be interpreted as adhering to Huntington's prescriptions. As Ikenberry (2004: 321) observed:

> sweeping new ideas ... that call for American unilateral and preemptive, even preventive, use of force ... form a neoimperial vision in which the United States arrogates to itself the global role of setting standards, determining threats, using force, and meting out justice. It is a vision in which sovereignty becomes more absolute for America even as it becomes more conditional for countries that challenge Washington's standards of internal and external behavior.

When examined in context of Huntington's earlier prescriptions and Ikenberry's later observations, Mr. Bush's pronouncements on the consequences of failure in Iraq indeed do convey a commitment to the inevitability of a clash of civilizations by shaping reality to fit the prediction. While therefore the motivations for the Bush foreign policy are in many respects anchored in the narrative of Huntington, the Bush narrative is decidedly crusading, situated in his "global war on terror." Evidence the grand assertion that the Iraq war is only a part of a larger ideological war. Moreover, if one were to listen closely to the narrative of the former Chairman of the National Defense Board Richard Perle one cannot help but come away with the impression that America is on a crusade; a crusade, however, that portends the end of coexistence attendant the mistaken belief in preemption as doctrine. Such a doctrine goes to the very foundation of international institutions, treaties, and covenants that until recently supported a pluralist world order which the Bush administration supported by its Christian coalition seems ready to sacrifice in furtherance of its territorial imperative.

But whilst the territorial imperative for Western peoples, especially Americans, translates to military prowess on the one hand, survival instinct, history, and cunning inform countervailing actions of non-Western peoples on the other. Clearly such asymmetrical challenges portend a quagmire for the US in the Middle-East and elsewhere; more so if it launched a military strike against Iran who has been a keen observer of events in Iraq. The Bush administration will be no more successful in Iran than in Iraq for the simple reason it does not now have nor will it ever acquire the support of the American people or with few exceptions the wider world. Hence, the danger for the Middle East and the wider world is that the Bush administration's frustration in Iraq could escalate the conflict to a level where nuclear devices are put into play. Recall, the rationalization for dropping two atomic bombs on Nagasaki and Hiroshima: "to save the lives of US combat troops" by bringing a quick end to the war with Japan. Recall also, Mr. Rumsfeld's reference to future use of nuclear weapons contained in the phrase: "bringing our conventional or *nuclear power* to bear in a regional crisis" (Suskind, 2006: 76), and France's President Chirac's not-so-veiled threat to "raze" Tehran if it were to use a nuclear bomb against Israel. The fault lines between the West and non-Western peoples could not be made clearer.

A Parallel Reality

As former Secretary of State Madeleine Albright tells it, the Bush team appears to be living in a parallel reality. From its approaches to the Israel–Palestine and Israel–Lebanon issues, it is a parallel reality derived from the US being the only superpower at the turn of the century, endowed with superior military assets and a perceived moral authority to remake the world. But, it is a parallel reality that has been rejected by the American people, as evidenced by the persistent low poll ratings of the President; wide-spread rejection of the ever-changing rationalization for the Iraq war which changes almost on a daily basis: from Saddam Hussein possessing WMD; to regime change; to bringing democracy to Iraq; to making Iraq the central front in the war on terror; and in January 2007, to preventing terrorists access to oil revenues.[11] Similarly, victory in Iraq has morphed in March 2007 to delivering an Iraq that can, according to Secretary of Defense Robert Gates, "govern itself, sustain itself and defend itself"; and in May 2007, to "reducing the violence in Iraq" rationalized on the basis that there will always be some level of violence. In July 2007, buoyed by reports that offer a glimmer of hope for success, the rhetoric has again changed to "complete victory" such is the state of the Bush Middle East "strategy." But it is a perception that is questioned by the former Commander of U.S. Central Command General John Abizaid who sees US troop presence in Iraq for at least another three to five years.[12]

Growing Republican Dissent

The growing distrust of the administration and the rejection of a Republican-controlled Congress and Senate that supported such a deception further speak to rejection. Seven years into his presidency and four years and counting in Iraq, President Bush is seen as the most isolated of American Presidents in the last fifty years. His demagoguery no longer resonates with the American people or with many members of his party. Writes Robert Novak, a conservative columnist: "Republicans in Congress do not trust their President to protect them."[13] In any other civilized country, Mr. Bush would have been obliged to demit office or at least be contrite. But, as George McGovern and William Polk observed: "Alien to Americans is the idea of making amends for our actions; we do not like ever to admit that we have been wrong" (quoted by Anna Quindlen).[14] Indeed, the phrase "mistakes were made" is often used in place of "I have made mistakes", which clearly convey very different meanings. While many would attribute such attitude to being strong, to matured societies it signifies weakness. Since Novak's observation, a number of senior Republican Senators have come out against continuing the war in Iraq. Many have come to the conclusion that the Iraqi government is not making any progress in reconciling differences and, therefore, the administration should think in term of troop withdrawal by March 2008.[15] Many of the Senators are due for re-election in November 2008 and have begun to disassociate from what is fast becoming a failed policy even with the surge. Even former advisers and Bush White House staffers have come out against the Bush administration; one, echoing President's Carter's take on the administration as being one of the worst in history.

Growing Global Disarray?

As told by former Russian President Mikhail Gorbachev: "The world is experiencing a period of growing global disarray."[16] "We lost 15 years after the end of the Cold War, but the West I think and particularly the United States, our American friends, were dizzy with their success, with the success of their game that they were playing, a new empire."[17] More critically:

> The Americans want so much to be the winners. The fact that they are sick with this illness, this winners' complex,. is the main reason why everything in the world is so confused and so complicated.... Under the current U.S. president, I don't think we can fundamentally change the situation as it is developing now.... It is dangerous.[18]

Who Lost Russia?

In many ways Mr. Gorbachev blames British Prime Minister Tony Blair for the strained relationship between the West and Russia. Mr. Blair, according the former Russian President, should have told Mr. Bush: "We know about empires, we know that all empires break up in the end, so why start again to create a new mess."[19] Mr. Gorbachev's observations find support in Kaletsky: "Despite all the past sentimental rhetoric of Western politicians describing Russia as a friend and "strategic partner" US and European behaviour has consistently treated Russia more as an enemy than an ally."[20]

Interestingly, according to Zbigniew Brzezinski, "Russia really has no choice but to become more gradually associated with Euro–Atlantic community, because if it isn't, it will find itself facing China all by itself.... The real destiny of Russia is to come closer to the West."[21] It is perhaps because of this perception of an inevitable subordinate relationship that the US and EU have adopted a somewhat patronizing approach to Russia. Indeed, Russia has been refused membership to the WTO, and many US pre-Cold War trade sanctions against it are still in place. At the same time, however, Russia's Ambassador to the UN Vitaly Churkin confirms that: "Russia will not be subordinated.... It is not feasible to think of Russian membership in the European Union or membership in NATO because we are not prepared to cede our sovereignty to anybody."[22] Moreover, according to Ambassador Churkin, "sometimes the United States is seen as working against some fundamental Russian interest."[23]

For his part, in his address at the *Democracy and Security Conference* held on June 5, 2007 in Prague, President Bush accused the Russian government of failing its people by backtracking on its promise of democracy and freedom: "In Russia, reforms that once promised to empower citizens have been derailed, with troubling implications for democratic development."[24] Mr. Bush was clearly responding to President Putin's barrage of accusations hurled at the US in the weeks prior to the Group of Seven plus Russia (G-8) meeting in Germany. More directly, Mr. Bush was seemingly obliged to respond to Mr. Putin's oblique warning issued to the Czech Republic and Poland on June 4, 2007. In addition to expressing concern over the US's plan to deploy a missile defense system in Europe, Mr. Putin warned that:

> If a part of the strategic nuclear potential of the U.S. appears in Europe and, in the opinion of our military specialists, will threaten us, then we will have to take appropriate steps in response. What kind of steps? We will have to have new targets in Europe.[25]

The targets, of course, are Poland where the US plans on deploying interceptor missiles and the Czech Republic, where it plans on having an advanced radar system installed. While the Bush administration seeks to reassure Russia that it is not the target of its enhanced missile defense program, according to the Russian president: "We are not satisfied with the explanations which have been presented to us. We think there is no reason to placing an anti-missile system in Europe."[26] Clearly, Mr. Putin has rejected the argument that it is intended to protect Europe from possible attacks by "rogue" states such as Iran and North Korea; the former not likely to have long-range missile capability within the next decade according to a state department official, and the latter currently in negotiation to abandon its nuclear weapons program. Interestingly, neither has ever threatened Europe. According to Ambassador Churkin, the US plan is seen as a threat to both Russia and China.27 Mr. Gorbachev has also come out in support of Mr. Putin.

The Widening Gap between the Rhetoric of Peace and the Reality of Militarism

While Mr. Putin's warning came as a surprise in terms of its harsh tone, it was long in the making, indeed since the run up to the Iraq war in 2003. Russia, then considered a budding ally of the US, together with Germany, and France vigorously opposed the invasion of Iraq. The US and the UK gambled their credibility on finding WMD in Iraq; they also are seemingly gambling their respective credibility in their assertions that Iran has a nuclear weapons program; and Mr. Bush and now Mr. Blair[28] are asking the Russian president to trust them on the missile defense system the US wants to erect in former member states of the

Soviet Union with whom the Kremlin had had problems when, according to the Russian president, "the anti-missile defense system is targeted against something that does not exist."[29]

Moreover, since the invasion of Iraq, the Vice President, the Secretary of State, and the President himself visited former Soviet Republics, lending support to their efforts to build democratic institutions while emphasizing their less than rewarding experiences as former Soviet Republics. Mr. Bush went so far as to praise the Hungarians for their revolt in 1956, seemingly oblivious to the fact that some nine years would elapse since the Budapest uprising before Black Americans gained their civil liberties and right to vote; and then only after mass protest and violence. Even then, injustice against Black Americans has been marked by violence since, with the Newark riots of 1967 in which 26 persons were killed and 715 others injured by police action. And then there are the Watts riots in Los Angeles, evidencing a less than exemplary form of freedom and democracy. Hence, despite the claims that the US is the "oldest democracy", in reality it began to function as a plural democracy only after the passage of the Voting Rights Act in 1965. Also, it was not until the passage of the McCarran-Walter Act in 1952 that non-white immigrants were allowed to become US citizens, having been barred since the passage of the Immigration and Naturalization Act of 1790. Not surprisingly, then, such seemingly ill-informed pronouncements by the Bush administration have prompted former Russian President Gorbachev to make the observation that: "the Russians were ready to be constructive, but America was trying to squeeze them out of global diplomacy."[30]

A Distrustful World?

This dissatisfaction with Mr. Bush's foreign policy extends beyond US–Russia bilateral political relations. In a BBC opinion poll of 26,000 people in 25 countries conducted in January 2007, seventy-five percent of those questioned disapproved of how the US government was dealing with the crisis in Iraq; a majority disapproved of the US "handling of *Guantanamo* detainees; the Israel–Hezbollah war; Iran's nuclear programme; global warming; and North Korea's nuclear programme." According to the BBC:

> This poll underscores conclusions drawn from several other surveys ... that anti-Americanism is on the rise, and the more the US flexes its hard power, the more it deploys troops abroad or talks tough diplomatically, the more it seems to weaken its ability to influence the world.[31]

Indeed, the Bush narrative which is clearly premised on the neoconservative notion that, to predict the future you have to shape it by whatever means, including the use of force, is of grave concern to other nations. Evidence the remarks of Russian President Putin:

> Nations are witnessing an almost uncontained hyper use of force in international relations.... One state, the United States, has overstepped its national borders in every way... This is very dangerous. Nobody feels secure anymore because nobody can hide behind international law.[32]

Interestingly, seven months earlier and two days before Israel declared war on Lebanon in July 2006, Mr. Putin was equally unequivocal about where he stands on the Bush narrative: "I made it clear [to Bush] that I would not be a party to any crusade or holy alliance"[33] Interestingly, this response to Hank Plant of CBS was little reported in the US, if at all, even though it clearly suggested that Mr. Bush was seeking to recruit Mr. Putin to his plan for creating a new Middle East and to supporting Israel's declaration of war on Lebanon on 12 July 2006. Recall Mr. Bush's Saturday radio address in which he characterized the invasion of Lebanon and the bombing of Qana as: "a moment of opportunity for a broader change in the Middle East." Recall further, Seymour Hersh's statement in a CNN interview that: "We worked closely with them months before, not necessarily knowing when it was going to happen, but when there was an incident they will take advantage of the incident, what I call a fortunate timing." The incident, according to Hersh, was the kidnapping of the two Israeli soldiers by Hezbollah in July 2006; an incident which Hezbollah's Nasrullah thought would result in negotiations not war. But, to his surprise Mr. Olmert was being true to one of the propositions of the Baltimore Program: "only *shlemiels* prefer truth and negotiation to propaganda and machine guns" (Feldman 1995: 181).

Moreover, with respect to the stand-off with Iran, any doubts about Russia's stance, and indeed China's, on these and other international issues are clarified by the statement of President Putin: "I would like to emphasize with satisfaction that the positions of Russia and China on all the issues discussed either coincide or are similar"; and that of China's President HU Jintao: "We have agreed that strategic cooperation between China and Russia has major importance for international affairs in creating a favorable atmosphere, in making international relations more democratic and ensuring global peace."[34] A follow-up statement by Russia's Foreign Minister Sergey Lavrov which states that the latest set of sanctions imposed by the UN on Iran was a "call for the resumption of talks rather than an instrument of punishment"[35] adds clarity to the statements with respect to Iran.

Pandora's Box

Beyond the damage to US image abroad and the polarization of Americans at home from pursuing its neoconservative agenda, the Bush team appears to have thoughtlessly and irresponsibly opened Pandora's Box in the Middle East, with consequences far beyond the capacity of the Bush administration—despite keeping "all options on the table"—and likely the West to resolve in the near future.

The conflicts in the Middle East, rooted as they are in religion, ethnicity, and other hitherto dormant distinguishing characteristics, will have to be resolved according to Vali Nasr (2006: 24), "before the Middle East can arrive at democracy." These views find support in Anthony Cordesman, Strategy Chairman of the *Center for Strategic and International Studies*.[36] Nasr further reminds us that: "Just as the settlement of religious conflicts marked Europe's passage to modernity, so the Middle East will have to achieve sectarian peace before it can begin living up to its potential"; a consideration that was clearly absent in the Bush team's grand strategy for prolonging US hegemony in the twenty-first century, and one that is slowly beginning to be realized by the Bush team as evidenced by Secretary Gates' comments.[37]

But more challenging than achieving sectarian peace in Iraq is the willingness of the West, particularly the US, to nurture acceptance by Muslims of a way of life that is anathema to Islam, not only in Iraq but in the Muslim world as a whole; curiously, a way of life that is being rejected by conservative Americans such as Newt Gingrich whose disgust at American children being allowed to, in his words, "dress up as pimps and prostitutes on Halloween" pursuant their freedom could hardly be contained,[38] and to the Christian fundamentalist led by the late Jerry Falwell who attributed partial responsibility for 9/11 to Gays, Lesbians, the ACLU, feminists, and others, and whose Moral Majority were believed to be responsible for re-electing Mr. Bush in 2004. Certainly, Jerry Falwell's appearance with the President when the presidential race became too close to call is widely believed as tipping the scale in favor of the incumbent.

It is this inherent contradiction or schizophrenia which manifests in the ideology of individualism constructed as it were in the plurality of language games and thus multifarious in interest and desire that is rejected by majority Muslims and, in a curious way, by former Speaker Newt Gingrich. Moreover, it should be recognized that John Locke's notion of virtue in selfishness or materialism upon which Western society turns does not have the same significance outside the West, especially in traditional Muslim communities despite attempts at various times in history to impose it upon the wider world. Islam, like Confucianism, speaks to family and to community and relegates individualism. Hence, the Bush administration's pronouncement that failure in Iraq would have disastrous consequence for America is not because the terrorists would invade our streets, as it would like Americans to believe, but rather because the US will have failed to persuade the Iraqis, indeed Muslims in general, to abandon a way of life that has been inculcated in their psyche for over 1300 years; and passively hand over control of their oil reserves to Western corporate interests, as was clearly planned for by the neoconservatives (see Suskind, 2004: 96). More than that, Mr. Bush and his team have opened Pandora's Box.

Materialism is not Everyone's Passion

According to Brink Lindsey, "the happiest people in the world are the richest people in the world." Not surprising, then, that materialism inherent in the notion of freedom and democracy is presumed to be everyone's passion is partly due to looking at the world through the prism of Western ideology as noted above and partly because capital accumulation—the defining characteristic of a capitalist world economy—has been pursued in the West as ineluctable over the centuries. It equally should be of no surprise that the former British Prime Minister Margaret Thatcher, the architect of British capitalist revival in the 1980s, should in 1987 declare: "There is no such thing as society. There are individual men and women, and there are families." Indeed, as the *sine qua non* of a capitalist world system capital accumulation depends crucially upon creating worldwide acceptance of individualism; if necessary by the exercise of condign power as implied in Mr. Bush's exhortation in Prague in June 2007: "Free nations must do what is necessary to prevail."[39]

Forgotten in these exhortations, however, is that the conduct of human interaction is bound up with the social, economic, and political conditions of their respective worlds in which they find themselves and that, in many areas of the world, human passions—"springs of human behaviour" in the vernacular of Jeremy Bentham—remain largely unaffected by the utilitarian desire for pleasure awakened by the Enlightenment that gives rise to Jean Francois Lyotard's "schizophrenic self" which, clearly, is not restricted to individuals. Furthermore, as the consciousness of the American people is awakened still further to the consequences of "our way of life" and begin to turn away from the excesses of individualism and conspicuous consumerism—consequences of the Enlightenment in the extreme to be sure—they increasingly question the motives behind condign power exercised in their name without transparency and accountability, notwithstanding the influence of those who cling to the shallow notion that there has to be some benefit to being a super power.

While, therefore, the Bush administration is entitled to make its pronouncements on good and evil, and to characterizing countervailing actions in the play-out of its Middle East policy as evil, evidencing the need for free nations to do what is necessary to prevail, it could hardly claim such narrative to be representative of the American people in an environment in which the President's job rating has been the lowest since he took office. Moreover, being characterized as "the worst" in US history by former President Jimmy Carter and as a "military monster"[40] by former Russian President Gorbachev are not exactly badges of honor. Clearly, America has been made, temporarily albeit, a haven for opportunists whose quest for significance predisposes them to rationalize the very essence of Americanism: a right to have rights. In this connection, it a curiosity that Mr. Bush should seek to lecture the gathering at the *Democracy and Security Conference* in Prague on government by the will of the people[41] while ignoring the will of the American people and assuming a paternalistic approach to governance at home and in international relations.

The Shia Revival

In addition to the shallow influence of Western political thought in the Middle East, according to Vali Nasr (2006: 251): "The Shia revival [which now plagues US and European policymakers] constitutes the most powerful resistance and challenge to Sunni extremism and Jihadi activism within the region"; indeed, to the West's quest for control of Middle East oil reserves on the one hand, and to implementing Huntington's prescriptions necessary to preserve, protect, and renew the unique qualities of Western civilization. Ironically, attempts at spreading freedom and democracy in the Middle East, which effectively is against the traditional Sunni-Arab allies of the US and the West, further serve to strengthen the Shia revival and thus evidences yet another significant consequential error in judgment by the Bush administration: characterized by Senator Chuck Hagel as the greatest foreign policy blunder in US history. As a result, the consequences will have to be borne by the West for generations to come if European history is anything to go by; and if Mr. Bush and his ideological extremist team were allowed to take the West down the road to perdition. With this in mind, the fundamental question thus becomes: How will the West treat with the consequences attendant the ill-advised opening up of Pandora's Box by the Bush administration after 2008 Presidential election? It could, of course, stay the course as the outgoing British Prime Minister Blair has advocated. But staying the course validates the notion that humans are locked in the cycle of historical determinism of which ideological extremism is central. In this connection, it is worth recalling that empires have failed because they made an enemy of change itself.

Environmental and Other Issues

Even when he tries, Mr. Bush seems unable to detach from what many in the Democratic-led Congress call a "confrontational foreign policy"; validating the notion that we live in a conflictual world. In addition to switching from a position of allaying the concerns of Russia over the proposed plan for a missile defense system in Europe, he openly criticizes Mr. Putin for "derailing" the progress of democracy in Russia. Curiously, he finds it necessary to label himself a "dissident." In similar contradictory fashion Mr. Bush expresses concern for the environment while rejecting the European proposal to reduce global carbon emissions by 50 percent by 2050.[42]

With respect to environmental issues, many American business leaders agree with Mr. Bush since it buys them time; not to find solutions but to find ways to transfer the burden to their competitors. To this end, many would likely point to a June 2007 report from Switzerland which states that China has surpassed the US as the number one emitter of carbon. But while this is true in terms of incremental addition to what currently exists, from a per capita perspective the US is still the number one emitter: by as much as five times that of the Chinese and two times that of the other Western industrialized countries. Hence, as observed by India's Foreign Secretary Shiv Shankar Menon: "The problem of global warming has been created by the industrialised countries.... Once our per capita emission levels reach the same as those of the industrialised countries, we'll be very happy to do our share too."[43] But even in the US, there is a growing number of states opposed to the Bush administration's stance on greenhouse gas. According to California Governor Schwarzenegger, "This is all bogus; because we won't have an economy if we destroy our environment.... We can grow the economy and still simultaneously protect the environment. It's not a choice, it's not either or; the two go hand in hand."[44] California has been joined by eleven other states that are seeking permission from the Environmental Protection Agency (EPA) to impose state law that would require automakers to reduce carbon dioxide emissions by 25 percent for cars and 18 percent for sports utility vehicles by 2009 year models.

Conclusion

The burning question arising from the above analysis is: why the inconsistency in the policy of peaceful transformation articulated by Secretary Rice and the confrontational rhetoric of the Administration since? One answer that readily comes to mind is that the President is being whipsawed by an ideologically-divided administration. One moment he speaks of peace and the next he sees himself as a "dissident" in a world beset by evil which he must put right by the exercise of condign power. Another, of course, is that since World War II America essentially has functioned as a war economy (Dator 2006: 124–125) and there are still those who blindly subscribe to the notion of empire. Indeed, given the increasing susceptibility of the American economy to both internal and external shocks, apparently Americans need to be distracted from the actual purpose of the war in Iraq and possibly beyond which is, according to former Secretary Rumsfeld, "to demonstrate what U.S. policy is all about ... [and] to dissuade countries from engaging in asymmetrical challenges to the United States (see page 144)."

From his articulated positions regarding Russia's concerns over his plans for a missile defense system in Europe which had heretofore been free of any nuclear threat, and the issue of global warming, Mr. Bush clearly has yet to extricate himself from the destructive influence of ill-informed neo-conservatism that has invaded his administration. Pinning his hopes on a reversal of fortunes in Iraq is once again taking the American people down the path of the existential and self-fulfilling prophesies with respect to the increasing threat of terrorism.

NOTES

1 "2008 State Department & foreign Operations Spending" House Budget Committee, www.appropriations.org, *C-SPAN*, March 21, 2007
2 President Bush address, June 1, 2002
3 Interview by Scott Pelly, '*60 Minutes*', cbsnews.com, March 4, 2007
4 Ibid.
5 Iraq War, Press Conference by Senate Majority Leader Harry Reid, *C-SPAN*, April 16, 2007.
6 Sheehan, J.J., "Why I declined to Serve", *Washington Post*, 16 April, 2007, p. A17
7 "The Case for War: In defense of freedom", included as part of "America at a Crossroads", *Frontline*, April 17, 2007
8 Excerpt from the President's Inaugural Address in January 2005
9 D'Souza, D., "In Praise of American Empire", *The Christian Science Monitor*, April 26, 2002.
10 Krane, J. "US warns Iran to back down", *Associated Press*, January 23, 2007
11 President Bush, press interviews in the run-up to his State of the Union address to Congress.
12 "Morning Edition", *NPR.org*, September 12, 2007
13 Novak, R.D., "A President All Alone". *Chicago Sun Times*, March 26, 2007
14 Quindlen, A., "Contrition as Leadership", *Newsweek*, January 8, 2007, p.56
15 Collinson, S., "Another Republican deserts Bush on Iraq", http://news.yahoo.com/s/afp/20070706/pl_afp/usiraqcongress_070706162139;_ylt=AmEDy_4Fy9ROcAmovLDxA22WwvIE
16 Nicholson, A., "Gorbachev blasts American 'imperialism'", *Associated Press*, http://news.yahoo.com/s/ap/20070727/ap_on_re_eu/russia_gorbachev
17 "Gorbachev criticises US 'empire", *BBC NEWS*, http://news.bbc.co.uk/go/pr/fr/-/2/hi/europe/6717037.stm, June 3, 2007
18 Nicholson, A., "Gorbachev blasts American 'imperialism'", *Associated Press*, http://news.yahoo.com/s/ap/20070727/ap_on_re_eu/russia_gorbachev
19 Ibid
20 Kaletsky, A., "It's the West that's starting this new Cold War, Russia's belligerency is hardly surprising", *The Times*, June 7, 2007, http://www.timesonline.co.uk/tol/comment/columnists/anatole_kaletsky/article1896029.ece
21 Brzezinski, Z., "Charlie Rose", PBS.org, June 15, 2007.
22 Churkin, Interview with Charlie Rose, "Charlie Rose", *PBS.org*, July 7, 2007.
23 Ibid.
24 "Bush criticises Russia on reform" http://news.bbc.co.uk/go/pr/fr/2/hi/europe/6723671.stm, June 5, 2007
25 News Hour with Jim Lehrer, PBS.org, 4 June, 2007; BBC World, June 4, 2007
26 "NATO condemns Putin's missile vow", *BBC NEWS*, http://news.bbc.co.uk/go/pr/fr/-/2/hi/europe/6719507.stm
27 Churkin's interview, "Charlie Rose", *PBS.org*, July 7, 2007
28 "Blair will be frank with Putin'', *BBC NEWS*, http://news.bbc.co.uk/go/pr/fr/-/2/hi/uk_news/politics/6724727.stm, June 6, 2007
29 "Nato condemns Putin's missile vow", *BBC NEWS*, http://news.bbc.co.uk/go/pr/fr/-/2/hi/europe/6719507.stm, June 4, 2007

30 "Gorbachev criticises US 'empire'', *BBC NEWS*, http://news.bbc.co.uk/go/pr/fr/-/2/hi/europe/6717037.stm, June 3, 2007
31 "Listen more is world's message to US", *BBC World News*, January 23, 2007
32 'Putin attacks 'very dangerous' US', *BBC World Service*, February 10, 2007
33 Joint Bush/Putin televised Press conference in St. Petersburg, July 10, 2006
34 Shchedrov, O., "China, Russia leaders reject force on Iran and N. Korea", http://news.yahoo.com/s/nm/20070326/wl_nm/china_russia_hu_dc
35 Isachenkov, V., "Russia slams U.S. global policy", http://news.yahoo.com/s/ap/20070327/ap_on_re_eu/russia_us
36 "U.S. Policy in Iraq", *Washington Journal*, *C-SPAN*, August 11, 2007
37 Baldor, L.C., "Gates: Iraq political reform difficult", *Associated Press*, http://news.yahoo.com/s/ap/20070802/ap_on_re_mi_ea/gates_iraq
38 "This Week", *ABC Television*, April 22, 2007
39 Mr. Bush address at the 'Democracy and Security Conference', Prague, June 5, 2007, C-SPAN
40 "Gorbachev criticises US 'empire'', *BBC NEWS*, http://news.bbc.co.uk/go/pr/fr/-/2/hi/europe/6717037.stm, June 3, 2007
41 "Democracy and Security Conference", Prague, June 5, 2007, *C-SPAN*
42 Hunt, T., "Bush says Russia won't attack Europe", *Associated Press*, http://news.yahoo.com/s/ap/20070606/ap_on_re_eu/bush
43 Majumder, S., "India, China under pressure at G8", *BBC NEWS*, http://news.bbc.co.uk/go/pr/fr/-/2/hi/south_asia/6725453.stm, June 6, 2007
44 "Schwarzenegger Speaks At Climate Change Summit In Miami", http://www.nbc6.net/news/13679407/detail.html?dl=headlineclick, July 13, 2007

Part Five

Israel's Territorial Imperative

Chapter Nine

Israel: A Dream on Hold?

Introduction

On April 1, 2007 Israel Prime Minister Olmert announced he is seeking a conference with Arab leaders to discuss a peace settlement to the Arab–Israel conflict. This announcement comes on the heels of the Arab League Summit held in Saudi Arabia on March 28, 2007, in which Arab leaders agreed to adopt Saudi Arabia King Abdullah's peace proposal of five years earlier. This proposal offers full recognition of Israel in return for its withdrawal to its borders prior to the 6-Day War in 1967, a separate state for the Palestinians, and an accommodation for those Palestinians who were displaced in the 1948 war. Accepting these terms could be too little too late for the embattled Israeli Prime Minister whose "incompetence" has been laid bare in the *Winograd Report* issued in April 2007. According to Judge Winograd, in "hastily" going to war with Lebanon in July 2006, Mr. Olmert showed, "a severe failure in judgment, responsibility and caution."[1] The Israeli people, pragmatists that they are have called for the resignation of Mr. Olmert along with that of the Minister of Defense.

Since the April announcement, the 18 month old Palestinian government of Fatah and Hamas unraveled in June 2007, with Hamas left in complete control of Gaza notwithstanding US and Israeli military and other support to the Palestinian president and leader of Fatah, Mahmud Abbas. The defeat of Fatah in Gaza by the "militant" organization Hamas provided yet another opportunity for Mr. Olmert to salvage his political career which he seized upon by declaring the newly appointed non-Hamas Cabinet of Abbas as one he can work with; one that signs on to "a non-binding declaration of intent.". Olmert was not alone in recognizing the new Palestinian Cabinet. The US and the EU both offered their support to Abbas and restored the flow of aid to the new government in the hope of overcoming the influence of Hamas in the West Bank. Prime Minister Olmert has also agreed to release 250 Fatah prisoners in Israeli jail and to flow US$500 million dollars, about one-half of collected taxes owed to the Palestinians, as goodwill gestures. Recall, Olmert had earlier refused to engage in any substantive negotiations with the Palestinians whilst Hamas was part of the Palestinian government even though Hamas offered to not insist on being a party to any talks between Abbas and Olmert. Moreover, in June 2006 he launched a military offensive against Gaza in an attempt to rescue an Israeli soldier kidnapped by another militant Palestinian group, holding Hamas responsible as the official government of the West Bank and Gaza.

To many on the outside, it is puzzling why successive Israeli governments have avoided reaching a settlement with the Arabs on the Palestinian issue, after all they were given 78 percent of Palestine in 1948 which they have expanded to about 92 percent by the occupation of the West Bank and Gaza, up to the point of their unilateral pull out of Gaza in 2006 (see Carter 2006). While most analyses offer explanations in terms of Israel's right to exist and the security threat posed by militant Palestinian movements and Hezbollah in Lebanon, the true reason are far more complex than the immediate conditions and current US–Israel narratives suggest. This chapter therefore seeks to explore some of the other reasons which include the now unspoken dream of "renewal of the Jewish homeland, destroyed 2,000 years earlier by the Roman Diaspora" (Hamilton 1995: 43) as primary, with the flow of foreign aid—partly discussed in chapter Four—as compensation for being de facto wedge for the Westernization imperative in the Middle East in the wake of the demise of the Soviet Union.

Renewal of the Jewish Homeland

Few analyses with respect to the Arab–Israeli conflict and negotiations have ventured outside the immediacy, with rocket-shelling and reprisals informing the sound bites that have come to define US media reports in the twenty-first century. Lost in the shuffle of discrete often interested perspectives and high-priced propaganda, is the desire for an all-Jewish state expressed by David Ben-Gurion at the Baltimore Hotel conference—*the Baltimore Program*—in New York City in 1942[2] (Hamilton 1995: 42; Feldman 1978) and reaffirmed by Israel Eldad (2007) in 1971. Moreover, political perspectives as observed earlier have come to replace facts in discourse in attempts to steer public and foreign policies towards predetermined self-serving goals. One such unspoken goal is for a "free and democratic Jewish Commonwealth ... [which] shall embrace the *whole* of Palestine, undivided and undimished", as spelt out in the *Atlantic City Resolution* adopted unanimously by the *American Zionists Organization* at their convention in Atlantic City in October, 1944. Not only was this resolution confirmed by the *World Zionist Conference* in London in August 1945 (Feldman 1978: 131), it remained the driving force behind Israel's unyielding policy towards peace negotiations with the Arabs with respect to the return of Arab–Palestinians. Indeed, though occupied by Arabs for centuries, from a Zionist perspective, according to Israel Eldad (2007: 18), "the Land of Israel had never been their patrimony and was never regarded as such." Not then, not today. Hence, with respect to the intention of establishing an all-Jewish state, John Mearsheimer and Stephen Walt's article that raised the issue of the Israel lobby and its influence on US–Israel relations is an exercise at dispassionate analysis, despite the apparent risk of misinterpretation by Nazi groups and anti-Semites. But before Mearsheimer and Walt there was Hannah Arendt.

Arendt, who sought to emphasize the cultural values of the kibbutzim, "saw the Zionist terror in the late 1940s as designed expulsion of the Arab population" with its "inherent principle of nationalism and its insistence on absolute sovereignty" as leading to the Balkanization of the whole region (Birmingham 2006: 138). As Arendt tells it in 1948, the *Baltimore Program* produced consensus on the following "more or less roughly stated propositions":

> The moment has come to get everything or nothing, victory or death; Arab and Jewish claims are irreconcilable and only a military decision can settle the issue; the Arabs–all Arabs–are our enemies and we accept this fact; only outmoded liberals believe in compromises, only philistines believe in justice, and only shlemiels prefer truth and negotiation to propaganda and machine guns; Jewish experience in the last decades–or over the last centuries, or over the last two thousand years–has finally awakened us and taught us to look out for ourselves; this alone is reality, everything else is stupid sentimentality ... in sum, we are ready to go down fighting, and we will consider any body who stands in our way a traitor and anything done to hinder us a stab in the back'(Feldman 1995: 181).

In light of the propositions of the *Baltimore Program* and the *Atlantic City Resolution*, as Arendt saw it:

> The land that would come into being would be something quite other than the dream of world Jewry, Zionist and non-Zionist. The "victorious" Jews would live surrounded by an entirely hostile Arab population, secluded inside ever-threatened borders, absorbed with physical self-defense to a degree that would submerge all other interests and activities (Feldman 1995: 187).

According to Peg Birmingham (2006: 139), Arendt's, "break with Zionism was in large part due to the creation of a refugee population through the forced expulsion of the Arab population in Israel and the minority status of those Arabs who remained; the latter, a proposition to the extent that it reflects history was deemed acceptable to Israel Eldad in 1971 (Eldad 2007: 131–2) and seemingly favored by Israel supporters and Mr. Olmert in 2007 as discussed below.

Whilst Arendt was castigated by the Jewish community for her views on modern Jewish history, her account supports the assertion of Mearsheimer and Walt—in response to Harvard Law Professor Alan Dershowitz—that Ben-Gurion wrote to his son Amos in October 1937 stating that, "the future Jewish state would have an 'outstanding army . . . so I am certain that we won't be constrained from settling in the *rest of the country*, either by mutual agreement and understanding with our Arab neighbors, *or by some other way*' (emphasis added)."[3] These perspectives of David Ben-Gurion as offered by Arendt and later by Mearsheimer and Walt would be understood far better when considered in context of the history of the Jewish people which is briefly outlined below.

Background

Many from a self-interested perspective have argued that it is the Arabs who have been prolonging the conflict, refusing to recognize Israel's right to exist as a state in the land that was "promised to them by God." But to the Arabs, it is a land from which the Jewish people had been expelled by conquering nations such as the Assyrians (721 B.C.E.), Babylonians (586 B.C.E.), and finally by the Romans in 135 C.E. Indeed, after 135 C.E. the Kingdom of Israel that was created by David around 980 B.C.E.—later split into the kingdom of Judaea and the kingdom of Israel after the death of Solomon in 926 B.C.E. because of internal disagreements—ceased to exist, except in the hearts and minds of the Jewish Diaspora. The Jewish people were dispersed throughout the region and the Mediterranean basin. Since then, they have really never been able to resettle in the Holy Land in any great numbers until the *Balfour Declaration* allowed for Jewish immigration into Palestine, and the eventual declaration of an independent Jewish state by Ben-Gurion in 1948, some 1,800 years after they were expelled by the Romans.

Contrary to the attempts at character assassination of the Prophet Muhammad by some who find it difficult to accept their own history, Middle Eastern Jews were allowed to return to Jerusalem as a "People of the Book" by the Prophet Muhammad who took control of it—yes, by the sword—in the seventh century, not from Jews but from other Muslims who were polytheistic. There they lived openly as Jews in peace and relative harmony with Muslims and Christians under conditioned power exercised by the Muslims until they along with all the other inhabitants were slaughtered by the Knights Templar in the First Crusade (1095-9). As discussed in Chapter Two, the first Crusade was authorized by Pope Urban II who took the opportunity to consolidate the political power of the Church by the exercise of its compensatory power. The Church never actually carried out any of the slayings but rewarded those who did by promising redemption.

Partitioning of Palestine

That the Holocaust should be the catalyst for establishing a state for the Jewish people in their historical homeland speaks in the first place to the importance of power in the game of territoriality, and in the second place, to the collective contrition of the Europeans and in a way, American Jews. As noted in Chapter Two, the Jews were constantly under attack by Arab–Palestinian who resented their return to Palestine under British sponsorship. At the same time, the British were also attacked by the Jews in response to the British government's *White Paper* which limited Jewish immigration to Palestine (Hamilton, 1995: 42). Hence, on November 27, 1947 the UN with US agreement partitioned Palestine into two states: one for Arab–Palestinians and the other for Jewish immigrants. The West

Bank came under the control of Jordan whilst the Gaza was administered by Egypt. The remainder of Palestine—about 78 percent—was given to the Jewish immigrants. But as noted above, even before the separation of Arabs from Jews, the idea of establishing a free and democratic Jewish commonwealth in all of Palestine was adopted by Ben-Gurion and the *World Zionist Organization.*

Despite the animus for Arabs expressed in the *Baltimore Program*, the creation of a homeland for the Jewish people in Palestine—formerly Judaea until the name was changed by the Romans—by way of the *Balfour Declaration* in the early twentieth century is not dissimilar to the gesture of the Persian king, Cyrus II in 538 B.C.E. who, after conquering Babylon (modern day Baghdad) where most of the Jewish people were enslaved by Nebuchadnezzar, returned them to Judaea to rebuild the temple destroyed by the Babylonians and required them to live by the "Book." These recorded facts of history are either overlooked, downplayed or even rewritten by those who now seek to ride the wave of opportunity in the aftermath of 9/11, as the invasion of Iraq evidences.

Navigating the Shallows

Succeeding Israeli governments and their advocates fully aware of the vulnerability of Europeans in the wake of the Holocaust have exploited it to the full since Ben-Gurion declared independence on May 16, 1948 just months after the US withdrew its support for the partitioning and proposed trusteeship for Palestine. In addition to which, the Arab–Palestinians rejected the partitioning which in retrospect was exactly what Israel wanted. Israel, according to Ardrey (1966), needed to legitimate its claim to the land, not by invoking a "long-ago deal with God" but rather by way of the territorial imperative as the binding agent for an all-Jewish state; and for which, as told by Arendt, it was both militarily and psychologically well prepared.

Driven by its own territorial imperative, and as anticipated and planned for by Ben-Gurion years before, the Arab Higher Committee, (Arab League) provided just what was needed to legitimize the state of Israel. Having rejected partitioning and trusteeship, "[t]hey bared their bodies, they died in piles" (Ardrey, 1966, 308); and a Jewish state was truly born again, this time out of "brutality that showed the dark side of the Jewish personality" which, like any other under siege, found expression in nationalism.

It was indeed the long-awaited expression of anger that had been accumulating for over 1800 years and made current by the atrocities of Hitler's Germany; and as articulated in the *Baltimore Program*, the Arabs paid the price (see also Eldad 2007). Years later, the founding father of Israel David Ben-Gurion is quoted by Mearsheimer and Walt as saying:

> If I were an Arab leader I would never make terms with Israel. That is natural: we have taken their country. . . We come from Israel, but two thousand years ago, and what is that to them? There has been anti-semitism, the Nazis, Hitler,

> Auschwitz, but was that their fault? They only see one thing: we have come here and stolen their country. Why should they accept that?[4]

It should be noted also that, although Alan Dershowitz and others dispute several assertions in Mearsheimer and Walt's article, none questioned the veracity of the statement attributed to Ben-Gurion or indeed the quoted excerpt from the October 1937 letter to his son. Moreover, according to Mearsheimer and Walt, "a number of Israeli historians have shown Ben-Gurion made numerous statements about the need to use force (or the threat of overwhelming force) to create a Jewish state in all of Palestine."[5] Also, in seeking to discredit Mearsheimer and Walt, Dershowitz claimed that, "Prince Bandar, a member of the Saudi royal family, was so astounded by the generosity of Israel's offer that he told Arafat: "If we lose this opportunity, it is not going to be a tragedy. This is going to be a crime."[6] Interestingly, *BAE Systems*, one of Britain's major arms company, and the *British Ministry of Defence* have been accused of making payments to Prince Bandar for a Saudi arms contract worth £43.0 billion. *BAE Systems* does not dispute making the personal payments (about £1.0 billion) to the Saudi prince but says they were with the "express approval" of the Ministry of Defense. Needless to say, Prince Bandar has denied any impropriety.[7]

In addition to expanding its territory in the 1948 conflict, Israel occupied the Sinai in consequence of joining Britain and France in attacking Egypt in 1956 in response to the nationalization of the Suez Canal by Egyptian president Nasser (Hamilton 1995: 42) and thus speaks to Arendt's expressed concern about an overly aggressive Israel. On demand of the US government, Israel relinquished the captured territory to the UN who maintained a peace-keeping force until 1967, days before the Six Day War. The invasion of Lebanon in 1982 in pursuit of militant Palestinians refugees was no less an extension of Jewish territorial imperative having found a base from which to build and having been buoyed by its military successes over the Arab states in the 1967 war.

Holding the Attention of the West

With a single focus and as an astute player on the international stage, Israel has been relentless if not ruthless in ensuring that the Holocaust remains uppermost in the minds of the West while exploiting every opportunity to extend its borders and seeking ways to justify its actions; again, an Arendt's expressed concern. To this latter end, Muslims who currently occupy lands once considered Judaea or Israel arguably are seen as legitimate targets for expulsion first, by labeling them terrorists and secondly, by pursuing a policy of seek and destroy with the approval and support of a Bush administration that is bent on situating its grand strategy in what it perceives as its justifiable war or terror, with a Europe still haunted by its recent past in support, albeit less enthusiastically so.

A Serving Current

To many westernized Jews in Israel and in the US who have been navigating the shallows since 1947, the time could not be more opportune; not only for cementing the territorial gains made against the Arabs but also to expand upon them in keeping with the dream of Ben-Gurion and the *Baltimore Program* (see Eldad 2007: 107). With the arrival at the White House of a US President whose messianic penchant is hardly contained, the sea could not be fuller and the current more serving. Hence, while it might be true that, "Israel's strategic value has declined since the end of the Cold War,"[8] its ability to capitalize upon opportunities to foster its own agenda has been made more sharp as evidenced by its ability to secure American and European aid, despite the fact that its economy is classified as middle-income.

Israel, to be sure, has done a credible job of exploiting America's desire to maintain its hegemony by making itself indispensable to a US administration committed to gaining control of Middle East oil reserves by whatever means. For example, in May 2006 the Israeli Ambassador to the UN Dan Gillerman proclaimed John Bolton, the US envoy to the UN, as a "secret member of Israel's own team at the United Nations."[9] While the comment was passed off as a joke, Ambassador John Bolton in reality proved to be just that, opposing any and all proposed resolutions that censured Israel and, indeed, vigorously condemned Hezbollah during the Israel–Lebanon war in the summer of 2006 without attributing any responsibility to Israel despite the evidence of disproportionate military response and the use of cluster bombs. At the same gathering in May 2006, Ambassador Gillerman "warned that Iran is months not years away from acquiring nuclear weapons"; a warning that has been the mantra of the Bush administration such is the cooperation between the two states and the level of confidence in their respective agendas.

But the US envoy is not alone in defending Israel's actions. In her statement to the UN Security Council in support of UN Resolution 1701, Secretary Rice not only blamed Hezbollah for the conflict but also failed to recognize Israel's disproportionate use of force in which over 1000 Lebanese civilians were killed and many more injured by US-supplied bombs. Moreover, the Israeli naval blockade that was designed to foment an uprising by the Lebanese people against Hezbollah by causing a humanitarian crisis was never mentioned. Nonetheless, the outrage expressed by the world was an embarrassment to both Israel and the Bush administration.

That the neoconservatives in the Bush administration were able to initiate two aspects of their Middle East strategy by first invading Iraq and secondly by seeking a conflict with Iran with the intent to invade it as a means to bringing it under Western control, provide the best chance for the Israeli government to achieve its dream of regaining the Promised Land after an absence of some 1800 years. Indeed, as a people who have maintained their Jewish identity, customs, and culture over the centuries by strict adherence to the Five Books of the Bible—given back to them by Ezra at the behest of Cyrus II of Persia—the opportunity to re-establish the kingdom of Israel cannot be squandered for the fourth time. And Ehud Olmert like every other Israeli leader knows this. In this connection, it is instructive that today's Israel is mainly located in the former kingdom of Judaea and that Lebanon, an artificial state, occupies part of the old kingdom of Israel. Equally instructive are the oblique reference to this fact by Ambassador Dan Gillerman during the debate on UN Resolution 1701 in August 2006 and his offer of assistance to dismantle Hezbollah and to rebuild Lebanon even in the face of Arab and Lebanese condemnation of Israel's brutality.

Quid Pro Quo

At the same time, Israel is totally embraced as a friend of the West for what it offers in return, the quid pro quo, if you will. This should surprise no one. The Israel of today is essentially an extension of Western philosophical indoctrination: its population of European Jews has experienced the Enlightenment and the formation of the interstate system in lock step with the Europeans. Indeed, despite the derision heaped upon the Jewish people over the centuries their contribution to European culture and development is inescapable. Hence, Israel's commitment to democracy is not only undeniably trustworthy but in consequence is accessed by the US as a base from which to proselytize freedom and democracy in the Middle East as part of its long-term strategy to bring that region under Western if not US control. Under this scenario, Israel gets its "Promised land" back—its *rasion d'ětre*—whilst the US and the West get control of Middle East oil reserves, with the Arabs and Iranians left to ponder the consequences of their errors in judgment. Recall, centuries earlier the Jews provided the technical knowledge and skills to a Christian-Spain, that is, until they became dispensable. The lessons of history clearly have not been lost on Israel.

The Israel–Palestine Issue

Given the contentious nature of the subject matter, it bears reiterating here that the following discussion is not to advance any one position but rather to show that, irrespective of how property rights are acquired, they will be fiercely defended in keeping with the territorial imperative. Moreover, as it applies to the Israel–Palestine issue it is worth remembering that sovereignty is a political concept recognized within the interstate system that has its grounding in the Treaty of Westphalia and, therefore, has very little applicability outside that framework. Therefore, sovereignty for any group is a function of international consensus within the interstate system and not simply by unilateral declaration by it, a point often overlooked by dictators and other interested perspectives but a point not lost on Israel (see Eldad 2007: 106–7).

Clearly, with respect to the Israel–Palestine conflict, then, failing a successful international-brokered peace accord the violence will continue. Driven by the territorial imperative, both Israelis and Palestinians appear unaccommodating of the other, invoking their respective historical claims and counterclaims backed by a hi-tech military on the one hand, and suicide bombing on the other; both seeking to have its claims validated in the court of world opinion. But the attendant rhetoric and polemics are the machinations of politicians within and without, motivated by notions of power aided by those who perceive themselves as beneficiaries in the game of territoriality. They, however, are not of the minds and hearts of the people, Jews or Palestinians, who are paying the price.

A Question of Nationalism?

The Israel–Palestine issue has for too long festered at the expense of both Israelis and Palestinians, a condition that was foreseen by Arendt who questioned Israel's approach to according citizenship. According to Peg Birmingham (2006: 39–140): "For Arendt, nowhere was the repetition of [European nation-state criteria for] nationalism more clearly seen than in the conditions of Israeli citizenship, and nowhere was the principle of the right to have rights more clearly absent." Arendt, further argued that, "Chauvinism ... could use the religious concept of the chosen people and allow its meaning to degenerate into hopeless vulgarity" (Feldman 1995: 39) in consequence of a state of perpetual military preparedness which seemingly defines the current Israel experience. Be that as it may, it should be recognized that the Jews are a people fiercely driven by the territorial imperative and, much like the salmon returning to its historical spawning ground, must overcome all obstacles or perish such is the determination.

Jews are not new to the Middle East. Indeed, they share a common heritage with the Arabs; they walked the same land centuries ago. Why and how they were ejected from the Holy Land is not for this book to ponder; there are many scholarly works that speak to this aspect of history. This said, it has to be recognized that, as a people mainly scattered in Europe after 135 C.E. the Jews have been persecuted and disparaged throughout history mainly because their strict adherence to what is undeniably a highly-disciplined way of life devoted to "preserving the identity of a de-territorialized man" proved incorruptible throughout the centuries (see Ardrey, 1966: 306–7), with the Holocaust as the last failed attempt to destroy it; something the Arabs should have given more thought to in 1947 and again in 1967. In both instances the territorial imperative was very much in evidence.

That the Arabs should consider the establishment of a Jewish state in the Holy Land an affront to their perceived historical rights speaks equally to their notion of territoriality rooted in history and not in any recent privilege bestowed by former European colonial masters acting in consort. Some would argue they traded one colonial master for another at the collapse of the Ottoman Empire and, as such, are expected to adhere to the rules of interstate behavior established by the Treaty of Westphalia, 1648. Indeed, most former colonies, now independent states, have found ways of complying with the established rules of interstate behavior. Yet, as evidenced by the Arab–Israel wars and the continued refusal to recognize Israel as a legitimate state created by the very institution that granted most of them international legitimacy as sovereign states with all the rights and protection of the international community, the Palestinians and some Arab states stridently defend their perceived historical rights even against their political creators. But as noted above, the Israelis paid for the land with their blood, and thus in their minds and indeed by the customs of the region are de facto owners. Indeed, control of Jerusalem has historically been on the basis of conquest. The Arabs know this only too well. History tells them that when the Muslims controlled the Holy City the Jews were obliged to live under conditioned power (*dhimmi* status) exercised by the Arabs. Israel Eldad (2007) and others have argued that the Palestinians in Jerusalem should expect to live under conditioned power exercised by Israel in keeping with this historical precedent, or leave.

Arendt and others notwithstanding, the Israeli government is seemingly unwilling to return to the *status quo ante* 1967, utilizing every available diplomatic and legal means to hold onto lands captured during the 1950s and 1960s, which includes exploiting the vulnerabilities of the West. Evidence the distinction made between "occupied territories" and "*the* occupied territories" and the argument that expanding settlements to accommodate off-springs of the original settlers though deemed illegal is not in violation of UN resolutions calling for a halt to further expansion of settlements, the Negev people's experience notwithstanding. On the basis of the latter argument, settlements in the West Bank increased by five percent in 2006 bringing the total to 270,000[10]; with only one settlement dismantled since Olmert promised unilateral withdrawal prior to the war with Lebanon.

"Other", no More

As noted above, the Jewish people have paid for being Europeans too much in lives and dignity; for being "Other" in foreign lands and their return to the Holy Land after so many centuries represent the primal instinct to survive as a people and would be fiercely defended as the propositions resulting from the *Baltimore Program* clearly evidenced. Both instinct and resolve were tested most decidedly by the Six Day War in 1967 which many claimed was an act of aggression by Israel. However, as Moshe Raviv, Political Secretary to former Israeli Foreign Minister Abba Eban tells it, the massing of Egyptian troops in the Sinai posed an immanent danger to Israel and had to be addressed directly in keeping with its policy of responding to situations that are perceived as threatening; curiously, giving rise to the notions of preemptive and preventive actions which now inform the Bush doctrine.

To the Israelis, the closing of the Straits of Tiran to Israeli shipping by the Egyptians was de facto declaration of war. Official Egyptian documents allegedly discovered after the war revealed that the Egyptian president had indeed plan on attacking Israel. According to Raviv, Battle Order 3/67 issued by the Egyptian High Command on May 18, 1967 read as follows: "An offensive operation is planned for the cutting off of the South and Negev area and to conquer Ellet."[11]

What prompted the Egyptians to mass troops in the Sinai was the alleged false information supplied by Russia that Israel had 12 divisions in place ready to attack Syria. Also, the Arabs saw the earlier Israeli action of diverting water away from Arab lands as a provocative action that could not go unchallenged. Moreover, the pan-Arab ambitions of Egypt's Nasser could hardly be contained and found support in an Arab world intent on destroying Israel. But, while the Arabs were celebrating victory even before the war began, the Israelis did what those threatened with annihilation do: they drew on their primal instinct, the territorial imperative, if you will, and the rest is history. In ex-post analysis, the Israelis unsure of its own military performance appeared to have tried every diplomatic means to avoid war with the Arabs but in the end the evacuation of the UN peace-keeping forces that had kept the peace between the two sides for ten years left them with no other choice: they did what the territorial imperative compelled.

But however great the price the Israelis have paid over the centuries, recompense does not reside in perpetuating the differential logic in language that derives the binary distinction of superior–inferior, rich–poor, enlightened–unenlightened, Jew–gentile from which the notion of "Other" is derived and of which Arendt was fearful; to do so serves only to validate a hierarchal social structure and the perpetuation of conflict. Likewise, hatred and inflexibility do not reside in Islam; they are cultivated and nourished by extremists on both sides who see a benefit in prolonging the conflict albeit at the expense of the people. Both Arabs and Jews need to recognize that their historical conflict dates back to at least a thousand years before the Prophet Muhammad and Islam despite attempts by opportunists to link the current conflicts in the Middle East to Islam. Moreover, Muhammad recognized the Jews as "People of the Book."

With these observations in mind, the Israel–Palestine issues as highlighted by President Carter are analyzed in terms of the forces behind them, that is, the play out of the territorial imperative. Also included are the perspectives of Harvard Law Professor Alan Dershowitz offered as rebuttal to Carter's advocacy for peace which has been interpreted as advocacy for the Palestinians.

Carter's Observations and their Discontent

According to former President Carter (2006: 208–9), Israel's illegal occupation of Palestinian lands on which a network of settlements has been constructed since 1967 in defiance to UN Security Council Resolution 242; the connecting of these illegal settlements by highways prohibited to Palestinians that also serve to cut-off access to their farmlands; and the building of a 40 foot wall with electronic sensors on both sides on Palestinian farmlands which, again, cuts off access to other parts of Palestine, all with the tacit approval of the Bush administration and US aid, are no less deprivation of basic human rights.

As President Carter further tells it, the walls restrict the free movement of the Palestinians and serve to isolate if not to imprison them in their own lands. These actions, according to President Carter, are not only illegal but serve to deprive the Palestinians the means to make a living. Moreover, President Carter appears to hold the view that a great injustice is being committed against the Palestinians with the tacit approval of the Bush administration. Recall, that Mr. Bush gave his approval for constructing the walls. It is instructive that the tactics adopted by Israel is not dissimilar to those used by the Inquisitors before driving the Jews out of Spain at the end of the fifteenth century. Then as now, the purpose is to "purify" the land (see Eldad 2007).

There are, of course, arguments to the contrary by supporters of Israel and of the Bush administration's US–Israel relationship and its policy in the Middle East. Many such arguments are strident and serve the neoconservative perspective of a new Middle East led by Israel; most focus on the daily rocket attacks on Israeli's towns and settlements; on the suicide bombings in Israeli cities; and on Israel's right to exist as the basis for Israel's use of force, albeit disproportionately so as seen through the eyes of the UN representative[12]. Moreover, it is argued the existence of such "threats" constitute terrorism.

There is, of course, no disputing the provocative and costly actions—in terms of life and property—of the Palestinians which, of course, cannot be allowed to go unchecked, Ben-Gurion's earlier expression of understanding of Arab reaction to Jewish occupation notwithstanding. Recall, the Jews were expelled by the Romans because they refused to accept Rome's hegemony. But dispassionate analysis necessarily requires a focus on proportionality, objectivity, and, of course, humanity in twenty-first century human interaction. As such, the disproportionate use of force by Israel speaks to violations of human rights; as does the approach to discourse on the Israel–Palestine conflict in the US speaks to question begging. With respect to the latter, it is commonplace for supporters of Israel, and the Israeli government itself to cherry-pick entry points in history or events to support their arguments and military actions by the latter in furtherance of its objective. Moreover, whilst UN-sponsored peace-keeping force is the recourse of choice for other similar situations, the international community seems not to think that the Israel–Palestine conflict justifies such intervention.

Desrhowitz's Rebuttal

Clearly, Carter's intervention must be seen in context of advocacy for the Palestinians. So, too, must be the rebuttal offered by Alan Dershowitz, be seen as advocacy for Israel. It is thus instructive that, in his attempt at rebuttal of President's Carter characterization of the Israel–Palestinian issue as *Palestine, Peace not Apartheid*, Dershowitz, should quote Israeli causalities from attacks perpetrated by Hamas in 2004 and 2005 as evidencing acts of terrorism by Hamas but seemingly challenged to offer evidence of any similar attacks by Hamas since it was elected to government in 2006, the point made by President Carter. Equally telling, is Dershowitz's silence on Palestinian deaths resulting from Israel's retaliation. Suffice it to say that, in terms of Palestinian casualties the ratio is greater than 10:1; in terms of property damage, Palestinians live in absolute squalor and are subjected to guided missiles and bombs, artillery fire, bulldozers, and sonic booms from low-flying fighter jets; all of which are rationalized as necessary to Israel's right to defend herself; and given that foreign aid is fungible, arguably financed by US foreign aid to Israel. Moreover, President Carter did not absolve Hamas from responsibility for deaths of Israelis as Dershowitz implied. What he did say is that, despite "Hamas had not accepted the PLO's commitments at Oslo that recognized the "right of the State of Israel to exist in peace and security ... their incumbent officials had been free of any allegations of corruption and, for sixteen months, had meticulously observed a cease-fire commitment" (Carter 2006: 178–9) and are supported by the evidence.

In proclaiming to be "pro-Palestine and pro-Israel" and as someone who wants to see Palestine as a state existing side by side with Israel, Dershowitz to a widely-cheering crowd at Brandeis University readily conditioned such a possibility not on the *status quo ante*—that is, pre1967 borders, which he considers representing "maximalist Palestinian position"—but on the basis of "reasonable compromise." In this, Dershowitz, while leaving the door open for removal of some settlements has avoided addressing the pronouncement by the George H. W. Bush White House: "The United States has opposed and will continue to oppose, settlement activity in territories occupied in 1967, which remain an obstacle to peace". This position was reaffirmed by Secretary Baker: "I don't think there is any greater obstacle to peace than settlement activity that continues not only unabated but at an advanced pace" (Quoted in Carter 2006: 131–2).

Dershowitz further suggested that the Palestinian refugees should stay where they are or be accommodated in the proposed Palestinian state and not be allowed to return to their original homeland in Israel because, as he puts it, "the return of four million Palestinians to the occupied lands would turn Israel into yet another radical Islamist state." Interestingly, in 1971, Israel Eldad (2007: 131) thought it would be a waste of time to talk about return of Arab–Palestinian to their original homes. At that time, Eldad expressed the view that just as the Jews in the Diaspora are encouraged "to leave and reunite in their own country", the Arab–Palestinian should be encouraged "to pick one of the numerous Arab states in order to live a full Arab life there"; their transfer to be financed by the international community. Those who remain should be kept as a minority element in Israel. Clearly, not much has changed in 36 years. In 2006, on the basis of a non-return, Dershowitz suggested the Palestinians will get not only a state of their own but also receive a US$ 35.0 billion Marshall Plan package that was part of the 1993 Oslo Accord which he further alleges President Carter advised against. It should be noted here that the PLO headed by Arafat did not recognize Israel as a state in 1993.

Dershowitz also observed that the Palestinians have had several opportunities for statehood since 1938 but squandered them. One such opportunity, to be sure, was in 1947 on the partitioning of Palestine by the UN with US agreement on the departure of Britain. As noted above, the Arabs rejected the partitioning and fought the 1948 war with Israel on the basis of their historical claims. Since then they have been at a military disadvantage against an Israeli military that has grown from strength to strength as the Six-Day War in 1967 and others revealed.

Critiquing Dershowitz's Propositions

What can be discerned from Dershowitz's narrative beyond its appeal to emotionalism? First, it must be recognized that Dershowitz is an advocate for Israel and must by reason of that relationship be seen as advancing the Israeli position. Hence, in context of the territorial imperative, to the winner go the spoils. Moreover, the Jewish imperative does not stop at the borders drawn by a body whose legitimacy and effectiveness has been in question since its formation. The inability of the UN to have any of its earlier Resolutions with respect to Israel complied with speaks to its ineffectiveness in the face of opposition from its more powerful members.

Secondly, in a world of *realpolitik* "reasonable compromise" suggests that Israel should continue to build on occupied territory until such time a solution is found with the expectation that, given the support of the US, UK, and the EU, it will be able to keep most of the occupied territory if and when the Palestinian leaders come to the realization that their people are better served by accepting an international peace settlement. Indeed, both President Bush and Prime Minister Blair in offering support for the wall in 2006 had indicated that it would be unrealistic to expect a return to the 1967 border. Prior to the building of the Wall in 2006, Mr. Blair had effectively supported Mr. Bush's position that, "the Palestinians must forego their right of return and that some Israeli settlements on the West Bank would not be part of a future Palestinian state", an idea that was at the time characterized as a "false impression" in 2004.[13] Also, as reported by Peace Now, some 200 settlements which were subsidized by the Israeli government still exist on Palestinian land in the West Bank at the end of 2006.

Thirdly, not only does the Dershowitz narrative feed into the idea that Islamist states are radical but also speaks to separatism as the ultimate goal of the Israeli government and its supporters, indeed vital to an all-Jewish state in keeping with the *1942 Baltimore Program* which some would argue is being kept alive by slow-walking the peace process; a tactic not lost on Professor Sharee Makdisi of the University of California[14]. Indeed, a two-state solution avoids embarrassing the purveyors of freedom and democracy in an Israel in which non-Jewish people would be the majority, overwhelmingly so if Palestinian refugees were allowed to return to Israel or should there be a single state of Israel, or Judea, that incorporates all of Gaza and the West Bank.

A single state, to be sure, would transform Israel into another South Africa where freedom and democracy in all its Black African glory reigns, but it is a model that is resisted and is perceived as contrary to the notion of an all-Jewish state in which the Torah reigns supreme (see Eldad 2007: Birmingham 2006: 139). In this regard, it is perhaps telling that Mr. Olmert, while expressing a readiness to hold talks with Saudi Arabia and other Arab states over their renewed peace plan, is adamant about not allowing the Palestinians to return: It is, according to the Israeli Prime Minister, "something we certainly can't agree to and we won't agree to.... I'll never accept a solution that is based on their return to Israel, any number."[15] Clearly, this position is anchored in the *Baltimore Program* and has not changed over the years (see page 191 above). Yet, an all-Jewish state is philosophically inconsistent with the notion of multi-culturalism and pluralism embraced by the US and the West in the twenty-first century; indeed, it is inconsistent with the ideology of freedom and democracy in which the Bush Middle East narrative is situated.

Fourthly, on the point of squandered opportunities for statehood, while it is true that Palestine was never a "state", Dershowitz seemingly has failed to consider the overarching influence on the Arab–Palestinian position of the proviso of the Balfour Declaration which states that: "In the establishment in Palestine of a national home for the Jewish people ... nothing shall be done which may prejudice the civil and religious rights of existing non-Jewish communities." That he has failed to do so is perhaps because the *Balfour Declaration* lost currency when Britain relinquished its Mandate and referred the Palestine issue to the UN in early 1947. Hence, that Arab–Palestine is not a state is because it lost that right in battle in 1948 and again in 1967. Clearly, the issue has now morphed to being a matter of Israel's security that first must be satisfied before it can be expected to relinquish control of occupied territories. The alternative, of course, would be for an international peace-keeping force in the West Bank and the Gaza.

The above said it is instructive that in response to the question on what should be the basis for a two-state solution, the British Foreign Secretary Margaret Beckett suggested that, "the basis of consideration should be along the lines of the 1967 borders."[16] Equally instructive, according to former Prime Minister Thatcher, the policy of the Conservative Party at that time was for a Middle East settlement based upon U.N. Security Council Resolution 242, which stressed two fundamental requirements: "withdrawal of Israeli armed forces from territories occupied in the recent conflict (i.e. the 1967 Six Day War); and the recognition of the right of every state in the area 'to live in peace within secure and recognized boundaries free from threats or acts of force'" (Thatcher 1995: 374). These conditions are rooted in rationality and give no consideration to the influence of history which exerts a tremendous influence on the passions of and interaction among the peoples of the region.

With respect to the two-state solution, according to President Carter 80 percent of Palestinians polled were in favor of a two-state solution supported by 67 percent of Israelis who think that having a separate state for the Palestinians would be an acceptable proposition. This view is supported by King Abdullah II of Jordan.[17] Despite such expressions, the leaders of both sides appear not to be responsive to the sentiments of their respective peoples but rather are engaged in the game of territoriality informed by "the convergence of threat and opportunity."

Management of Information

The not-so-tacit dehumanization of the Palestinians to a US–media audience by compliant reporting ensures minimal objection if not acceptance of the label as terrorists to be wiped out by the "good guys" flying the flag of freedom and democracy. With respect to the managing of information reaching the American public, as pointed out by President Carter the unconditional acceptance by the Palestinians of the Road Map to Peace, and Hamas' implicit acceptance of Israel's right to exist if it were to return to its pre-June 5, 1967 borders have been under-reported in the US and are conspicuously absent in discourse on the Israel-Palestine issue.[18] Evidently, territory captured by Israel in war is seen in context of the primitive notion of conquest for reasons noted above.

The Narrative of Peace

Peace is in the narrative of all interested parties. But, behind the declared support for peace are certain actions that are inconsistent with peace and betray hidden notions of territoriality: First, the withholding of payment of revenues collected by Israel on behalf of the Palestinian government to the democratically elected Hamas-led government; and secondly, the withholding of humanitarian aid to the Palestinians by Western donors as collective punishment because, as President Carter puts it, the Palestinians chose to elect Hamas which is branded by the Bush administration, pliant Europeans, and the Israeli government as a terrorist organization.

As seen through the eyes of Palestinians and their supporters, however, the Western philosophical notion that, "sovereignty—the right of a state to make autonomous decisions within its realm ... [resides] in the people who alone could legitimate a regime" (Wallerstein 2005: 4) is seemingly reserved for Western democracies and their friends and does not apply to non-compliant non-Western people. At the same time, however, given that Arab–Palestinians rejected the offer of sovereignty implicit in the proposed partition of Palestine by the UN in 1947, and having lost in battles against Israel since, it is not unreasonable for Israel to expect that the creation of a Palestinian state from what remain does not portend a stronghold for extremists. It is a price the Palestinians must now pay.

Not surprising, then, restoring the flow of aid to the Palestinians is conditioned on Hamas recognizing Israel's right to exist; renounce violence against Israel; and disband its militia. But even with a pliant Palestinian President and the agreement for a government of national unity between the two factions, the flowing of US$100.0 million to Abbas by the Israelis, as recognized by the British Foreign Secretary, falls very short of the revenues colleted by them, the with-holding of which is "creating a humanitarian crisis in Palestine."[19] Moreover, despite efforts to form a unity government between Hamas and Fatah at the urging of King Abdullah of Saudi Arabia,[20] with full support of the Arab nations, the US, EU, and Israel have signaled their unwillingness to lift the sanctions against the Palestinians and restore the flow of aid to the people through their democratically-elected government who after more than a year of deprivation of both means to earning a living and humanitarian aid are showing signs of malnutrition. But not all European countries have signed on to the Israeli narrative. The announcement of a Palestinian unity government was greeted by Norway's Foreign Minister as a first step to peace and thus has moved to normalize relations with the Palestinian government in an attempt to move the peace process forward.[21]

Perhaps it is this realization that the Palestinian people are unfairly punished has caused France to signal its willingness to provide humanitarian aid whilst the Russian Foreign Minister in a meeting with the Palestinian Prime Minister announced that Russia will push for an end to the boycott of the Hamas-led Palestinian government[22]. However, these two gestures of humanitarian concern and the aftermath of the Israel–Lebanon war in July–August 2006 have been interpreted by Dershowitz as weakening the prospects for peace. According to Dershowitz, "the prospects for peace are not good. The only way Israel could make peace is if it is a very strong country, militarily, economically, politically and in every other way" [23]; a classic expression of the territorial imperative when taken in context of the *Atlantic City Resolution*, and inconsistent with the notion of reasonable compromise. Dershowitz further accuses some European countries of undercutting Israel; and France of "essentially supporting terrorism", with "blood on its hands." Moreover, according to Dershowitz, "Israel has to know that when it makes concessions it will be perceived as a sign of strength not a sign of weakness." Meanwhile, with respect to the UN's role, it is instructive that its Ambassador DeSoto in Jerusalem should question its impartiality. In a leaked private memorandum to the *Guardian* newspaper, DeSoto is of the view "the U.N. no longer has an impartial role as a Middle East negotiator. He blames pressure from the United States."[24]

It is interesting that Dershowitz's conditions for peace, which is a very strong Israel, should mirror the conditions set by President Reagan in his "zero option" approach to negotiations with the Soviet Union. Suffice it to say Reagan was orchestrating the demise of the Soviet Union. Moreover, it bears remembering that the resounding victory by the Israeli military over the Arabs—Syria, Jordan and Egypt—in the six-day preemptive strike by Israel in 1967 brought not peace in Palestine but rather occupation of the West Bank and the Gaza, thereby adding to the 78 percent of land that was formally recognized by the UN as the state of Israel in 1949.

When taken in context of the differential logic of the signifying chain in language—good–bad; right–wrong; strong–weak, and the like—Dershowitz's observations reflect what the Arabs would likely consider unreasonable expectations from someone who speaks of "reasonable compromise" as essential for peace. Indeed, for Israel to be stronger than it is currently, the Palestinians must be made correspondingly weaker necessarily. Moreover, Dershowitz's observations say nothing to his earlier observation in January 2007 that, "making peace is the mark of a great leader."[25] More curious, is that these statements detract from a reality that speaks to an Israel that is highly-militarized, armed with nuclear weapons, with a perceived right to use cluster bombs against a civilian population;[26] is fully supported in every way by the US with deep pockets and a Europe committed to recompense as a means to salvaging its collective conscience. Moreover, Israel, as noted by its Prime Minister in December 2006, is more than able to defend itself against all enemies; and that while there is no desire for war with Syria, "that doesn't mean conditions are ripe for us to negotiate with them."[27] But, according to the ISG, "the US will not be able to achieve its goals in the Middle East unless the US deals directly with the Arab–Israeli conflict." Additionally, the embattled British Prime Minister Blair sees a restart of peace talks by his initiative as an opportunity to rescue his legacy, from a geopolitical perspective that is.

Peace from an Arab Perspective

From an Arab perspective, however, according to King Abdullah II of Jordan, the continued occupation of the West Bank and the Gaza by Israel, "is perceived as one of the great injustices of the past several decades" and that, "Israel must decide between being a fortress nation or having peace and security with its neighbors", that is, "whether or not it believes in a two-state solution." If it does not believe in a two-state solution, according to King Abdullah II, "there will never be an ability for us Arabs to create the framework to have peace with them unless we solve the future of the Palestinians."[28]

While not surprising, it is equally interesting that Palestinian refugees in Egypt, Jordan, and Lebanon are referred to as "exiles" by Israel and the US. The reason, of course, is that in addition to taking the focus off Israel's occupation, Jordan, Egypt, and Lebanon are recipients of US foreign aid and as such are expected to accommodate Palestinians who were evacuated in preparation for war with Israel in 1948 (see Feldman 1978) and who clearly would not be allowed to return to their homes in Israel for the reasons given above. Even then, there are refugee camps in the Gaza and the West Bank, the conditions of which are regarded as "ghetto like" by three visiting German bishops one of whom remarked, "I never thought I would have to see something like this ever again in my life"[29]; but no clamor for UN peacekeepers or United Nations High Commissioner for Refugees (UNHCR) presence by the international community. Of course, the director of the Holocaust memorial was "appalled and surprised" by the comments.[30] Yet, years earlier, before the six-day war in 1967, before Hamas, before Hezbollah, before bin Laden, Arendt in 1948 and Ardrey (1966: 309) made the observation that the Israelis were no different in their brutality against the Arabs who, as shown earlier, were accommodating of them throughout the centuries. These accounts of history while they may be ignored are beyond rewrites however inconvenient they may be to some.

A second reason perhaps is the idea of a Palestine state in "a confederation with Jordan" (Thatcher 1995: 374) as still a possibility. Jordan, it should be remembered had administrative responsibility for the West Bank before the Six Day War in 1967.

Israel–Lebanon War

In addition to the road blocks to peace mentioned above, Prime Minister Olmert's unilateral withdrawal from the Gaza which was fully supported by Mr. Bush as part of the strategy for the Middle East is seen by many observers as a major strategic blunder for both governments. But more telling was the failure of the Israeli military assault on Lebanon on July 12, 2006 which, again, had the nod and support of the US President who was shown clearly as refusing to call for a halt to hostilities in the expectation that Israel would be able to destroy Hezbollah in short order, the televised "Yo Blair!" *faux pas*, if you will. As noted by President Carter: "For five weeks, the United States government strongly supported Israel, encouraged their bombardment of Lebanon, and blocked the efforts of France and other nations to impose an immediate cease fire" (Carter 2006: 200). Recall, also, Mr. Bush's grand but unsubstantiated assertion: "Hezbollah started this war and Hezbollah was defeated."

Another reality that goes to the credibility of the Bush administration assertions is that, in an Israeli poll taken at the end of December 2006 and reported on by the *BBC*, 50 percent of Israelis polled says Mr. Olmert has no integrity, while over 75 percent sees him as having no leadership skills, and an equal percentage blames him for the results of the Israel–Lebanon conflict. Indeed, Mr. Olmert has since recognized his unpopularity and call for his resignation and that of the Minister of Defense Amin Peretz following the resignation of General Dan Halutz, Army Chief of Staff.[31]

What is more damaging to the Bush administration is the allegation as reported by Seymour Hersh of the *New Yorker Magazine* that: "Israel had devised a plan for attacking Hezbollah, and shared it with Bush administration officials, well before July 12." This revelation lends support to the theory that the invasion of Lebanon was part of the US grand strategy described earlier, whereby for its support in bringing Middle East oil reserves under US control Israel would be allowed to move on Lebanon as part of its dream of re-establishing the kingdom of Israel. Evidence Mr. Olmert's declaration of war not on Hezbollah but on Lebanon:

> I want to make clear that the event this morning is not a terror act but an act of a sovereign state that attacked Israel without reason. The government of Lebanon, of which Hezbollah is a part, is trying to shake the stability of the region.

The pretext for the war was, of course, the killing of three Israeli soldiers and the capturing of two others by Hezbollah (see also Carter 2006: 198). Curiously, a month earlier Israel kidnapped a Hezbollah official in Lebanon. Hezbollah's offer for a prisoner exchange was rejected by Mr. Olmert, much to the surprise of Hezbollah's leader Nasrullah.

There are, of course, denials from the Israeli government as well as from the Bush administration to Hersh's assertion. Suffice it to say that in the context of *realpolitik*, "Presidents [and Prime Ministers] lie."[32] However, any doubts about tacit US approval should be dispelled by the shuttling between Tel Aviv and Washington: Like clock work, there was always a "visit" by Olmert that foretells some kind of action either in Palestine, such as building a wall and launching an attack on Gaza in June 2006, or in Lebanon, such as, again, launching an all-out attack that killed over 1000 Lebanese many of whom were civilians. Equally interesting is that, not six months after launching an unrelenting and indiscriminate attack on Gaza in June 2006 at a cost of several Palestinian lives, Mr. Olmert should now find in the Israeli military the capability to target rocket launchers with "pin-point" accuracy in both the West Bank and Gaza. These revelations speak to the level to which territoriality is deterministic and the importance of condign power in asymmetrical relationships.

Financial Support

It is interesting that Hannah Arendt should have been concerned about Israel's dependency on financial support from American Jewry to fund its large expenditure on national defense:

> If the Israeli government cannot win its economic independence from such money it will soon find itself in the unenviable position of being forced to create emergencies, that is, forced into a policy of aggressiveness and expansion (Feldman, 1978: 39).

Prior to breaking with Zionism, Arendt was concerned that the result of an uneasy Armistice—which still defines Arab–Israel relationship to date—rather than a peace agreement would compel an Israel that focuses its entire energy on self-defense, with the likelihood that, "political thought would center around military strategy; economic development would be determined by the needs of war" (Feldman 1978: 187) which clearly are being financed by the US. Given that about one-fifth of US aid goes to Israel (see Chapter Four), the question whether it serves the economic and security interests of Israel to brand any dissident group a terrorist organization so as to maintain the flow of foreign aid from the US for fighting terrorism is not without merit in the light of Arendt's observation.

Needless to say Arendt's assertions have been vehemently disputed.[33] Be that as it may, Arendt assertions border on the prophetic.

US and European Aid

According to Mearsheimer and Walt:

> Since the October War in 1973, Washington has provided Israel with a level of support dwarfing that given to any other state. It has been the largest annual recipient of direct economic and military assistance since 1976, and is the largest recipient in total since World War Two, to the tune of well over $140 billion (in 2004 dollars) ... one-fifth of total US aid budget every year. [34]

Indeed, in August 2007 the Bush administration announced a US$30.0 billion aid package for Israel over the next ten years. It is US$10.0 billion more than the package announced for the Gulf States which as noted earlier includes arms for Saudi Arabia. Interestingly, while no adverse comment was voiced for the Israel package which has been approved, many in Congress are opposed to the arms package for Saudi Arabia, and thus speak to Mearsheimer and Walt's contention.

As revealed in a *BBC World Service* report on December 13, 2006, the Israeli Prime Minister has at long last implicitly acknowledged that Israel possesses nuclear weapons, despite its silence and that of the US and the Europeans over the years. Clearly, this revelation comes on the heels of the challenge by the Iranian President to the facts surrounding the "Holocaust" and his reiteration of what is regarded as threatening the existence of Israel. More revealing is that France is alleged to have built the nuclear reactor in Israel whilst the UK provided the plutonium in 1967 as part of their respective aid package to Israel.

The use of American-made and supplied bunker-busting and cluster bombs by Israel in largely civilian-populated areas of Lebanon is yet another example of compensatory power exercised by the US. Israel takes the responsibility for their use whilst the US takes the benefits from their use. In a seemingly act of desperation to inflict as much damage as possible before the cease-fire took effect, Israel resorted to the use of cluster bombs in largely civilian areas while those who have the power to put an end to the carnage buys times for their de facto wedge in the Westernization process. Indeed, that these bombs were US made did nothing for the credibility of the Bush administration, especially when as noted earlier Israel used US-made cluster bombs in its war on Lebanon in 1982.

Conclusion

That the Arab–Israel conflict should be included in this book is only to provide evidential support to the proposition that the territorial imperative is deterministic and that the foreign policy of the US supported by the West with respect to the Middle East is by design in keeping with the overarching grand strategy to contain China as driven by the territorial imperative; it is not to advance any one position.

The above said the debate of the issues rages on and is unlikely to reach an acceptable conclusion until those in power come to the realization that reasonable compromise is the language of diplomacy, if such were to enter the language of the territorial imperative. Indeed, some might even argue that what is required is a framework that consciously avoids absolutisms and is amenable to accommodating "difference" within a political system that is cognizant of history and loosely constructed on the principle of democracy and freedom, bearing in mind that "choice" is central to both, and that, in the long run, Arabs and Jews must arrive at their own peace agreement without either side dependent on some outside power for protection. In this connection, recognizing that giving voice to those victimized by the logic of the status quo not only is preferable to conversion by way of the bomb, but could prove foundational to a lasting peace in the Middle East, albeit the most difficult proposition for the dominant voices to accept almost six decades into the struggle for an all-Jewish state in all of Palestine.

Strangely enough, these sentiments were expressed by Hannah Arendt decades ago (Feldman 1978: 37). In this regard, the pain felt by every Israeli family for the loss of a single life should not be minimized but rather for the sake of our common humanity be recognized as ten fold for the Palestinian and Lebanese people, for there are at least ten times as many Palestinian and Lebanese families whose mourning as human beings is indistinguishable from that of the Israeli family. Not to recognize this is to squander the opportunity to prove to the world that as a people of the book the Jews are not only deserving of their return to the Promised Land but also are willing to share their intellectualism, their discipline, and their many unrivalled achievements honed over the centuries in exile. Not to recognize this as the ultimate in human achievement is to be no different from those who in earlier times believed in and promoted the notion of a hierarchy of man. The alternative, as we are obliquely yet poignantly reminded by King Abdullah II of Jordan, is a condition of enduring insecurity. Indeed, while it is incumbent upon the Arabs to recognize Israel's right to exist, it is equally incumbent upon Israel to disavow the propositions of the *Baltimore Program* and the *Atlantic City Resolution.* It is perhaps this realization for mutual retraction of extremist narratives that now compels a return to "shuttle diplomacy" previously rejected by Secretary of State Rice. In this regard, former British Prime Minister Blair and now Middle East Envoy has the unenviable task of creating a framework for peace that is free from the baggage accumulated over five decades. In this is connection, it is ironic that a former British Prime Minister should have the task of finding a lasting peace 60 years after the Mandate for Palestine was relinquished by Britain in turmoil. With this in mind, it is perhaps better for one to read history rather than talk history.

NOTES

1 "Israeli leaders rush to war", *BBC News*, 30 April, 2007, http://news.bbc.co.uk/go/pr/fr/-/2/hi/middle_east/6608649.stm
2 Mearsheimer J., and Walt, S., "The Israel Lobby", *London Review of Books, Vol. 28, No 6.* 23 March, 2006.
3 Mearsheimer, J., Walt, S., "The Israel Lobby" Letters, *The London Review of Books, Vol. 28, No. 9*, 11 May, 2006.
4 Mearsheimer J., and Walt, S., "The Israel Lobby", *London Review of Books, Vol. 28, No 6.*, 23 March, 2006.
5 Mearsheimer, J., Walt, S., "The Israel Lobby" Letters, *The London Review of Books, Vol. 28, No. 9*, 11 May, 2006.
6 Dershowitz, A., "The Israel Lobby", Letters, *The London Review of Books, Vol. 28 No. 8*, 20 April, 2006
7 Oliver, M., and Tempest, M., "Blair: Blame me for BAE", *Guardian Unlimited*, http://www.guardian.co.uk/baefiles/story/0,,2102023,00.html#article_continue, June 13, 2007
8 Mearsheimer J., and Walt, S., "The Israel Lobby", *London Review of Books, Vol. 28, No 6*, 23 March, 2006.
9 "Israel's UN Ambassador slams Qatar, praises U.S. envoy Bolton", *Reuters*, informationclearinghouse.info/article13161.htm, May 23, 2006
10 Statistics provided by Peace Now, *National Public Radio*, March 11, 2007
11 Raviv, M., "1967 Arab-Israel War, Israeli Diplomacy", *C-SPAN2*, June 4, 2007
12 "Gaza offence 'disproportionate'", *BBC NEWS*, July 25, 2006.
13 Everts, S., and Grant, C., "Blair can unlock the Middle East impasse", *The Financial Times*, August 18, 2004, p. 17.
14 "Israel-Palestine Conflict", Palestine Center, *C-SPAN2*, January 29, 2007
15 Entous, A., "Olmert reaches out to Saudis over peace plan", http://news.yahoo.com/s/nm/20070330/wl_nm/israel_arabs_dc
16 "Debate on Iraq and the Middle East", British House of Commons, *C-SPAN*, 24 January, 2007

17 Interview by Jim Lehrer, "News Hour", *PBS.org*, 7 March, 2007
18 Carter, J., "In Depth" , *Book TV C-SPAN* , December 3, 2006
19 Interview by Jim Lehrer, "News Hour", *PBS.org*, 7 March, 2007
20 "Saudis seek Palestinian dialogue", *BBC NEWS*, 28 January, 2007
21 BBC News, *BBC World Service*, 20 March, 2007
22 BBC News, *BBC World Service*, 27 February, 2007
23 "Mosaic", *WXEL*, www.WXEL.org , March 1, 2007
24 Inskeep, S., "Morning Edition", *National Public Radio*, http://www.npr.org/templates/transcript/transcript.php?storyId=11007437
25 Address by Dershowitz, Brandies University, 23 January, 2007
26 The use of cluster bombs in the later stages of the Israel assault on southern Lebanon was not the first time such bombs were used. In 1982, Israel used US made and provided cluster bombs in Southern Lebanon, prompting President Reagan to impose a six year ban on the supply of such bombs to it.
27 "Israel rejects Iraq study ideas", *BBC NEWS*, http://news.bbc.co.uk/go/pr/fr/2/hi/middle_east/6217656.stm (2006/12/07)
28 Interview by Jim Lehrer, "News Hour", *PBS.org*, March 6, 2007
29 "German bishops rile Holocaust memorial", http://news.yahoo.com/s/ap/20070310/ap_on_re_mi_ea/israel_germany_bishops
30 Ibid
31 Anidjar, P, "Unpopular Israeli PM in fight to survive", http://news.yahoo.com/s/afp/20070316/wl_mideast_afp/mideastisraelpolitics_070316113128
32 Wilentz, P. "Tribute to Historian Arthur Schlesinger", *C-SPAN*, November 27, 2006
33 See Dershowitz, A., "The Israel Lobby", Letters, *The London Review of Books, Vol. 28 No. 8*, 20 April, 2006
34 Mearshimer, J. and Walt, S., "The Israel Lobby", *The London Review of Books, Vol. 28, No.6*, 23 March, 2006

Part Six

The Peace Imperative

Chapter Ten

Universalizing Peace through Acceptance of "Other"

Introduction

As revealed in the preceding chapters, territoriality is a defining characteristic of human interaction; with condign, compensatory, and conditioned powers instruments to a global relationship predicated on order. Territoriality has been at the center of conquests and empires past; and permeates existing institutional frameworks that regulate economic and political relationships between states in an interstate system that is reflective of the relative power of international actors. Hence, as can readily be discerned from the account of experience, only the rhetoric has changed over time. The underlying objective of order remains unchanged, and depending upon the nature of the countervailing response will elicit condign power as the disciplinary mechanism exercised either in consort with others of like mind or unilaterally. Therefore, Thucydides' observation that the strong will do what it will and the weak what it must continues to have currency in the twenty-first century. However, if, as observed by John Gaddis (2003: 156), the twentieth century ended, "as far as US foreign policy was concerned, very differently from the way it began", so too must be the hope for the twenty-first century, absent the trauma of the intervening years that characterized most of the twentieth century.

Even as this manuscript goes to print, the controversy over the invasion of Iraq in March 2003 pursuant the Bush doctrine of preemption rages on while Americans pay with their lives—over 3,800 at the time of writing, with many still in their teens—and thousands more with missing limbs and post-traumatic stress disorder. All, for a policy the effects of which this and future generations will likely have to endure just because of the convergence of a perceived threat and opportunity: the "serving current" from the perspective of neoconservatives and dreamers who have hijacked the political process at the turn of the century and whose ambitions are perceived rooted in the notion of empire, as former Russian president Mikhail Gorbachev charged, and former Speaker of the US House of Representative Newt Gingrich unabashedly acknowledges separately.

Interested Perspectives

Frighteningly, despite the failed Bush doctrine of preemption and prevention, many continue to defend it stridently and with passion. All have argued from the perspective of perceived hatred for Americans by Muslims by way of *ex-post* rationalization to validate their perverse policy preferences predicated on remaking the Middle East and of reinstituting a world order predicated on power. In this connection Robert Kaufman's arguments are particularly telling. He argues, for example, that preemption is a necessary strategy because there is inherent hatred for Americans, that is, there are terrorists, "who seek to destroy us not for what we have done but for who we are"—whatever that means but clearly evidencing the "schizophrenic self"—and, therefore, he continues, "we need to attack them before they attack us." Moreover, according to Kaufman:

> After 9/11, we don't have stability and the search for stability is an illusion.... The issue is not whether there will be change in the Middle East but what direction the change will take.... President Bush has wisely and courageously decided to take a proactive role in shaping that change by necessity, not utopian impulses. By the convergence of threat and opportunity, he is pushing it in a benign rather than a destructive direction.[1]

Kaufman's implicit rejection of the notion that what we do often defines who we are is particularly instructive from the perspective of perversity. On the other hand, according to Hannah Arendt (1952), to live in a society where rights are upheld, is to be judged by one's actions and opinions. As such, many would argue that if the terrorists do indeed hate who we are (whoever "we" is) then it is because of what we have done from being who we have become, which is even more despicable because of attempts to pervert the US Constitution which defines who we are.

Kaufman notwithstanding, there is overwhelming recognition if not agreement that the stationing of US military in Saudi Arabia was a contributing factor if not the primary reasons for 9/11. For example, in arguing against Mearsheimer and Walt's assertion that the Israel Lobby influences US foreign policy, Alan Dershowitz countered:

> In fact, bin Laden was primarily motivated by the presence of American troops in Saudi Arabia. Saudi Arabia, recall, had asked the United States to defend the Arabian Peninsula against Iraqi aggression prior to the first Gulf War. So it was America's ties to and defense of an Arab state—from which 15 of the 19 9/11 hijackers originated—and not the Jewish state, that most clearly precipitated the events of 11 September 2001.[2]

There are countless others who have come to the same conclusion, including *Hudson Institute* Senior Fellow Hillel Fradkin who referred to the stationing of

American troops in Saudi Arabia as a probable cause of the terrorist act on 9/11.[3]

It is equally interesting that Kaufman should consider the implementation of the Bush doctrine in the Middle East as "benign" rather than "destructive." The *Oxford dictionary* defines benign as: "1, genial and kindly. 2 favorable; not harmful." Destructive, on the other hand is defined as: "1 causing destruction. 2 tending to refute or disparage; negative and unhelpful." Hence, to remotely suggest that the Bush Middle East policy and rhetoric are benign and not destructive is to live in a parallel universe or worse still to be guilty of blatant dehumanization of another, that is, to deny others the "right to have rights" (see Arendt, 1952). Fortunately for the world, as indicated by the recent polls on the popularity of their respective leaders in the US and Israel, 70 percent of Americans and 90 percent of Israelis find the perspective of Kaufman and others of similar persuasion unacceptable if not repulsive.

Clearly, we in the West live in a world of discrete perspectives in the twenty-first century; all informed and compelling for their respective audiences; all competing with one another for national recognition; few transcending the enticement of self-interest; with fewer still holistic in analysis in consequence of the limited attention span given to any issue and to the high place specialization holds in American political and economic thought.

In playing to their respective audiences, however, those in positions of power and influence, including the popular news media, wittingly or unwittingly engage in the psychology of language games, often sacrificing fundamental principles and, more importantly, truth, in support of interested view points. But, as the Librarian of Congress, James Billington counsels:

> If you want to reach the unimagined question and learn to accept the unwelcome answer, you have got to get back into books; and you have to get back into developing the qualities of judgment, wisdom, and imagination that is internally generated and not defined by somebody else's picture on the screen.[4]

At the foreign policy making level, there is a tendency for American policymakers to arrogate to themselves everything that is good and virtuous while approaching other cultures with ignorance, arrogance, and disdain. As a result, "WWW" is a constant in foreign policy statements, discourses, and commentaries. The WWW in this instance is not an acronym for the "World Wide Web" with which most if not all are familiar; rather it is: What We Want. Almost every statement of or on foreign policy is prefaced with WWW: what we want the Iraqis to do ...; what we want the Pakistanis to do ...; what we want the Palestinians to do ...; what we want the North Koreans to do …, and so on. But a foreign policy predicated on what we want is by definition a contradiction of "freedom", the mantra of President Bush; indeed, it is nothing less than a denial of the freedom of choice or the right to have rights.

In consequence of taking the WWW approach, those in authority consider themselves endowed with the moral authority to act preemptively; to be judge, jury, and executioner. With such a mindset, they are prone to commit errors in judgment and disclose weaknesses that never were as consequential as they are today: the unknown unknowns, if you will, as evident in the conflicts in the Middle East and by the heuristic quality of the Bush administration's policy. In this connection, it is particularly instructive that Retired Lt. General Ricardo Sanchez should consider the planned invasion and occupation of Iraq as "unrealistically optimistic and catastrophically flawed." That:

> There is no question that America is living a nightmare with no end in sight.... The administration, Congress, and the entire inter-agencies, especially the State Department, must shoulder the responsibility for this catastrophic failure and the American people must hold them accountable.[5]

Clearly, as is being played out in the Middle East, game-theoretic models that are grounded in Western ideology are often incapable of estimating with the degree of certainty necessary to understanding the motivating forces behind countervailing actions of the foe who have largely escaped the Westernization process. Such models often fail primarily because there is no Western model to accurately predict the territorial imperative at a basic level; and defeat of the enemy, the desired outcome, effectively informs input: "Shock and Awe", for example. In this construction, weaknesses resulting from being inattentive to the value system of the wider world and an over-emphasis on winning, a discernible personality trait inculcated at prestigious tertiary American institutions are revealed. With such mind-set, we are our own worst enemy; and rather than attract rightly-deserved admiration for the many good things that are American, we elicit distrust and contempt, yes, for what we have momentarily become; not for "who we are" fundamentally.

A Paradigm Shift

As articulated by Republican Representative Ron Paul: "We need a humble but strong foreign policy.... We cannot go around the world telling other people how to live."[6] Clearly, Congressman Paul has in mind a paradigm shift in current US foreign policy: one that is design to win back the trust, respect, and silent authority once the exclusive domain of America after World War II. While these views are shared by Republican Senator Chuck Hagel and several others from both sides of the political divide and from without, there are others whose disdain for "difference" are hardly contained in discourses and debates at the highest level—such is their perception of a full sea and a serving current—and, therefore, should be recognized for their destructive rhetoric. Even then, there is a glimmer of hope: the consequences of the Bush doctrine in the Middle East could be made to serve as the basis for constructing a peace paradigm that recognizes the need for accommodating "difference" in a pluralist global society, and for avoiding the extremists within. It is what real freedom is all about. Moreover, democracy requires that the will of the majority be respected: nationally, by a change in policy as demanded by the people—as evidenced by national polls or by referendum where allowed—and internationally, by adhering to established covenants, and not be flouted by reason of being a superpower.

"Ethical" or "Moral"?

The necessity for President Bush to accommodate if not to play to a particular constituent demonstrates well the risks of becoming philosophically inconsistent when issues are treated discretely, devoid of any consideration of the implications for other policies equally discretely derived, with their own rationalization and ethical underpinnings. For example, in vetoing for the second time the Embryonic Stem Cell Research Bill (247–176) Mr. Bush spoke of the need to uphold "the sanctity of human life." According to the president, "destroying human life in the hopes of saving human life is not ethical ... and it is not the only option."[7] Many would wholeheartedly agree with the sentiments expressed by the president. However, on closer analysis, it is instructive that "ethical" and not "moral" was the choice of adjective since the latter would call into question policies that have resulted in hundreds of thousands of lives taken since March 2003. But, then, the constituents were different, such is the contradiction of politics as we know it.

The irony in the Bush administration's expression of indignation at the thought of destroying a human embryo whilst willing to have children of foreign lands killed and maimed as collateral damage, ostensibly to save American lives sometime in the future but in reality in support of hegemony, is inescapable to all but the power mongers and opportunists; and speaks to the need for a paradigm shift in policymaking: from the discrete to the holistic; from the selfish to the humane; from doing order to doing right. Some would argue that the issues are entirely different: that one is about the ethical values of Americans while the other is all about preventing the smoking gun coming in the form of a mushroom cloud which the Iraqis were bent on perpetrating by seeking uranium from Niger, according to the Bush team, that is. Others seek to rationalize the philosophical inconsistency that defines the Bush narrative on the spurious notion of the existence of a bunch of men in cave planning to establish a caliphate from India to Iberia, as if we were back in the Dark or Middle Ages. But such differentiation even if it were remotely valid leads inevitably to the conclusion that in terms of the value system of the Bush administration, the value of a life is relative.

But a life is a life, whether it is white, black, brown, yellow, blue or green; whether it is American, British, French, Chinese, Israeli, Arab, or African; whether rich or poor; or whether it is Christian, Muslim, Jew or other. This is the reality of a pluralist world in the twenty-first century. This is the reality in which our children and grandchildren were born into and with which the Bush administration will have to come to terms to be credible in the eyes of the majority of Americans and the rest of the world, and indeed posterity, rewrites of history notwithstanding. Strangely enough, America has been down this road before. In 1967, for example, referring to the Vietnam War Senator Robert Kennedy asked: "Do we have the right here in the United States to say we are going to kill tens of thousands, make millions refugee, as we have; kill women and children, as we have?" Once again Americans must address that fundamental question. Robert Kennedy's answer was: "I seriously question whether we have that right." Then as now, most Americans seriously question whether they have.

The Geopolitical Challenge

From a geopolitical perspective, there is a perceived decay in the geopolitical solidarity in the West since the demise of the Soviet Union; and this might be of grave concern to the US who perceives the need for yet another binding agent to support the military industrial complex upon which American prosperity was built and continues to depend. Indeed, since 1992 the EU has been pursuing its own political and economic interests, during which time many of its members have found themselves free to be critical of the US and even to ignore America's leadership on many international issues: Iraq for example. But for the US who has become accustomed to being the leader of the West since World War II such state of affairs could signal the need for renewal of solidarity against a common foe. Perhaps the first to recognize this symptom was Mikhail Gorbachev who in the mid1990s expressed the view that, "America needs an enemy." In this context some might be tempted to regard Mr. Bush's war on terror as an attempt at therapy.

While there might be some validity in Gorbachev's prognosis, the Bush administration, having earlier consigned diplomacy to the trash heap in favor of preemption, is visibly struggling to fully come to terms with the new reality in diplomacy; that is, it has yet to learn that approaches which portray philosophical inconsistency have no currency in a world of instant knowledge and information transfer: not in America and certainly not around the world except perhaps in those states seemingly beholden to the US; and even then there is no certainty.

Prior to the internet as a primary means in the transfer of information, knowledge, and ideas, it was relatively safe for politicians and diplomats to engage in the fine art of being long on rhetoric and short on specifics, with several cleverly devised points of exist. Today, however, ordinary citizens around the world have become better informed and are able to recognize relatively easy the shallowness and ever-widening credibility gap in the pronouncements of policymakers. It is what derives activism at every G-8 meetings and WTO trade conferences; it is what informs resistance to universalizing self-serving notions.

With respect to the Israel–Palestine issue, it speaks to the notion of philosophical inconsistency that Olmert should speak of humanitarian concern for Palestinians while being partially responsible for orchestrating a humanitarian crisis in the first place. Not only has he withheld taxes collected on behalf of the Palestinian government on the election of Hamas in January 2006 but also sought to block others from providing humanitarian aid. Also, in addition to arresting Hamas parliamentarians and cabinet ministers as officials responsible for acts of violence committed by splinter groups of Fatah,[8] the Israeli air force was seen acting in behalf of Fatah by degrading Hamas positions in Gaza during the fierce fighting between Fatah and Hamas in early June 2007. These military actions continue after Hamas seized control of the Gaza and Mr. Olmert has once again visited with Mr. Bush and arguably received support for his plans.[9] Be that as it may, Mr. Olmert, it should be clearly understood, is acting in the interests of Israel and his actions as such evidence Israel's territorial imperative.

But, Mr. Olmert is not alone in his overt support for an all-Fatah Palestinian government. The US and EU have played their part by freezing aid to the Palestinians while Hamas remained in control of the Palestinian Parliament and government. In addition, the US reportedly provided financial and military support to Fatah following Secretary Rice's meeting with Palestinian president Abbas in Jordan in December 2006. To the majority of observers, these external interventions are clearly contrary to the notion of freedom and democracy, especially at a time when bringing freedom and democracy has been offered as one of the reasons, albeit ex post, for the invasion of Iraq. But, like Israel, the US is also manifesting its territorial imperative.

But despite the dismissal of the Hamas-majority cabinet and the appointment of an emergency Cabinet acceptable to Israel, the US, and the EU, and the partial resumption of aid to the PLO-led government, the fundamental issue of settlements—and their protection—in the West Bank, as former Israeli negotiator Daniel Levy points out, remains. Moreover, both Levy and former US State Department official Dennis Ross see the inclusion of Hamas as necessary to arriving at a durable peace: Whilst Levy envisages a "power-sharing" arrangement with Hamas, Ross foresees some form of "triangular approach" without legitimizing Hamas.[10] What is more, irrespective of their political colors Palestinians are still suspicious of Israel. As several analysts have pointed out, most notably Robert Malley, Middle East Program Director of the *International Crisis Group*, there have been opportunities for Olmert to work with Abbas before.[11] Hence, despite Olmert's rhetoric of working with the new Palestinian Cabinet, which he regards as a "genuine partner"[12] many would recall his widely-reported offer on November 27, 2006 to release Palestinian prisoners "even those who have been sentenced to lengthy terms" for "Gilad Shalit's [the Israeli soldier captured by the Palestinians in June 2006] release and his return safe and sound to his family", and to dismantle many settlement in the occupied West Bank to bring about "real peace", as he puts it. Recall, also, Mr. Olmert was deemed to have no credibility in Israel and that they were calls for his resignation including by the Israeli Foreign Minister. Not surprisingly, then, as reportedly remarked by Mr. Abbas's national security chief, Mohammad Dahlan: "Israel is releasing money not because they are honorable but they just want to entrench the divide between the West Bank and Gaza."[13]

Given this obvious disconnection between rhetoric and reality it is a curiosity that, rather than seek to narrow the credibility gap many politicians continue to engage in philosophical inconsistency. In the US for example, whilst the official line of the Bush administration is for a peaceful solution to the Israel–Palestine conflict, based on the evidence it is abundantly clear to the world that the Bush administration has lost its standing as an honest broker in the Middle East, especially in the Israeli–Palestinian issue.

Beyond the Middle East

Beside the Middle East, even when Mr. Bush tries to portray the US as a superpower concerned about poverty in developing countries, and about the environment, his administration's self-interested agenda precedes him. In this regard, Mr. Bush's 2007 Latin American trip was not only ill-planned and ill-informed but also unsuccessful. For example, while the Bush team was promoting the "year of engagement"[14] and Mr. Bush was talking-up US aid to the region, the Congress was debating the administration's proposed reduction for fiscal year 2008 to the existing US$1.4 billion aid package, of which US$567 million is allocated to Columbia to eradicate cocaine production and trafficking. Moreover, when compared with the US$3.0 billion a year foreign aid to Israel of which approximately 25 percent is for military expenditure[15]—the equivalent of all the humanitarian aid to Latin America—Mr. Bush's expression of concern for human lives rings hollow to those who are closely examining US foreign policy, a process that seems to be sadly lacking in the White House. Such inconsistencies provide fodder for America's detractors such as Venezuela's president Hugo Chavez, Iran's Ahmadinejad, and Zimbabwe's Mugabe. With respect to Zimbabwe's policy towards white farmers, some supporters of Robert Mugabe find drawing a parallel with Israel's policy towards Arab–Palestinians irresistible.

With respect to the environment, to many observers the Bush administration is seen as engaging in double-speak: Concern for the environment is predicated essentially on protecting the troubled American economy. To this end, Mr. Bush has included China and India in his rhetoric, knowing full well that neither would agree to the European proposal for fixed cuts in carbon emission.[16] Indeed, the Chinese who are opposed to fixed targets while lauding Mr. Bush's proposal as "a positive change," agree with the Europeans for a single policy.[17] Nonetheless, the Chinese and Indians already are suspicious that the Bush administration is seeking to unfairly spread the burden of carbon emissions reductions in ways that would slow their economic growth, and have articulated their respective positions, drawing attention to where the historical responsibility should be placed.[18]

China's Normative Power

As shown in Chapter Five, the Chinese economy is growing at a rapid pace not because its currency is undervalued but because of its abundant supply of labor which it makes available to FIEs interested in investing in China. In this connection, China's trade surplus with the US does not operate to the full benefit of the Chinese economy as many policymakers and analysts are wont to believe. Indeed, China runs a trade deficit on a consolidated basis. In other words, China's actual trade surplus with the US is but a minor proportion of its total world trade after discounting the activities of the FIEs. More than that, the Chinese economy is more integrated into the world economy by the policy initiatives of the Chinese government than US policymakers and others fully realize. In this regard, it is particularly interesting that James Fallows of the *Atlantic Monthly* magazine found that for every US$1,000.00 item produced in China by an American firm only about US$100.00 remain with the Chinese; the balance of US$900.00 goes to the US company doing business in China.[19] Hence, it would be foolhardy for US policymakers to take a simplistic and wholly self-interested bilateral approach to its trade relations with China without fully understanding the implications of their actions for the world economy and indeed for the US economy.

According to *Johns Hopkins University's* David Lampton (2005: 317), China's "normative power" is growing in consequence of a posture that speaks to "economic engagement, security assurances, opposing superpower domination, championing a level playing field for developing countries and being economically successful." This perspective is shared by John Ghazvinian whose account of the African experience speaks of a "Beijing Consensus" which stands in contrast with the *Washington Consensus* of the 1980s and 1990s that speaks to private-public partnerships and liberalization of economies in developing countries[20] (see also Ghazvinian 2007). It is a posture that resonates with many in Asia and the developing world, and one that contrasts most strikingly with the Bush doctrine of preemption and the archaic core-periphery paradigm that heretofore served the developed Western economies; one that is more likely to be embraced as the more acceptable of the two by an informed Third World. It is also a posture that is grounded not in communism as we know it but rather in Taoism:

> Cultivated in the individual, Virtue will become genuine;
> Cultivated in the family, Virtue will become abundant;
> Cultivated in the village, Virtue will multiply;
> Cultivated in the state, Virtue will prosper;
> Cultivated in the world, Virtue will become universal. ("Lao tse, The Book of Tao")

Notwithstanding this contrast in approaches which many Chinese emphasize, Chinese officials contrary to the administration's rhetoric regard the US as the world's sole superpower and a source of advance technology and, of course, market for its products. Hence, according to Zhang and Tang (2005), China's power diplomacy is oriented necessarily towards the US and to the region thereafter. Even so, China's posture on championing a level playing field for developing countries and opposing superpower domination has brought it criticisms from the West who, having written off over US$40.0 billion of Third World debt, believe that there should be some strings attached to Chinese aid to developing countries. But from the Chinese and indeed developing countries' perspectives, there needs to be a paradigm shift with respect to foreign aid: from the long-established core–periphery framework to one fully supportive of sustainable development.

From Condign Power to Compensatory Power

The above said, while the West is exercising its condign power with respect to Iran's refusal to suspend uranium enrichment, there is overwhelming evidence that condign power today could be replaced by compensatory power tomorrow. The case of North Korea discussed in Chapter Four stands in evidence. Indeed, it is worth noting that Ambassador Christopher Hill now not only speaks of establishing "bilateral US–PRK working group" with a country that was not too long ago labeled one of the "Axis of evil" but also holds out the possibility for "cross-recognition and normalization" as an end-game issue for 2008.[21]

In addition to North Korea, the case of Libya also stands in evidence of what could happen if a country gives up its nuclear ambitions and belligerency. Libya is now well on its way to benefiting from Western investments and in the fullness of time is likely to be treated as an important trading partner of the West. This said it needs to recognize that the door was not slam shut to Libya despite its belligerency. It remains to be seen whether the same would be true for Iran. Recall, both North Korea and the US went through a period of hurling insults at each other before coming to the realization that they both needed to make a shift in their respective perspectives.

The Geo-economics Challenge

In addition to philosophical inconsistency in the geopolitical arena, adjusting to a condition of diminishing marginal returns is equally challenging to the West in general and to the US in particular. Indeed, one of the challenges arising from China's normative power goes to the root of classical economic doctrine, that is, Adam Smith's invisible hand of the market. Since it was first articulated in 1776, theories have been constructed upholding the power of individualism in economic affairs; to the point where it has become *sine qua non* for the capitalist economic system, with economic determinism the inevitable outcome.

The West rode the train of abundance, building institutions in recognition and support of its Promethean will to conquer the environment and non-Western peoples whilst its citizens compete with one another in the "endless accumulation of capital"; reinforcing the notion of individualism in the process, neither knowing nor caring how much they affect the public good, as evidenced by global warming. Few paid attention to the fact that Adam Smith's observations were just that: observations of eighteen-century man on the verge of one of man's greatest achievements in an essentially abundant and un-spoilt world, the Industrial Revolution. Indeed, Smith's invisible hand of the market was an inevitable conclusion which unfortunately has been largely misinterpreted to be prescriptive, the consequences of which the world is only now beginning to experience. In other words, the law of diminishing marginal returns is beginning to manifest in the several economic indicators in the advanced industrialized economies, thus forcing them to return to less benign means of interaction with the resource-rich countries and potential competitors, as discussed in the preceding chapters and above.

But besides observing the invisible hand of the market, Adam Smith also made this unheralded observation:

> In the restraint upon the importation of all foreign commodities which can come into competition with those of our own growth, or manufacture, the interest of the home-consumer is evidently sacrificed to that of the producer. It is all to the benefit of the latter, that the former is obliged to pay that enhancement of price which this monopoly almost always occasions.

Based on this passage from Adam Smith's *Wealth of Nations*, it should be clear that those who are inclined to protectionism do so not to benefit the American consumer but rather to serve their political ends. They should also realize that tariffs and quantitative restrictions take away from the notion of the "invisible hand" which so many have convinced themselves defines the American economic system. Hence, few are ready to accept that America needs a paradigm shift in its consumption pattern and in its international economics relations, if only because the truth has been kept buried in ideological rhetoric. However, the time has come for a reality check on the direction of the US economy, the bastion of Western capitalism and avowed purveyor of individualism.

Before Adam Smith

Interestingly, about 1,850 years before Adam Smith the Chinese historian Szema Chien in his essay *On Wealth and Commerce* made this observation of the interaction of humans in production and trade in China:

> The farmers produce them, the wholesalers bring them from the country, the artisans work on them, and the merchants trade them. All this takes place without

> the intervention of government or of philosophers. Everybody exerts his best and uses his labor to get what he wants. Therefore prices seek their level, cheap goods going to where they are expensive and higher prices are brought down.... All things are produced by the people themselves without being asked and transported to where they are wanted. Is it not true that these operations happen naturally in accord with their own principles? (Lin Yutang 1960: 208).

From this translation by Lin Yutang, the invisible hand of the market was not only fully understood and indeed articulated by the ancient Chinese but also was seen in terms of a harmonious relationship between humans and the environment and thus a phenomenon of nature. That this interaction of demand, supply, and price with the environment seemingly has escaped successive policymakers speak to a world economic system that has become more exploitative over time.

New Reality; Old Rhetoric

According to George Will, the American economy has never been stronger than it is today.[22] The question thus becomes: For whom? Certainly not for ordinary Americans who do not share in the all-important "intellectual capital" that he perceives is driving the US economy. And they are not likely to do so any time soon if the cut back in education and other productivity-enhancing social services on the one hand, and the readiness of the Central Bank and the Treasury to bail-out Wall Street and Hedge Funds on the other hand, is anything to go by. Hence, despite the positive spin the administration puts on the state of the US economy, it is headed in the wrong direction. Indeed, according to United Nations Conference on Trade and Development (UNCTAD) Report, the US economy not only will not achieve the lofty growth rates for 2007 predicted by the Federal Reserve Chairman but also will lag both the EU and Japan whose GDP growth rates for 2007 are estimated at 2.8 percent and 2.3 percent respectively. Moreover, the rest of the world will likely achieve GDP growth rates at least double that of the US.[23] Clearly, the danger for Americans in the twenty-first century is the ease with which ideology clouds judgment and spin becomes reality for most.

It is not the emergence of China or its positive trade balance with the US that is responsible for the current predicament of the US economy either; rather, it is the unbridled high consumption rate of Americans and the growing national debt burden that are chiefly responsible, as discussed in Chapter Six. Indeed, contrary to the rhetoric the growth of the Chinese economy over the last ten years has been the mainstay of the world economy and hence the US economy. Therefore, there is no discernible causal relationship between China's economic growth and America's decline, even though China is now a net buyer of energy. Rather, imports from China have served to keep US inflation rates in check while the latter struggles to contain labor and energy costs and to stimulate production in other areas.

China, as we have seen indirectly shares its trade surplus with America—which is about 25 percent of the total US trade deficit—with other trading nations who in turn are able to trade with the US thereby returning such surpluses in the form of products cheaper than what it would cost to produce in America while providing a market for American-made goods and services. The US trade deficit, on the other hand, is a pure trade deficit in consequence of: a) its dependency on foreign oil; b) its extraordinarily high domestic consumption which is necessary to sustain US economic growth, and; c) its declining relative competitiveness in consequence of its cost structures. In terms of the latter, the only significant cost in common with the Chinese economy is the cost of energy. But, whereas the Chinese demand for energy is primarily a function of increasing production, in the case of the US it is a function of private consumption, our way of life, if you will.

Interestingly, Americans are well ahead of the curve in per capita energy consumption as with everything else; but as pointed out by Representative Roscoe Bartlett, they are not happier than those who are part of the curve.[24] Hence, unless US policymakers address these issues directly and with honesty, the risk for the world and indeed the American people is that the resort to condign power becomes an irresistible alternative. Recall, Mr. Blair's proposal to include hard power as an integral aspect of Britain's foreign policy. Therefore, America as the superpower needs to effect a paradigm shift not only in its geopolitics but also in geo-economics posture. Never in its history has the requirement for a shift in foreign policy been greater; the "old" thinking must give way to a "new" thinking that is respectful and accommodating of "Other"; and for coexistence instead of universality of an ideology predicated on hegemony.

From the evidence, we clearly need to recognize that our socio-economic and political philosophies do not reflect the geo-economics and geopolitical reality of the twenty-first century and the advances in information technology: both have rendered our approach to international economic and political relations outmoded and thus ineffectual. Indeed, the actions and attendant consequences of US foreign policy in the Middle East evidence the dangers of relying heavily on condign power—in rhetoric as well as deed—and less on accommodating other political systems. Clearly, the quiddity of cultures in a world community that values pluralism requires a global political system that is accommodating of difference while recognizing that there will almost always be dominant voices in any society. Indeed, as Samuel Huntington (1966: 310) reminds us: "the belief that non-Western peoples should adopt Western values, institutions, and culture is *immoral* because of what would be necessary to bring it about" (emphasis added). The challenge, then, is to adopt a heterogeneous set of rules that not only fosters unity without the universalizing process but also, and equally important protects against the tyranny of the majority or indeed of the powerful as alluded to by Harvard's Bryan Hehir (see page 31) and by Haris Silajdzic, former prime minister of Bosnia (see page 9).

NOTES

1 "In Defense of the Bush doctrine", *Book TV, C-SPAN2*, May 17, 2007

2 See Dershowitz's letter "The Israel Lobby", *London Review of Books, Vol. 28, No 8*, 20 April, 2006

3 Book TV, *C-SPAN2*, May 7, 2007

4 Billington, J., Librarian of Congress, "Q&A", *C-SPAN*, July 1, 2007

5 "Ex-Commander Sanchez Faults Iraq Strategy", *All Things Considered*, NPR, October 13, 2007, http://www.npr.org/templates/story/story.php?storyId=15257952

6 Paul, R. "Washington Journal", *C-SPAN TV*, March 12, 2007

7 The President's Press Conference, White House, June 20, 2007.

8 Daraghmeh, A., "Israelis arrests Hamas leaders", *Associated Press*, http://news.yahoo.com/s/ap/20070524/ap_on_re_mi_ea/israel_palestinians

9 See Press Conference on June 19, 2007, *BBC World News*; see also al-Mughrabi, N., "Israel attacks Gaza; contacts new Abbas govt.", *Associated Press*, http://news.yahoo.com/s/nm/20070620/ts_nm/palestinians_dc

10 Interview with Margaret Warner, 'News Hour', *PBS.org*, June 19, 2007

11 Washington Institute for Near East Policy, *C-SPAN2*, June 18, 2007.

12 "US EU restores Palestinian ties", *BBC News*, http://news.bbc.co.uk/go/pr/fr/-/2/hi/middle_east/6764541.stm, June 18, 2007.

13 al-Mughrabi, N., "Israel attacks Gaza; contacts new Abbas govt", *Associated Press*, http://news.yahoo.com/s/nm/20070620/ts_nm/palestinians_dc

14 See Beale, J., "US fights Latin America's suspicions", *BBC News*, http://news.bbc.co.uk/2/hi/americas/6432185.stm, March 8, 2007

15 Mearsheimer, J., Walt, S., "The Israel Lobby"

16 Mason, J., "Europeans cool to Bush plan on climate change", http://news.yahoo.com/s/nm/20070601/ts_nm/climate_bush_dc_4; see also, "US seeks new greenhouse gas goals", *BBC News*, http://news.bbc.co.uk/go/pr/fr/2/hi/americas/6708995.stm, May 31, 2007

17 Graham-Harrison, E., Buckley, C., "China says climate policy must make room for growth", http://news.yahoo.com/s/nm/20070604/ts_nm/china_climate_dc

18 Majumder, S., "India, China under pressure at G8", *BBC News*, http://news.bbc.co.uk/go/pr/fr/-/2/hi/south_asia/6725453.stm

19 Fallows, J., interview with Jeffrey Brown, "News Hour", *PBS.org*, June 25, 2007

20 Ghazvinian, J., 'Book TV', *C-SPAN 2*, March 27, 2007

21 Hill, C., Assistant Secretary of State for East Asian and Pacific Affairs, Press Conference June 25, 2007, *C-SPAN.*

22 "This Week", *ABC News*, September 2, 2007

23 Jordans, F., "Report Says U.S. Economy Will Slow Sharply This Year and Fall Behind Growth in Most of World", *Associated Press*, http://news.yahoo.com/ap/070905/un_us_economy.html?.v=2

24 U.S. House of Representative, C-*SPAN*, June 25, 2007.

Bibliography

Adem, S., 2005, *Hegemony and Discourse: New Perspectives on International Relations*, Lanham, Maryland: University Press of America Inc.

Albright, M., 2003, *Madam Secretary, a Memoir*, New York: Hyperion.

Amin, S., 2006, *Beyond US Hegemony? Assessing the Prospects for a Multipolar World*, Lebanon: World Book Publishing.

Amsden, A.H., 1989, *Asia's Next Giant, South Korea and late industrialization*, NY: Oxford University Press).

Andrea, A.J., 2003, *Encyclopedia of the Crusades*, Westport, Conn: Greenwood Press.

Ardrey, R., 1966, *The Territorial Imperative, A Personal Inquiry into the Animal Origins of Property and Nations*, New York: Atheneum.

———, 1961, *African Genesis, A Personal Investigation into the Animal Origins and Nature of Man*, New York: Atheneum.

Arendt, H., 1952, *The Origins of Totalitarianism*, New York: Harcourt Brace.

Armstrong, K., 2006, *Muhammad: a prophet for our time*, New York: Atlas Books.

Bell, M.W., et al., 1993, "China at the Threshold of a Market Economy", *IMF Occasional Paper 107*, (Washington, DC: IMF).

Bhagwati, J. and H.T. Patrick, 1990, *Aggressive Unilateralism:. America's 301 trade policy and the world trading system*, An Arbor, Michigan: University of Michigan Press.

Bhagwati, J., 1988, *Protectionism*, Cambridge, Mass: The MIT Press.

Birmingham, P., 2006, *Hannah Arendt and Human Rights, The Predicament of Common Responsibility*, Bloomington, Indiana: Indiana University Press.

Bok, D., 1996, *The State of the Nation, Government and the Quest for a Better Society*, Cambridge, Mass: Harvard University Press.

Bloom, A., 1987, *The Closing of the American Mind: How Higher Education Has Failed Democracy and Impoverished the Souls of Today's Students*, New York: Simon and Schuster.

Briestweiser, K., 2006, *The political education of a 9/11 widow*,

Brown, D., 2001, *Bury my Heart at Wounded Knee: an Indian history of the American West*, 13th edition. New York: H. Holt.

Buchanan, P., 2002, *The Death of the West*, New York: Thomas Dunne Books, St. Martin's Press.

Bundy, McG., 2004, "The Unimpressive Record of Atomic Diplomacy" in *The Use of force, Military Power and International Politics 6th Ed.*, R.J. Art and K.N. Waltz eds., Lanham, Maryland: Rowman & Littlefield Publishing, Inc., 85–93.

Buzan, B., 2004, "How and to whom does China matter?" in *Does China Matter? Essays in memory of Gerald Segal*, B. Buzan and R. Foot, eds. London: Routledge.

Cardarelli, R., and Kose, A., 2004, "Economic Impact of U.S. Budget Policies", in *IMF Occasional Paper 227: U.S. Fiscal Policies and Priorities for Long-run Sustainability*, M. Mühleisen, and C. Towe, C. eds. Washington, DC: IMF.

Carter, J., 2006, *Palestine, Peace not Apartheid*, New York: Simon & Schuster.

Chang, C.V., 2006, *Privatisation and Development, Theory, Policy and Evidence*, Hampshire, England: Ashgate Publishing Limited.

Chow, R., 2001, "King Kong in Hong Kong: Watching the "Handover" from the USA" in *Whither China? Intellectual Politics in Contemporary China*, X. Zhang, ed. Durham, NC: Duke University Press, 211–228.

Chung, J.H., 2005, "China's Ascendancy and the Korean Peninsula", in *Power shift: China and Asia's New Dynamics*, D. Shambaugh, ed. Berkeley, California: University of California Press, 151–169.

Clarke, R.A., 2004, *Against all Enemies: Inside America's War on Terror*, New York: The Free Press, Simon & Schuster.

Compton, J.R., 2005, "Shocked and awed: the convergence of military and media discourse" in *Global politics in the Information Age*, M.J. Lacy and P. Wilkins eds. Manchester, UK: Manchester University Press.

Donaldson, T., 1989, *The Ethics of International Business*, New York: Oxford University Press.

Craig, C., 2002, *The Good men: a novel of heresy*, New York: Riverhead Books.

Dillon, D.R., 2007, *The China Challenge, Standing Strong against the Military, Economic, and Political Threats That Imperil America*, Lanham, Maryland: Rowman & Littlefield Publishing, Inc.

Eldad, I., 2007, Updated version, *The Jewish Revolution: Jewish Statehood*, Jerusalem: Gefen Publishing House

Feldman, R. H., 1978, *Hannah Arendt, The Jew as Pariah: Jewish identity and politics in the modern age*, New York: Grove Press, Inc..

Foot, R., 2002, "Introduction", in *Order and Justice in International Relations*, R. Foot et al., eds., Oxford: Oxford University Press, 1–23.

Fukuyama, F., 1999, *The Great Disruption, Human Nature and the Reconstitution of Social Order* New York: The Free Press, Simon & Schuster.

Gaddis, J.L., 2004, "Implementing Flexible Response: Vietnam as a Test Case in *The Use of force, Military Power and International Politics 6th Ed.*, R.J. Art and K.N. Waltz eds., Lanham, Maryland: Rowman & Littlefield Publishing, Inc., 221–246.

———, 2003, "Order versus Justice: An American Foreign Policy Dilemma" in *Order and Justice in International Relations*, R. Foot et al., eds., Oxford: Oxford University Press, 155 – 175.

Galbraith, J.K., 1983, *The Anatomy of Power*, Boston, Mass: Houghton Mifflin Company Boston

Garver, J.W., 2005, "China's Influence in Central and south Asia, Is it Increasing?" in *Power shift: China and Asia's New Dynamics*, D. Shambaugh, ed. Berkeley, California: University of California Press, 205–227

Grandin, G. 2006, *Empire's Workshop: Latin America, the United States, and the rise of the new imperialism* New York: Metropolitan Books.

Haber, H. F., 1994, *Beyond Postmodern Politics: Lyotard, Rorty, and Foucault*, New York: Routledge.

Halprein, M.H., 2004, "The Korean War" in *The Use of force, Military Power and International Politics 6th Ed.*, R.J. Art and K.N. Waltz eds., Lanham, Maryland: Rowan & Littlefield Publishing, Inc., 181–196.

Hamilton, N.A., (1995), *Founders of Modern Nations, A Biographical Dictionary*, Santa Barbara, CA: ABC-CLIO.

Harding, H., 1981, "China and the Third World", in The American Assembly, Columbia University and Council on Foreign Relations, Inc.

Heidenreich, L., 2007, *"This Land was Mexican Once"*, Austin, Texas: University of Texas Press.

He Ping, 2002, *China's Search for Modernity, Cultural Discourse in the Late 20th Century*, New York: Palgrave Macmillan.

Huntington, S. P., 1996, *The Clash of Civilizations and The Remaking of World Order*, New York: Touchstone, Simon & Schuster.

Ikenberry, G.J., 2004, "America's Imperial Ambition" in *The Use of force, Military Power and International Politics 6th Ed.*, R.J. Art and K.N. Waltz eds., Lanham, Maryland: Rowman & Littlefield Publishing, Inc., 321–332.

Jenkins, B.M., 2004, "International Terrorism" in *The Use of force, Military Power and International Politics 6th Ed.*, R.J. Art and K.N. Waltz eds., Lanham, Maryland: Rowman & Littlefield Publishing, Inc., 77– 84.

Kaarsholm, P., 2006, "States of Failure, Societies in Collapse? Understanding of Violent Conflicts in Africa", in *Violence Political Culture & Development in Africa*, P. Kaarsholm, ed. Oxford, UK: James Curry Limited.

Karl, R., 2001, "The Burdens of History: *Lin Zexu* (1959) and *The Opium War* (1997)", in *Whither China? Intellectual Politics in Contemporary China*, X. Zhang, ed. Durham, NC: Duke University Press, 229–262 .

Kaufmann, C., 2004, "Intervention in Ethnic and Ideological Civil Wars" in *The Use of force, Military Power and International Politics 6th Ed.*, R.J. Art and K.N. Waltz eds., Lanham, Maryland: Rowman & Littlefield Publishing, Inc., 394–414.

Kesselman, M., et al., 1996, *Comparative politics at the Crossroads*, Lexington, Mass: D.C. Heath and Company.

Keynes, J.M., 1964, *The General Theory of Employment, Interest and Money*, New York: Harcourt Brace Jenovich

Krueger, A.O., 1993, *Economic policies at Cross-purposes: The United States and Developing Countries*, Washington, DC: Brookings Institution.

Krugman, P., 1999, *The Return of Depression Economics*, New York: W.W. Norton & Company.

Lacy, M.J., and Wilkins, P., 2005, *Global politics in the Information Age*, Manchester, UK: Manchester University Press.

Lampton, D.M., 2005, "China's Rise in Asia Need Not Be at America's Expense" in *Power shift: China and Asia's New Dynamics*, D. Shambaugh, ed. Berkeley, California: University of California Press, 306–328.

Laqueur, W., 2004, "The Changing Face of Terror" in *The Use of force, Military Power and International Politics 6th Ed.*, R.J. Art and K.N. Waltz eds., Lanham, Maryland: Rowman & Littlefield Publishing, Inc., 450–462.

Lentner, H.H., 204, *Power and Politics in Globalization*, New York: Routledge

Lin, Yutang 1960, *The Importance of Understanding, Translations from the Chinese*, Cleveland, Ohio: The World Publishing Company.

———, (1949), *The Wisdom of China, An Anthology*, London, UK: Michael Joseph LTT.

Luke, T.W., 2005, "Developing a new speech for global security: exploring the rhetoric of evil in the Bush administration response to 9.11.01", in *Global politics in the Information Age*, M.J. Lacy and P. Wilkins eds. Manchester, UK: Manchester University Press.

McCelland, J.S., 1996, *A History of Western Political Thought*, London: Routledge.

McNair, B., 2005, "The global public sphere: fourth estate or new world information disorder?" in *Global politics in the Information Age*, M.J. Lacy and P. Wilkins eds. Manchester, UK: Manchester University Press.

Misra, B.B., 1990, *The Unification and Division of India*, New Delhi: Oxford University Press.

Mitter, R., 2003, "An Uneasy Engagement: Chinese Ideas of Global Order and Justice in Historical Perspective" in *Order and Justice in International Relations*, R. Foot et al., eds., Oxford: Oxford University Press, 207–235.

Morton, L., 2004 "The Decision to Use the Atomic Bomb" in *The Use of force, Military Power and International Politics 6th Ed.*, R.J. Art and K.N. Waltz eds., Lanham, Maryland: Rowman & Littlefield Publishing, Inc., 165–180.

Mühleisen, M., 2004, "Overview: Returning Deficits and the need for Fiscal Reform", *in IMF Occasional Paper 227: U.S. Fiscal Policies and Priorities for Long-run Sustainability*, M. Mühleisen and C. Towe eds. Washington, DC: IMF.

Murray, A.V., 2006, *The Crusades, an Encyclopedia, Vol. 1: A-C*, Santa Barbara, CA: ABC-CLIO.

Musharraf, P., 2006, *In the Line of Fire, a memoir*, New York: The Free Press, Simon & Schuster.

Nasr, V., 2006, The Shia Revival, how conflicts within Islam will shape the future, New York: W.W. Norton & Company.

Naughton, B., 2007, *The Chinese Economy, Transitions and Growth*, Cambridge, Mass: The MIT Press.

Nicolaidis, K., and Lacroix, J., 2003, "Order and Justice Beyond the Nation–State: Europe's Competing Paradigms" in *Order and Justice in International Relations*, R. Foot et al., eds., Oxford: Oxford University Press, 125–154.

Ohashi, H., 2005, "China's Regional Trade and Investment Profile", in *Power Shift: China and Asia's New Dynamics*, D. Shambaugh, ed., Berkeley, California: University of California Press, 71– 95.

Pape, R.A., 2006, *Dying to Win: the strategic logic of suicide terrorism*, New York: Random House.

Peck, J., 2006, *Washington's China, The National Security World, the Cold War, and the Origins of Globalism*, Boston, Mass: The University of Massachusetts Press.

Piscatori, J., 2003, "Order, Justice and Global Islam" in *Order and Justice in International Relations*, R. Foot et al., eds., Oxford: Oxford University Press, 262–286.

Prasad, E., ed., 2004, *China's growth and Integration into the World Economy, Prospects and Challenges, IMF Occasional Paper 152*, Washington, DC: IMF.

Prasad, E., and Rumbaugh, T., 2004 'Overview," in *China's growth and Integration into the World Economy, Prospects and Challenges, IMF Occasional Paper 152*, Prasad, E. ed. Washington, DC: IMF

Pye, L.W., 1981, "The China Factor in southeast Asia", in *The American Assembly, Columbia University and Council on Foreign Relations, Inc.*

Read, P.P., 2005, *"Alive"*, New York: Harper Collins.

Roberts, A., 2003, " Order/Justice Issues at the United Nations", in *Order and Justice in International Relations*, R. Foot et al., eds., Oxford: Oxford University Press, 49–79.

Rubin, R. E., 2000, *Foundations of Library and Information Science*, New York: Neil-Schuman Publishers Inc.

Rumbaugh, T., and Blancher, N., "International Trade and the Challenges of WTO Accession" in *China's growth and Integration into the World Economy, Prospects and Challenges, IMF Occasional Paper 152*, Prasad, E. ed. Washington, DC: IMF

Sansom, G. (Sir), 2004, "Japan's Fatal Blunder, in *The Use of force, Military Power and International Politics 6th Ed.*, R.J. Art and K.N. Waltz eds., Lanham, Maryland: Rowman & Littlefield Publishing, Inc., 153–164.

Segal, G., 1999, "Does China matter?" in *Does China Matter? Essays in memory of Gerald Segal*, B. Buzan and R. Foot, eds. London: Routledge.

Sen, A., 2002, *Rationality and Freedom*, Cambridge, Mass: The Belknap Press of Harvard University Press)

Seo, Y., and Takekawa, S., "Waves of Globalization in East Asia: A Historical Perspective" in *Fairness, Globalization, and public institutions, East Asia and beyond*, J. Dator, et al, eds. Honolulu: University of Hawai'I Press, 219–248.

Shambaugh, D., 2005, "The Rise of China and Asia's New Dynamics", in *Power Shift: China and Asia's New Dynamics*, D. Shambaugh, ed., Berkeley, California: University of California Press, 1–22.

———, 2005, "Return to the Middle Kingdom?" in *Power Shift: China and Asia's New Dynamics*, D. Shambaugh, ed., Berkeley, California: University of California Press, 23–47.

Sigmund, P.E., 1988, *St. Thomas Aquinas on Politics and Ethics*, New York: W.W. Norton & Company

Sklair, L.1995, (2nd Ed), *Sociology of the Global System*, London: Prentice Hall Harvester Wheatsheaf

Slack, C.K., 2003, *Historical Dictionary of the Crusades*, Lanham, Maryland: Scarecrow Press Inc.

Solomon, R.H., (Ed.), 1981, *The China Factor: Sino-American Relations and the Global Scene*, New Jersey: Prentice Hall Inc.

Spodek, H., 2006, *The World History, Volume 1. Prehistory to 1500*, 3rd ed., Upper Saddle River, NJ.,

Sum, N., 2005, "Global financial markets and the ICT revolution: perfect market or (im)perfect domination?", in *Global politics in the Information Age*, M.J. Lacy and P. Wilkins eds. Manchester, UK: Manchester University Press.

Stewart, G.R., 2002, *Ordeal by Hunger, the story of the Doner party*, Salem, NY: Adventure Library.

Suskind, R., 2004, *The Price of Loyalty: George W. Bush, the White House, and the Education of Paul O'Neill*, New York: Simon & Schuster.

Talbott, S., 1981, "The Strategic dimension of the Sino-American Relationship", in *The American Assembly, Columbia University and Council on Foreign Relations, Inc.* New Jersey: Prentice Hall Inc.

Thatcher, M., 1995, *'The Path to Power'*, New York: Harper Collins Publishers.

Tussie, D., 1987, *The Less Developed Countries and the World Trading System*, London: Frances Pinter Publishers.

Van Evera, S., 2004, "Offense, Defense, and the Causes of War" in *The Use of force, Military Power and International Politics 6th Ed.*, R.J. Art and K.N. Waltz eds., Lanham, Maryland: Rowman & Littlefield Publishing, Inc., 44–69.

Wallerstein, I., 2005 (2nd Printing), *World Systems Analysis*, (North Carolina: Duke University Press

Wang, G., 2005, "China and Southeast Asia, The Context of a New Beginning", in *Power Shift: China and Asia's New Dynamics*, D. Shambaugh, ed. Berkeley, California: University of California Press, 187–204

Weaver, R.K., (2000), *Ending Welfare as We Know It*, Washington, DC: Brookings Institution Press.

Woods, N., 2003, "Order, Justice, the IMF and the World Bank, in *Order and Justice in International Relations,* R. Foot et al., eds., Oxford: Oxford University Press, 80–102.

Woodward, B, 2006, *State of Denial*, New York: Simon & Schuster.

World Bank, 2005, *World Development Report 2006, Equity and Development*, Washington DC: IBRD/World Bank

———, 2004, *World Development Report, 2005, a Better Investment Climate for Everyone*, Washington, DC: IBRD/World Bank.

Yahuda, M.B., 2004, "Gerald Segal's Contribution", in *Does China Matter? Essays in memory of Gerald Segal*, B. Buzan and R. Foot, eds. London: Routledge.

Zhang, X, 2001, "Nationalism, Mass Culture, and Intellectual Strategies in Post-Tiananmen China" in *Whither China? Intellectual Politics in Contemporary China*, X. Zhang, ed. Durham, NC: Duke University Press, 315–348.

Zhang, Y., and Tang, S., 2005, "China's Regional Strategy" in *Power Shift: China and Asia's New Dynamics*, D. Shambaugh, ed., Berkeley, California: University of California Press 48–70.

Index

About the author:

Claude Chang is an independent International Development Economics and Business Consultant, and Adjunct at Johnson and Wales University. Dr. Chang was Secretary to the Treasury of Guyana and member of the Board of the Guyana Central Bank. He served as a Member of the Governing Council of the University of Guyana. His research interest includes: development economics; privatization, competition and regulation; and international economics relations.

Chang is the author of *Privatisation and Development, Theory, Policy, and Evidence*, (Ashgate Publishing, 2006) and has contributed a book chapter to *Leading Issues in Competition, Regulation and Development* edited by Cook, P. et. al (Edward Elgar, 2004), a DFID-funded project of the Centre on Regulation and Competition at the University of Manchester. He has contributed two background papers on the opportunities and challenges with respect to African infrastructure to the African Development Report 1999, and was lead contributor to the "*Declaration of the Geneva 2nd HIPC Ministerial Meeting, Geneva, June 6–8, 2000.*" Dr. Chang was an invited Commentator, at *Centro De Estudios Monetarios Latinoamericanos* (CEMLA) Seminar on *Financing Sustainable Growth and Development in Latin America*, Mexico City, (September 7th–8th 2000).

Chang, a former UNDP consultant, was also Adviser to the Public Accounts Committee, Guyana Parliament, and has over 20 years experience in the telecommunications industry in the US, Guam, Guyana, and the Caribbean.

www.ingramcontent.com/pod-product-compliance
Ingram Content Group UK Ltd.
Pitfield, Milton Keynes, MK11 3LW, UK
UKHW041142300926
15471UKWH00011B/99

9 780761 83981